Other works by John Suler

The Psychology of Cyberspace

Photographic Psychology: Image and Psyche

Contemporary Psychoanalysis and Eastern Thought

Madman

Strange Adventures
of a Psychology Intern

John R. Suler

True Center Publishing

Instructor resources are available at truecenterpublishing.com. You can also visit John Suler's *Teaching Clinical Psychology* website. Author Contact Information: suler@rider.edu

Published in the United States of America
By True Center Publishing, Doylestown PA
truecenterpublishing.com

This book is a work of fiction. Names, characters, places, and incidents either are the product of the author's imagination, or are used fictitiously. Any resemblance to actual persons, living or dead, events, organizations or locales, is entirely coincidental.

Suler, John R., 1955–
    Madman : strange adventures of a psychology intern /
John R. Suler.
    p. cm.
    LCCN 2009938984
    ISBN-13: 978-0-9842255-3-8
    ISBN-10: 0-9842255-3-6

    1. Interns (Clinical psychology)—Fiction.
    2. Clinical psychologists—Training of—Fiction.
    3. Psychiatric hospitals—Fiction. 4. Psychological
    fiction. 5. Medical fiction. 6. Bildungsromans.
    I. Title.

    PS3619.U4M33 2010   813'.6
                               QBI09-600197

Manufactured in the United States of America

First Edition Published June, 2010

Cover photographs and jacket design by John Suler and Kira Suler
Map of unit by Debra Finnegan-Suler
All other clip art ©2010 Jupiterimages Corporation

For Debra, Asia, and Kira

With gratitude for my mentors and teachers:
Nancy McWilliams and Arlene Burrows who opened
the door to exploring the intrapsychic realm; Ed Katkin,
Joe Masling, and Lloyd Silverman, for teaching me
what it means to be a scientist; Howard Tennen, for his
guidance through the world of psychiatry; and
Thomas Altizer who revealed what lies beyond psychology.

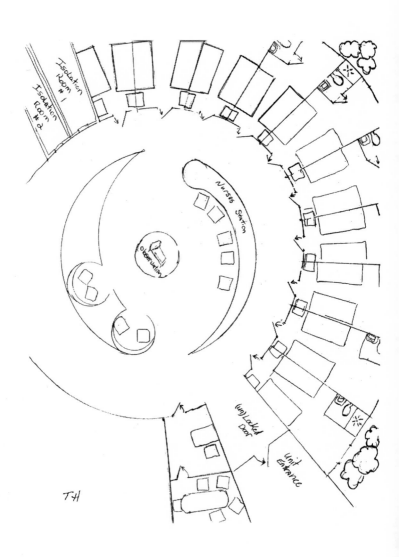

Isolation Room #1

Isolation Room #2

Nurses Station

Observation

(un)Locked Door

Unit Entrance

T.H

Madman

Chapters

CHAPTER 1

– Up –

I SHIFTED THE OLD NOVA into second gear, splashed it through a muddy puddle, and started up the hill. Weary from many years of loyal service and abuse, the rusty hand-me down gasped for more fuel to grapple with the climb. My prayers that it would not stall — a recent symptom of its senile rebellion — would be answered today. The road curved gracefully around the hill as might any scenic route through these mountains, but this path bore a more serious and practical intent: to guide the faithful to the Medical Center at the top. Midway up I caught a glimpse of the distant city through a brief clearing in the late autumn trees. Snuggled into the valley that stretched to the edge of the horizon, the city glowed unnaturally in the oblique rays of the early morning sun, singled out from the wooded landscape by a stream of light descending through a small, temporary break in the overcast sky.

Despite the scenic beauty, that familiar tiny feeling of depression seeped into the back of my head — an almost imperceptible affect nagging for attention. I searched for its source and settled on an explanation: the long day ahead of me.

Internship. Doesn't "intern" mean "to imprison?" We're expected to work our butts off, all in the name of Training. It seemed more like a grueling rite of passage than anything else — the establishment's last chance to test the limits of the student's psyche before welcoming him to the club. I thought of Dr. Hapling, my psychopathology professor at graduate school, with his tenured feet perched atop his desk and a smile of retrospective content spread across his face. He offered his rationale, "I went through it too. We all did."

Do unto others as was done unto you.

Even graduate school was easier than this internship, and those four years at the university were no picnic. Blockbuster courses that terrorized and infantilized us; comprehensive exams that roused suicidal panic; slave labor as research assistants to tenure-hungry faculty; and, of course, the interminable dissertation, the final hurdle, the last of the Herculean tests of one's determination to overcome all the eccentricities of the academic system and its faculty. Not to mention the frustrations of dealing with professors who had complete power over the student's destiny, who with a casual comment in faculty meetings could inflate or pop a student's reputation. Then, of course, there were the nightmarish stories of the doltish professors who purposefully undermined students who were smarter than they were, or the narcissistic, fame-crazed superstars who sucked students dry and then tossed them aside, or the sleeze-buckets who subtly hinted that you had to sleep with them to graduate. The real horror show occurred when you put several of them together on your dissertation committee. Meetings became a game of "can you top this" where the most important objective was not the candidate's work — and the need to graduate — but rather proving who was smarter than whom. Select the wrong mix of professors for your committee and the group dynamics grind you to bits.

Graduate school was a real education.

I looked at myself in the rearview mirror. "Oh, aren't we the cheerful spirit today, Tom? Are we the runner-up for the Norman Vincent Peale Award?"

After all, there was a positive side to graduate school. Some of the professors actually were Teachers in the truest sense; they cared about your personal and professional development. And we students did secretly find satisfaction in the bohemian student lifestyle of impromptu partying and discussing psychology over bottomless cups of coffee at the all-night diner. Despite all the work, there was some freedom to be unconventional and slightly irresponsible — wearing thread bare jeans to every social event, using a fruit crate as a coffee table, catching a matinee movie. We guys could let our hair and beards grow without anyone blinking an eye. Come to think of it, almost everyone grew a beard at one time or another. It was an unconscious homage to Freud, maybe even an unconscious requirement to receive your Ph.D.

Of course, there were positive aspects to this internship too — new people and new ideas, the excitement of working in the Real World of Medicine, a steady supply of tongue depressors.

I love my work. I hate my work. There it is — that Old Ambivalence, the never-ending toss-up between contradictory feelings, the weighing of the positives and the negatives, the to-be-or-not-to-be's that trouble us all. Life could be so much more enjoyable, so much simpler, without the crippling "but." Exceptions and qualifications. Are animals so indecisive? Is a frog ever conflicted about diving into a pond? Do geese draw up a mental list comparing the pros and cons of flying south for the winter? Only humans seem to be tormented by the powers of reason and self-awareness that knot our will and make us waver between this and that. There is no escaping ambivalence. Freud said that opposites lie close to each other in the unconscious: love and hate, pleasure and pain, desire and fear. The healthier of us are aware of our contradictory feelings, can accept and verbalize our conflicts. We try to smooth over the internal brawl and heave our will in the chosen direction. Often, we're only partially successful. The only solution may be to force the conflict out of our mind, leaving conscious the tolerable half, burying the other. But buried ideas and feelings don't lie dormant. They creep and crawl in darkness; they go bump in the night. They seek out the cracks in our armor and make our lives miserable in disguised ways. For some poor souls, the conflict tears open the psychological gut — and out spills madness.

Why are we humans so afflicted and unhappy? It's sort of pathetic. What did we do wrong to deserve this? Is it the accumulation of bad karma? Is it payback for having picked the sacred apple, or for knocking off the Neanderthals?

The Nova started to gasp and shudder as the incline became more steep. It needed more power. I realized I was going uphill in fourth gear. Duh! As I tried to downshift, and momentarily took my eyes off the road, something swept passed the front of the car. I slammed on the brakes while swerving towards the inside of the hill. Did I hit it? Was that a thud? The car stopped short and I banged my head on the steering wheel. I looked around, but didn't see anything. My hands shaking and heart pumping, I reached for the door handle and quickly got out of the car. There was nothing there — uphill or downhill. A bird sitting on a nearby tree branch stared at me curiously, "What's the problem, human?"

Dare I look under the car? Scared about what I might find, I got down onto my hands and knees and peered below… Nothing. Rubbing my bumped and now puzzled noodle, I stood up and leaned back against the car door. I could have sworn I saw something in the road and would have pondered this mystery a bit longer, if not for the fact that something was pulling steadily at the back of my pants. I turned around, half expecting to catch some practical joking person or animal in the midst of giving me a wedgie — but I was greeted by something a bit more alarming. My belt loop was caught in the door handle of the Nova that had now begun to roll slowly backwards down the hill. As the car began to pick up speed, with me being half dragged and half running backwards alongside it, grabbing unsuccessfully to free my pants, the insight suddenly struck me that this could be a serious situation. What if the car rolled right off the side of the hill, yanking me with it down onto the rocky terrain below? The bird, still staring at me from its perch, quizzically cocked its head.

You would think I would have panicked and screamed like a lunatic, or been catapulted into one of those superhuman adrenaline highs in which I could have lifted the car right off its wheels. But I just laughed. It's called dissociation, old boy. "This is ridiculous," I said to the bird while trying to control my backward stumbling prance. "I'm going to be wedgied to death."

Suddenly, the car came to an abrupt halt, sending me into a reverse somersault onto the grassy shoulder. Green and cloudy blue chased each other round and round for a moment or two, until I finally tumbled to rest in a seated position at the rear bumper of the car. The Nova was only a few feet from the edge of the hill and from my precipitous fate, but there was nothing else there — no tree or rock or guardrail that could have stopped the car's rolling. What the hell? I stood up and looked around. Just me and the car standing there in the middle of a patch of grass alongside the road. "I guess there really must be a God," I said jokingly to the bird — but my little cohort was gone.

When I got back into the car I just sat there for a minute. Did that really happen? After taking a quick inventory of my now trembling body, I realized I was uninjured — not even a grass stain on my clothes. But on second examination, I did discover one sequela. The belt loop on the back of my pants was torn. "Well, we're off to a good start today, aren't we?" I pronounced unconvincingly to the sky as I gave the broken loop a quick tug and started back up the hill.

Finally, despite fate's warning to the contrary, I reached the top, where the residual anxiety from my comical near-death experience began to fade. Slowing down at the gate, I spotted Jon sitting in his booth, his nose pressed into a paperback book, probably some sci-fi novel like "The Attack of the Cabbage People." He consumed these stories like the rest of us drink water. Technically, he might be labeled as a schizotypal personality. He was eccentric, superstitious, pre-occupied with peculiar topics, interpersonally odd. In plain English — a Space Cadet. Tall, thin, with stooped shoulders and a slightly too large head, he perfectly fit Sheldon's body type of the "ectomorph." The Hospital Rules of Convention, as he called them, forced him to wear a uniform — white shirt and dark pants — but with those pink high-top sneakers and a green paisley tie pulled to a mutated 45 degree angle from his midline, you knew from a mile away that it was Jon.

He was totally oblivious to my car idling no more than four feet away, so I tapped the horn. He nearly fell off his stool. Some security guard.

"My word! A rude awakening! How are you faring this fine day, Dr. Holden?"

If you didn't know Jon, you would swear that he was being cynical, or mocking you with such formal expressions — which would be consistent with his history as a former Berkeley philosophy student, counterculture radical, and perpetual intellectual prankster. He once stole the department chairman's favorite book — Aristotle's Metaphysics — replaced the entire text with blank pages and returned it to the professor's shelf.

But he was sincere, even when he was joking.

"Well, actually, coming up the hill I almost hit a ghost… and a miracle saved me from being dragged over a cliff by my car."

"Hmm, I'd say that kismet is on your side." He seemed only mildly surprised, as if these sorts of things happened in his world all the time. "Which reminds me…" He paused and cautiously looked from left to right, as if someone might overhear our conversation out here in the middle of the road! Tilting precariously on his stool, he leaned towards my window until his back curved into the shape of a question mark. His eyelids drooped slightly, covering half his pupils, giving him that quasi-conscious, burnt-out look so typical of those sensation seekers who dropped a few too many hits of acid during their college days.

"Officially, it is quite impossible to get a staff sticker for the A-lot up here at the top of the hill. But I have some underground connections. I might be able to get you a visiting clinician sticker. As long as you don't park up here every day, they probably won't notice."

"That'd be great, Jon. But if you're gonna get into trouble doing it, please, don't take the risk."

For a moment his eyes opened wide. "Risk? I am thoroughly enamored of risks, especially when it involves stratagems to thwart administration. It's my most preferred avocation."

"Just be careful, Jon. Someday they're going to catch you and they'll force you to reveal all your escapades — and all your secrets."

His body straightened up to military attention. "Not even if they locked me into a room and forced me to listen to cable news!"

"O.K. Just trying to look out for you. After all, if you were fired from this job, when would you find time to read?"

Jon laughed. He leaned towards me again and spoke in a whisper, "If I lost this position, I might have to become a psychologist, read their science fiction, and trick my patients instead."

I never could outwit him. He was the master of passive-aggressive joking and one-upmanship. It was his sense of humor, as well as his offbeat mind, that I enjoyed most about him.

"Very funny, Jon. See you later."

"Before you go, Dr. Holden, I have a riddle for you. What happens when you mix a dyslexic, an agnostic, and an insomniac?

I reflected on this for a moment, but nothing came up, except a brief thought of what it would be like flying through the air while shackled to my car. "I give up."

"You get someone who stays up all night worrying, 'Is there a DOG?'"

I laughed. "Your mind is not normal, Jon."

"Thank you," he replied, pleased with himself.

As I drove away he called out to me, "Dr. Holden, bid my fond greetings to Barb!"

"Will do," I shouted back.

I parked near a black Jaguar, which probably belonged to some surgeon, in hopes that it would catch the security patrolman's eye and divert his attention from my decrepit Nova. A very long shot, but I was willing to try anything. I couldn't afford any more tickets. Parking in P-lot at the bottom of the hill and taking the shuttle bus up — the only alternative — was extremely inconvenient. Even chief residents were forced to ride the shuttle from P, or "Peon" lot as we affectionately called it. Being allocated a sticker to the upper lots required payment with your testicles or your firstborn child. Only one other privilege was considered more precious by the hospital staff, a privilege for which some would lie, cheat, and steal: an office with a window.

I leaned forward, reached behind me, and felt the broken belt loop. My heart started racing again. I can't afford that right now. Can't dwell on it. Got to get going. Three deep breathes — and onward.

As I walked towards the medical center I forced my mind to focus on its architecture. Constructed of steel and mirror-glass that distorted the nearby trees, its two front surfaces swept away from the main entrance in graceful curves suggesting a large circular structure. Yet the impression of size and circularity was deceptive, for just beyond the edges of the building, out of view from the front entrance, the walls turned sharply inward and ended abruptly. An illusion of grandeur. No doubt this location was also chosen to magnify the building's visual impact. Perched on top of a hill amidst rural surroundings, it seemed to herald the power of medical knowledge rising above the untamed wilderness. If only they could keep the mindless geese from shitting on the sidewalks, it would all be so perfect.

I leaned against the rails of the escalator that sympathetically carried me up to the third floor. At the end of the hall stood the gray metal doors with wire-mesh windows that marked the entrance to the inpatient unit. In such a modern and esthetically designed building, these institutional looking doors were an anomaly. Why not wood, or even a pleasing coat of paint on the metal? The patients were rarely violent, so there was no need for wire mesh to guard against projectiles. The doors, in fact, were never locked. Nevertheless, this ominous entrance stirred the almost palpable sensation that something dangerous lurked just beyond: the nightmare of insanity, the bedlam of the present-day possessed, the horror of souls gone awry. I suddenly remembered my old high school friends and our favorite joke as we drove by the antiquated mental institution just outside our small hometown. It was a huge gothic building with smoke bellowing from tall brick stacks. "How many do you think they're burning today?" I laughed off my medieval thoughts, but as I approached the entrance to the unit, I noticed again the tension in my throat and accelerated heart rate that betrayed anxiety. Summoning up a half-hearted confidence, I pushed through the double-doors and strode onto the unit.

CHAPTER 2

Changing of the Guard

THE PSYCHIATRIC INPATIENT UNIT looked futuristic. The room was circular, with the exception of the entrance hallway that briefly disrupted its continuity, a short stem reaching to the outside world. The ten patient rooms — each containing two beds, a small bathroom, and a tinted window overlooking the countryside — were lined up around half the circumference. The remaining half consisted of a dining area and recreation lounge, a large room for group meetings, the two isolation rooms, and the director's office, one of the privileged few to have a window. A green-carpeted walkway formed a ring that followed the contour of the circular wall. Dim track lights in the ceiling created a feeling of twilight, of being enclosed and contained. Two apostrophe-shaped counters were located in the middle of the unit, their outer surfaces paralleling the walls of the circumference, their inner surfaces perfectly positioned so that the bulbous portion of one counter fitted neatly into the tapering tail of the other, like two fish swimming gracefully around each other. One counter contained the nursing station, strategically located to allow the staff an unobstructed view of the entire unit. Windows looking into each patient's room also gave the staff visual access to activities inside, although patients were allowed to close their curtains at night and while dressing. The other counter contained two small cubicles for conducting therapy and psychological testing. They were often referred to as the "libraries" because their shelves were stacked with a collection of miscellaneous paperback books donated by the staff over the years.

At the focus of the circular room, located between the two counters, in the very heart of the unit, was the slightly elevated Center Circle. If necessary, suicidal, obstreperous, and unpredictable psychotic patients could be seated there so the staff could keep an eye on them. A preliminary precaution. The last resort for dealing with a dangerous patient was Isolation — a locked room containing only a mattress. Most patients never required these features of the unit's clever architecture, although people suffering from agitated depression would take advantage of the unit's circular design by pacing around and around on the outer walkway. Manic patients liked to jog, sometimes fully attired in sneakers and sweat suits.

If, by magic, an unsuspecting citizen was swept off the streets and popped onto the unit, he might not even realize he was standing in a psychiatric ward. Very few psychiatrists wore the traditional physician's lab coat and none of the nurses wore the standard white uniform. The patients seldom acted bizarrely, or became violent, or actively hallucinated, thanks to the miracles of modern medications. If the visitor spoke to the inhabitants, he would not suspect them mad. After several minutes conversing with a schizophrenic, he might feel uneasy about the unusual quality of his acquaintance's ideas or manners, but he probably would not realize the person was schizophrenic. Most people, even some mental health professionals, tend to underestimate psychopathology. It would take a while for our visitor to catch on; he might even mistake his surroundings for an innovative hotel for the eccentric.

Because the unit was a short-term facility, patients stayed only two to four weeks. Symptoms were treated swiftly, if possible. Patients who were severely disturbed, dangerously suicidal, or violent, were taken by ambulance to more secure institutions and involuntarily committed. They might stay there for months, years, or in the case of some schizophrenics, a lifetime. The financially distraught state institutions and the maximum security hospitals for the criminally insane were places you would rather not visit — and where you would dread to live. Simply mentioning these hospitals to unruly chronic patients, who knew the system inside and out, would snap them into compliance. To them, "We'll have to send you to Elmcrest" was like saying "We're sending you to the Black Hole of Calcutta." By contrast, the medical center was the luxury edition of medical treatment. So pleasing were the accommodations, so helpful and supportive were the staff, that many of the patients from poor neighborhoods balked when it was time for discharge. They never had it so good.

As I walked onto the unit I glanced at the clock. Three minutes to eight. Still enough time to skim through the charts to see how my patients fared through the night. I had learned one lesson on this internship: Always be prepared for morning report. Getting caught off guard without an explanation for setbacks in a patient's progress, even in your absence at night or on the weekend, was an embarrassing faux pas. Any reasonable explanation would do. Even all-purpose buzzwords like "regression due to family conflict" or the handy "discharge anxiety" were better than saying "I don't know." That was the equivalent of saying, "My brain is mush and I don't know what I'm doing." When confused, in doubt, or just plain ignorant, a doctor nevertheless must speak with unswerving conviction.

A tap on my shoulder pulled my attention out of the stack of progress notes. It was Marion. She smiled warmly — a spark of youth lighting up her aging, wrinkled face. "Sorry to interrupt. I just wanted to congratulate you for the fine job you did with Elizabeth. She made so much progress while she was here."

"She worked hard," I replied, "and really responded quickly to medications. And thanks to your work with the family, her husband finally realized how he contributed to her depression."

"True," she answered gently as she touched me on the arm, "but don't forget to give yourself a little credit too. See you inside." Hobbling, but in her strangely graceful way, she hurried off to the group room. Thank God for Marion. She was the old mother hen of the unit — warmhearted, caring, nurturing — attributes that did not exactly flourish among some of the other staff members. Somehow the training of social workers like Marion spared their humane, down-to-earth qualities, rather than effectively stamping them out as in the highly intellectualized education of the psychologist, or in the medically mechanistic shaping of the psychiatrist. In her forty years as a social worker, Marion had developed a different kind of knowledge, a quiet but hardy wisdom gained through a lifetime of work with the sick and poor.

I checked the time. Thirty seconds to 8:00. All the staff members were converging on the door to the group room, as if someone had tilted a chess board and all the pieces, big and small, were sliding toward one corner. I quickly popped the charts back into the rack and plunged towards the meeting, lest I be the one who was embarrassed by arriving late.

Suspecting I was the last in, I quietly closed the door behind me and slipped into the nearest chair just as the head nurse began her report of the previous night's events. The usual stuff: a few patients requested some sleeping pills, Mr. Pinkton had an upset stomach, Mrs. Watts again was repetitively packing and unpacking her suitcase while sleepwalking. As I had deduced from the absence of new entries in the charts, my two patients had slept through the night without mishap. I felt spared, and grateful.

Safe, at least for the moment, I sat back and observed the ritual of morning report. During this transition from the night to day shift, the staff passed along information according to a strict protocol as orchestrated by Fred Cooling, the chief resident, also known as the "Chief." At the head of the room he sat tall, straight-backed, with squared off shoulders, like a true warrior presiding over the rituals. He deferred only to Dr. Stein, the director of the unit, who sat quietly off to the side, brushing and straightening his Armani ritual dress. He was the Really Big Chief, the keeper of the sacred bones of psychiatric wisdom. He also possessed more gold than anyone in the room.

I imagined an anthropologist from the 24th century, sitting behind the one-way mirror, watching us, writing notes for a thesis about primitive tribal rites. The medicine men wear stethoscopes rather than bone necklaces, and they quote the Diagnostic and Statistical Manual of Mental Disorders rather than chant lyrics about spirits in the trees and sky.

And how could the ritual be complete without the caffeinated sacrament to wash away the sins of physical and mental lassitude? Some say the western world runs on oil, money, or the narcissistic quest for power. Wrong. The life blood, the source of all energy and motivation, is coffee. I looked around the lopsided circle of staff members. Everyone was holding a styrofoam cup. The Chief drank several quarts of the stuff each day. He had a cup pinned to each sleeve and embossed into his favorite mug were the words "Caffeine Psychosis." No doubt the lining of his stomach looked like the inside of his mug — brown and crusty.

Not that I'm being critical. I too would have been quietly quaffing if I had had a few more minutes before morning report to suckle at the pot. How many businessmen and professionals would be thrown into a state of uncontrolled panic if coffee mysteriously vanished? Without its grounds, western civilization would collapse. And it's because the stuff is more than just a stimulant to gear-up the mind and body for work. Coffee is a social lubricant. Just think of all the conversing and laughing around the coffee pots of the world, or about the unspoken sense of community among people who imbibe together. Coffee means group cohesion. Let's also not forget how it lends emotional support. When in doubt at work or in a uncomfortable social gathering, when you don't know what to do or say, when you're feeling insecure, you can always pause to take a sip; or simply stare into the cup, as though an answer might appear in the floating artificial creamer.

Coffee helps us feel complete.

Let me put it this way. Our early social training, when we are one or two years old, leads us to think we reside within the boundaries of our bodies. "Me" is everything from the skin and in. "Me" is mostly organic tissue with some mental and emotional stuff clinging to the inside. Rarely do we consider that our identity, both psychological and physical, projects outward beyond our mortal frame, how it is connected intimately to the material world around us. Coffee may seem like a silly example, but it's not far off target. Consider your feelings about your very first car, or why you just can't bring yourself to throw away those old clothes, or the house where you grew up as a child, or why humans since the dawn of time have been possessed with producing artistic and scientific doodads that will live beyond them. The traditional psychoanalyst would say that such possessions are hypercathected with libidinal energy; more contemporary theorists would call them "selfobjects." The basic message is the same: We surround ourselves with satellites of our sense of self, each an external manifestation of some crucial aspect of who we are. We cling to them because they wield the power to make us feel more tangible, real, complete. They soothe our inner confusion as we struggle to stand on the shifting sands of our identity.

When I was in high school I had a small note pad. I used it to jot down homework assignments, ideas about class projects, and miscellaneous reminders to myself. One day I discovered it was gone! I turned my locker and every pocket inside out, my anxiety mounting with each passing minute that my search failed. I retraced my steps of that day, but to no avail. Ironically, only when I accepted that it was really, truly gone, forever, did my panic fade. Cold reason gave a helping hand, because, logically, it was no great tragedy. But on a deeper level there was a relentless feeling of loss. Something had been torn away. A piece of me had been squirted out of the universe, unexplainably. For other people it might have been a set of keys, a wallet, eyeglasses. In each case the anxiety about the lost object would signify the same predicament: a hole in identity that longs to be filled.

I forced my attention back to the meeting. One of the medical students was finishing up his sweaty explanation of why Mrs. Watts again was packing and unpacking her suitcase in the middle of the night. The Chief looked displeased with the student's rationale. He looked towards Dr. Stein, who was either bored or indifferent. He sat quietly on the outer edge of the circle of chairs, working at his fingernails with a gold file. Sensing that he was up the medical creek without a tongue depressor, the medical student looked down into his styrofoam cup. His two peers sitting next to him, similarly dressed in white shirts and ties, simultaneously raised their cups to their lips. I could swear their hands were shaking. Having admitted patients the day before, they knew they were next at bat.

"That's enough," the Chief grumbled, "let's talk to Mrs. Watts during rounds and find out what's going on." Fred set his stopwatch to zero and looked up. "The admission summaries have been running overtime. Let's keep them down to exactly three minutes." He paused his index finger over the start button and looked out across the room with an automated expression. "Rachel Finski was admitted yesterday."

The second medical student sprang to life, as if the Chief's announcement punched a button hidden somewhere on his chest. He straightened his spine and firmly gripped the clipboard on his lap. In a crisp, dry voice he read his admission summary.

"Rachel Finski is a 30 year old, single, white, unemployed female. She has had numerous hospitalizations in the past. This is her second hospitalization here. Her presenting complaints included feelings of depression and thoughts about suicide. Although suicidal ideation was present, no specific plan was mentioned. There was no homicidal ideation. Some of the vegetative signs of depression were hyposomnia, including early morning awakening, a decrease in concentration and memory, and a recent increase in appetite resulting in a slight weight gain. No significant psychomotor retardation or agitation was noticed. On the mental status exam the patient showed adequate remote and recent memory; judgment and abstraction were good; attention and concentration were somewhat impaired since the patient had difficulty with serial 7's but not multiplication or serial 3's; insight was fair; her salient thought content centered on suicide. The patient appeared to be above average in intelligence and she demonstrated considerable knowledge about psychiatry. A significant thought disorder was indicated by her thinking that was often tangential and circumstantial. Her ideas were bizarre and delusional. She believes her outpatient therapist was plotting to kill her and that she has been poisoned by contaminated tap water. The physical exam was unremarkable. Two years ago at the state hospital…"

The budding psychiatrist. I imagined what it was like being in his shoes, being a medical student, learning the ropes of the medical world. The psychiatrist's training is quite different from a psychologist's. It focuses on biological treatments of mental disorders, especially psychopharmacology. For that reason, when you ask the average person about the difference between a psychiatrist and a psychologist, the light bulb flashes and they answer, reflexively, "A psychiatrist can prescribe drugs." Very true. But people suffer from the mistaken notion that this privilege is icing on the cake for the psychiatrist, all other things being equal with the psychologist. The truth is that psychiatrists do not have the same expertise as psychologists plus more. Psychologists too have their own unique skills. Their training in graduate school emphasizes statistics and experimental research. They are the masters of diagnostic testing, including intelligence and personality tests. And unlike psychiatrists, they hold an academic degree, which means they have been doused with theories from a variety of fields in psychology — cognition, perception, memory, learning, personality, development, social processes, biopsychology — to name a few. They are expected to think like scholars. Perhaps that's why some mental health professionals perceive psychologists as overly intellectual and analytical. They're probably right.

Psychologists and psychiatrists often find themselves mired in professional competition with each other. Who is more qualified to do psychotherapy? One particularly sore spot concerns the coveted access to the secrets of psychoanalysis. Since the time of Freud, the psychiatric profession has jealously guarded this territory. Many orthodox analytic institutes, which are, supposedly, the most elite bastions of training in insight-oriented therapy, once refused to accept psychologists into their programs. Why? Because psychologists have no medical background. Other institutes have a more lenient philosophy and greater financial crunches: they welcome psychologists and even social workers into the fold. But the elitist medical analysts from the big-time schools consider these institutes watered-down imitations of the real thing. Only when pressured by the goliath American Psychological Association in an emotionally charged and historic lawsuit, did the orthodox institutes finally relent and open their doors.

Ironically, Freud, the founder of psychoanalysis and a physician himself, believed that of all the people seeking to be analysts, physicians are probably the least qualified. Why? Because they are too biologically-minded. Those with a liberal arts background, Freud suggested, can resonate better with the psychological, emotional, and interpersonal issues that make up psychoanalysis. Somehow many medical analysts have forgotten the great master's opinion. They have substituted other rationales. They claim that physicians, having worked with people who are ill and dying, better understand human suffering and loss. I wonder about that. If anything, their training may push their heads into the sand so they don't acknowledge suffering, especially death. Death is defeat, failure. And that rubs the M.D.'s omnipotent ego the wrong way. When Elisabeth Kübler-Ross, the renegade physician who pioneered the study of death and dying, asked her colleagues about patients who had passed away, some denied that anyone in their hospital died!

There's a parable about a peasant who pleaded with a guru to cure his grief over his wife's death. The guru agreed, but insisted that the man first find someone in the city who had not experienced the loss of a loved one. The man went from door to door, family to family, but every household had its own tales of death and bereavement. Finally, the peasant realized that he was a member of the universal community of human suffering. That was his cure.

That familiar demanding voice reached into my mental diatribe. I was just barely conscious of it: "Elizabeth Baso was discharged yesterday". Someone's elbow surreptitiously jabbed my forearm. A bolt of panic shot through me. "Elizabeth Baso was discharged yesterday," the Chief repeated, now with a distinct tone of irritation.

"Oh!" I crackled. Instinctively, I raised my hand to bring a coffee cup to my mouth. I needed to wash the frog — and the anxiety — down my throat. But there was nothing in my hand. I didn't have a cup of coffee! I cleared my throat and faked a confident voice.

"Elizabeth Baso was discharged yesterday after spending four weeks on the unit. Many of the vegetative signs of her depression were cleared by Prozac during the hospitalization. Family therapy was successful in clarifying some of the family dynamics that contributed to her depression. Her follow-up treatment will be individual psychotherapy with Dr. Benjamin Levinson, a private psychiatrist in Flemington. Family therapy was strongly recommended and the patient was given a referral to the Carrington Clinic."

"Thank you," the Chief sighed. "The new admission today will be Richard Mobin. I'm assigning him to Dr. Holden. From what his parents told me on the phone, it sounds like a psychotic episode. He might be suicidal. His mother will be bringing him in sometime this evening." He paused to scan the room." Are there any other issues or questions?"

The staff looked at each other, then turned towards the director sitting in the back of the room, slightly outside the circle of chairs. He was clipping his nails and did not look up. There would be no pronouncements today.

"Right," the chief resident tossed into the silence. He glanced at his watch and tried to suppress a smile of satisfaction. We were on time. "Let's get on with it."

CHAPTER 3

Rounds

B Y THE TIME I PULLED MYSELF out of my chair, most of the staff had hustled out the room. Still sitting next to me, Barb, one of the younger nurses, was jotting down a note in her appointment book.

"Thanks for giving me a poke," I said to her. "I drifted off for awhile. Fred must think I'm an idiot."

She smiled from ear to ear, as she often did, even when she was nervous or embarrassed. Her glowing white teeth marched along her lips. Small drops of spittle stuck in the corners of her mouth — an unattractive glitch in a woman who had the body of a porno star, but was too innocent to even know it. "Oh, I'm sure he's an understanding person," she answered cheerfully, "although he doesn't always seem that way." She paused to think. "He must be understanding — he's a chief resident in psychiatry."

Talk about naive optimism. I tried to disguise my basically cynical constitution. "Well, let's hope so. We better get going before our empathic leader starts rounds without us."

She followed me out, her corduroy pants ruffling through two steps for each one of mine. For a moment I could not see the group. Then, out of the corner of my eye, I spotted across the unit one of the medical students, at the tail end of the rounds-roundup, being herded into a patient's room. We hurried around the outer perimeter of the unit, slipped through the half-closed door, and came to an abrupt halt at the back of the group. Barb almost collided into me. I suddenly realized I had forgotten to convey Jon's hello to her. No matter. It was just an idle promise, another of those social amenities we all use to smooth out the rough edges of our day-to-day interactions.

Barb listened intently to the Chief, unaware that I was watching her. How strange, I thought, that she was engaged to Jon. The spaced-out, rebellious, intellectual radical and the sweet, naive homebody. There is a great deal of validity to the "odd couple" phenomenon. Opposites attract. They balance and compliment each other's strengths and weaknesses. Take, for example, women with a histrionic personality style — highly emotional, flighty, and impressionable — who marry compulsive, overly intellectualized men. They need each other to feel more whole. Yet beneath the surface of each person, pressed into some forgotten corner, too uncomfortable to acknowledge, hide the characteristics of the mate. Perhaps this more than anything else is the source of the attraction between them.

"Well now, Miss Finski, I've heard this is your second visit with us." Fred spoke confidently — maybe too confidently for a chief resident — and with a bit of pedantry. "So what has brought you back to us?"

Rachel sprang up in her bed and slicked back her short, dirty hair. "My water is blocked." Her oddly narrow face was nearly expressionless, but she spoke with urgency.

"Now you see, I don't understand that. Explain what you mean."

"My water is blocked. It cannot flow freely. Water must be able to change from liquid to solid, from solid to liquid. It must be able to sublimate, to create the atmosphere that protects us all. It must be free to flow in me, and through me, and out me, below and above me. The water in the air is the projection of my aura. Your EEG and catscan will show you that. Water is the essence. It doesn't care. Water has no concerns. It just wants to flow."

Scratching his head, Fred donned his impatient, skeptical expression. "Now Rachel, let's forget about the water for a minute. Your outpatient therapist told us there have been some problems in his therapy with you. Tell me about that."

"We got along well at first. He was empathic and supportive, and some of his interpretations were quite accurate. I felt like I could trust him. He was a good object. He studied psychoanalysis at Austin-Riggs, you know. A real top-notch. But then he tried to take me apart, like some kind of car mechanic. He tried to take away my essence by rearranging my braindikes. But the water got blocked. The right hemisphere of my brain flooded. The axons sprang leaks, and he didn't have enough fingers to plug up the holes. He tried switching my anti-psychotic medications. That just made me worse. My water got so contaminated that it couldn't seep through my neurons. It was like neuroplasmic sludge. My brain short-circuited. I had epileptic seizures. I was afraid the fire in my belly would go out because the water couldn't get to it. I need that fire, you know. Winter is coming. It is the neurochemical energy of my soul. He's trying to take away my essence, but I won't let him."

The medical students' eyes spun in their heads. But Fred was undaunted, "Rachel, let me interrupt you." He placed his index finger against his temple, as if pointing inside. "Now you realize there is no flooding in your head, no leaks, no fire in the belly. These are things you have imagined. After all, it isn't even logical that a fire would go out if water didn't get to it. Water extinguishes fire, now doesn't it?"

Rachel frowned and fell back, frustrated, against her pillow. "This is why I'm not getting better. I'm drowning in fossils. Is there a shaman in this hospital?"

"Rachel, now listen to me carefully. Your outpatient therapist told us that the problem was that you stopped taking your medications. You were beginning to hallucinate again."

"Hallucinate, hell yes! And what a regression, or is it progression, or concession? A vision a day keeps the doctor away, you know."

"Rachel," Fred interjected, shaking his head, "you were beginning to hallucinate again. Your therapist told us you were starting to feel very depressed. He said you started talking about suicide. Now Rachel, are you still thinking about killing yourself?"

"You're the one who's killing me with this reality testing. Can't you see that water can't be created or destroyed? It just changes form. From solid to liquid to gas to spirit."

"Rachel," Fred interjected again, even more insistently. "It's important that you answer my question. Are you still thinking about killing yourself?"

She paused for a second. Her chin dropped. She looked defeated. Softly, she responded, "I thought about it last night, some. I couldn't sleep. They gave me a sleeping pill but it didn't help."

The Chief was satisfied with himself. "The nurses told me you were awake most of the night. Were you thinking about suicide the whole time?"

"Not all the time. I was worrying about fire and water too because —"

Fred quickly interrupted. He stared right into her eyes. "Did you think of any specific way of hurting or killing yourself?"

"Well, no," Rachel replied thoughtfully. Then, suddenly remembering, she reached under her pillow and pulled out a book. "I thought maybe I would crumple up these pages and swallow them, one by one, until I choked to death." I looked at the title of the book as she held it out towards Fred. It was Fenichel's *Psychoanalytic Theory of Neurosis*.

That was a new one. Fred was momentarily caught off guard. "Uh, yeah. Do you just think about doing this, or will you actually try it, or some other way of hurting yourself?"

"I don't think I'll do it. I'm sure this book tastes awful. I'd probably just get sick and puke it up." She held her stomach with both hands and looked out the window towards the sky. "I still think about it though. It makes me nervous."

"About killing yourself."

"About kicking the big bucket." She continued to gaze outside, her eyes unfocused. "All that water. Where will it flow to?"

Fred peeked at his watch. "You're in good hands here, Rachel. Your primary therapist, Dr. Lawrence, started you on some medications that should help. It's important that you take them and that you talk to your therapist, let him know when you're feeling depressed, or when you're thinking about hurting yourself. O.K.?" Fred grabbed Bob Lawrence by the arm to pull him forward from the group. An unassuming guy with a perpetual deer-caught-in-the-headlights look on his face, Bob almost fell over from the yank. But Rachel didn't move her eyes from the sky.

"Medical students are OK," she mumbled through her trance. "They're only half-baked."

"Do you understand me, Rachel?" Fred said.

"Yes, Dr. Cooling."

"Right." Fred did an about-face and marched out the door, the entourage trailing behind like imprinted ducklings. Halfway to the next room he stopped abruptly, folded his arms across his chest, and waited for us to flock around him. We quickly settled into our silent formation. For one dramatic moment, he paused.

"Well now, doctors, what did you observe?"

We all hesitated, except for Ron Peri, the resident who supervised Bob. With his nose slightly elevated, he adjusted his glasses and spoke with confidence that bellowed up from his discrepantly pudgy, short-limbed body. "I think it's clearly a schizophrenic process. There were loose associations and tangential thinking, and obviously paranoid beliefs in the form of her fear that her outpatient therapist was trying to poison her. Also, I believe the ideas about fire and water in her body qualify as somatic delusions. In fact, there was considerable perseveration on those ideas."

I wanted to throw up all over his white lab coat. He was the only physician on the staff who wore one. If there's one thing I can't stand, it's a know-it-all. If there's one thing that makes me absolutely livid, it's a know-it-all doctor. I wished that all motion in the world, except me, would magically freeze for one minute, so without anyone knowing, I could tie his shoe laces together.

Fred nodded, "That's correct. But let's not forget that there were also signs of depression, as Dr. Lawrence mentioned in morning report — for instance, suicidal ideation and her trouble sleeping last night. So we have to consider the diagnosis of depression superimposed on schizophrenia. Order a DST."

"Yes, definitely a DST," Ron echoed, "to determine whether an endogenous depression is superimposed on the schizophrenia."

A favorite expression of my old high school teacher hissed subvocally through my throat: "Obsequious sycophant" — the most grimy of Brown-Nosers. No doubt Ron hoped the chief resident would join him in mutual preening. But Fred, forever focused on business, was impervious to Ron's toady entreaties, which made Ron even more desperate for attention.

"What else did you observe?" Fred asked as he scanned our faces. Barb hesitantly poked her head between the shoulders of the two residents and started to speak. But Ron interrupted her. "Wouldn't you agree, Dr. Cooling, that the patient's expression 'braindike' is a neologism?"

"Well, I guess it could be considered a neologism in the sense that it's a word you wouldn't find in any dictionary, a word that has a special meaning only to the patient. But neologisms usually are more nonsensical, more gibberish. Usually it's a condensation of two or more words rather than simply the idiosyncratic linking of two words."

Ron looked down and shuffled his feet. Not being exactly right irritated him. I imagined his singed little ego when Dad told him he didn't screw the top of the jelly jar on tight enough.

"I was just thinking that…" Barb paused self-consciously, realizing she had succeeded in breaking into the conversation. She smiled nervously. "I was just thinking that Rachel seemed to be sad."

"We've already determined that depression is present," Ron answered sharply. "Experience in working with these patients will tell you that they often describe depression as feeling sad, blue, or low. It's in the DSM."

I wanted to wrap my hands around his neck. If he couldn't keep his self-doubts and self-deprecations to himself, if he couldn't contain his attempts to project them onto others, I was more than willing to help stop up his mouth.

"Oh, I'm sorry," Barb said. "I've only read parts of the diagnostic manual. I guess I didn't mean depression. It was just that Rachel seemed sad, or mournful, like she felt she was losing someone, or something."

"Interesting," Fred mused. "No doubt her worry about losing her capacity for intellectual thinking. She seems to know something about psychiatry, which is partly the result of her being in and out of mental hospitals for the past ten years. She's also very bright and she uses her intellectualizations as a defense. But it's starting to give out under the strain of her decompensation. It doesn't work too well as a defense anymore, and she's worried. You could see her struggling to maintain control over her thinking, without too much success. She couldn't cope with my open-ended questions at the beginning of the interview. Her thinking was unfocused and almost nonsensical. But then what did I do to change the interview?"

Everyone looked down into their coffee. I cursed myself again for not having grabbed a cup before morning report.

Fred's patience quickly wore out. "I provided more structure," he continued tenaciously. "I was more direct and asked more specific questions. I helped her reality test by trying to show her that her delusions were false. This is what schizophrenics need: Structure and reality testing. And when I was persistent with this she responded well. She became more logical and coherent."

"But wasn't she also a little incoherent towards the end of the interview?" Bob asked. Anxiety rippled through him when he realized he had just questioned the chief. After all, he was only a medical student.

"Yes, good!" Fred answered. "Now why was that? What issue did I focus on that made her unravel?"

Bob hesitated.

"Suicide," I mumbled, the word tumbling out so automatically that I did not even have time to worry about possibly being wrong.

"Correct." Fred riveted his eyes to me. "And what was the result of the lethality assessment?" Everyone turned to look at me.

Now I was nervous. An image of tumbling over a cliff briefly skirted across my mind. "Well, uh, there were some suicidal thoughts, although she didn't seem to have strong intent, and no specific plan, or at least no plan that would be considered really lethal. Unless you consider Fenichel lethal."

No one laughed.

"True," Fred said, "choking on paper isn't exactly a very lethal method of killing yourself. But I'd rather play it safe, at least for today." He turned to Bob, who was listening intently. "Put her on 30 minute checks." Bob nodded obediently.

"Right. Let's move on."

I started after Fred as he strode off to the next patient's room, but someone held my arm. It was Marion.

"You've got a call on 09. It's Mrs. Mobin."

"Who?"

"Mrs. Mobin. Your new patient's mother."

I had completely forgotten about the admission. Rounds pushed forward without me. I stepped into the nursing station and picked up the phone. "Hello, Mrs. Mobin. This is Dr. Holden."

"Hello, Doctor. They told me you'd be takin' care of my son Richard."

"I'll be his primary therapist while he's here on the inpatient unit. Is there something I can do for you?" As she started to answer, I heard the click of another receiver being lifted off the hook.

"I just wanted to know if you was gonna shock him."

"What do you mean?"

"Somebody told me that when people get sent to the sanitarium, you know, when they ain't really actin' right, the doctors give them an electric shock to the brain, to snap them out of it. I don't want my son to get no shock!"

"I don't know exactly what kind of treatment we'll be giving Richard. We have to wait until he gets here to see how he's doing, then we'll decide. From what Dr. Cooling told me — you remember him, you spoke to him on the phone — from what he told me about Richard, it doesn't sound like we'll be giving him any shocks. We only use that as a last resort, and usually only for people who are very depressed."

"I don't want him to get shocked. He's a good boy, you know. He's been into trouble lately, he's been a little wild and actin' funny sometimes, but even if he seems bad on the outside, on the inside he's a good kid, a kind kid. I never used to have any problems with him. It's those other kids on the block. They needle him, just because he's big and a bit slow. They keep doin' it, tryin' to trick him, and they won't let up. He don't really want to hurt nobody. If they would just leave him alone. He can't help bein' different. People just make him out to be bad."

"Has he physically hurt anyone?" I asked.

"He's gotten into some scruffs, but nothin' bad. Are you gonna shock him if he does?"

Before I could answer, I heard a voice ringing loudly in the phone, too loud to be coming from her end of the line. I turned around. On the extension at the opposite end of the nursing station was Ron Peri. "Your son is psychotic, Mrs. Mobin. We need to treat him as soon as possible. I suggest you bring him into the hospital as soon as you can."

"Who's this? Dr. Cooling?"

I tried to wave Ron off the phone, but he ignored me. "No, Mrs. Mobin, that's Dr. Peri on the other line. He's the —"

"What do you mean my son's psychic? He don't read minds."

"Your son is having a psychotic episode," Ron continued. "That means he's losing contact with —"

"Please let go of the line, Dr. Peri," I interjected.

" — reality. There is a disintegration of his —"

"What? Reality?"

"Mrs. Mobin, I apologize for —"

" — ego."

I amplified my voice to drown out the chatter. "Mrs. Mobin, I apologize for this confusion. I'd like to speak to you in private this afternoon when you bring Richard in. What time do you think you will be here?"

"I don't know about this."

"It's important that I see Richard so I can help him. What time will you be here?"

She hesitated. "About three o'clock."

"Fine. I'll see you then."

As I hung up the phone I spotted Ron leaving the nursing station. I intercepted him. Oblivious to having committed an incredibly tactless transgression, he jumped with surprise when I grabbed his stumpy arm. I tried to control myself and act rational, but my voice quivered with anger, "Why did you do that?"

"Do what?"

"Interrupt my phone call."

"I didn't interrupt. I picked up the phone when you did. It was important that I talk to the patient's mother."

"But I'm the primary therapist. There's no reason for you to talk to her."

"I was with Fred when he spoke to Mrs. Mobin. He assigned me as medical backup, so I'm responsible for the patient."

Primitive impulses bubbled up from my id, a murderous rage pressurizing my gut. My eyes watered. My stomach tightened. The fight-or-flight response. I tried to steady myself. "I'm the primary therapist. I'm responsible for the patient. When I need your help, when I need medical backup, I'll ask for it. Otherwise, don't interfere with my work."

Ron seemed unruffled, even indifferent. "I'll give him a physical when he comes in. After I talk to Fred I'll decide what meds would be best. I'll make an entry in the chart."

He walked away, leaving me standing there. The white noise of rage buzzed through my brain. A block of wood. I just had a conversation with a block of wood. I wanted to chase after him, grab him by the collar, and tell him to his face what I really thought of his stupid, small mind.

But I didn't.

"Why are you looking so gloom and doom?" Barb was standing next to me, beaming her naive smile. "Be happy! Fred was just called down to E.R. The rest of rounds are canceled."

CHAPTER 4

Respite

GOOD FOLLOWS BAD.
This unexpected free time greeted me like an oasis. I picked up my knapsack in my office and headed straight for the elevator. With rounds curbed I had exactly 25 minutes free until my next appointment. Images of lounging in the cafeteria, a cup of coffee warming my hand, flashed between my thoughts of revenge against Ron. During case conference I could undermine his comments with fancy theoretical objections. In the staff meeting I could toss out an innuendo about his incompetence. But verbal challenges are mere sublimations of much more primitive urges. On the elevator I could spit in his face and knee him in the groin.

As I turned the corner I sighed with relief. Ron was not standing by the elevator. Surprisingly, the doors opened without my rapping the button. Manna. I stepped in, avoiding eye contact with the other passengers, and pressed G. As the doors closed I realized I had forgotten to check the up/down arrows. Which way was the elevator headed? Several of the floor indicators glowed with the desires of the pilgrims standing behind me, so it could go either way. My stomach, floating towards my ribs, informed me that it was down. Perfect!

To be an elevator, wandering aimlessly in the vertical, dispassionately carrying harried passengers who for a few short moments in their travels must cope with one another. Everyone always stares straight ahead, silent, trying their best not to see, hear, or smell the others, or be seen, heard, or smelled. It's like a bad existential play.

Standing there, immobilized, a pressure slowly mounted in my chest. Still pissed off at Ron? No, it was more than that. I never did like being in an elevator. Being enclosed in that tight box, with people's eyes on my back, made me ill at ease. It was a violation of personal space — the invisible zone surrounding our bodies that we do not allow strangers to enter. It's a zone reserved for intimate relationships. When anyone else penetrates it, we feel anxious and violated. Compressed personal space is like a pressure cooker. When the elevator doors finally opened, we would all ricochet out of this container like bursting popcorn.

Last in, first out. As soon as the doors parted enough for me, I squirted through like a watermelon pit. A wave of cool air greeted me as I popped out. Without looking back to see if the others made it, I hurried down the hallway to the cafeteria. It was nearly empty. I walked directly to the coffee dispenser and pondered the choice of a large or small cup, a decision that somehow soothed me.

"May I help you?" A short and plump kitchen aide, wearing a poorly fitted uniform stained by forgotten mishaps, stared at me with a void but content expression. Her servile grin exposed her gray, chipped teeth. She reminded me of those ambulatory schizophrenics you sometimes see in fast-food restaurants, usually sitting alone in the corner, dressed in old mismatched clothes, talking to themselves between sips of coffee and tokes on their cigarettes. If this woman was indeed a psychiatric patient, she was more fortunate than most.

Chronic schizophrenics may spend many years in rehabilitation programs designed to rebuild basic living skills, such as how to wash clothes, cook, keep a checkbook, or carry on a coherent conversation. Yet very few ever succeed at the ultimate goal of living independently and securing employment. Even holding down what most people consider a menial job would be a tremendous accomplishment for these poor souls. In the hospital's psychiatric day treatment program, the inspiration for all its members was the legend of one former patient who graduated and got a job as a kitchen helper in one of the fancier restaurants in town. Fear, anger, and a profound feeling of futility swept through the program when they learned a few months later that she had been admitted to the hospital. During an acute psychotic relapse she had tried to slice her wrists in a food processor.

"Just getting some coffee," I said as I handed her some money and prepared my cup.

She looked puzzled. "This one's a nickel, not a quarter. You're 20 cents short."

Embarrassed, I quickly dug some change out of my pocket and fumbled with it in my hand. Some of the coins jammed into my key ring, a few dropped to the floor. Now look at who needs rehabilitation! I finally managed to retrieve a quarter from the confusion and passed it across the counter. As I turned to leave, she called out after me, "Sir, you forgot your nickel!"

"Keep it," I mumbled and continued my escape. I sat down at a table on the periphery of the semi-circular cafeteria, next to a window. Before taking my long awaited sip of coffee, I noticed that I had forgotten to stir in the cream. Of course there was no useful implement nearby, except a chewed up plastic straw on the seat across from me. I left my pen upstairs and I sure didn't want to return to the serving counter. When there are no other options, be primitive. I deftly jabbed my finger into the solution, giving it a quick spin. It was much hotter than I expected. With a mind of its own the finger leaped out of the cup and into my mouth for relief. As I sucked out the pain I quickly surveyed the cafeteria: no one was watching. Now more determined than ever to overcome any obstacle, I wrapped my throbbing finger and its companion digits around the styrofoam container, fully prepared to enjoy this drink, even if it killed me.

Concentrating, I looked down into the cup. Streaks of cream swirled in circles through the dark liquid, slowly breaking off into disconnected chains that curved back on themselves as they continued their revolution. Attracted by some unseen force, they began to weave through each other, exchanging parts, dancing intricate and rhythmic patterns. Independent worlds colliding, fusing, separating as they traveled in unison around an invisible center. Clouds that wandered thoughtlessly through a mocha sky.

My trance was broken by the wind whistling through a small gap in the window. The trees outside swayed in response to the breeze, their nearly bare branches rippling in a series of waves, beckoning the change of seasons. Hopefully, the approaching winter would not be as harsh as the last. I remembered Jon's story of a schizophrenic patient who had been delivered to the inpatient unit by the police. They had found him at the shore trying to suck up the beach with his mother's vacuum cleaner. On the third day of his stay on the unit, he wandered out of the hospital and into the surrounding woods during the peak of a blizzard. Hospital security searched for him for several hours, but to no avail. Eventually, despite their wounded pride, they called on the state police for help. When the rescue party finally found him, he was deep in the woods, lying on his back in the snow, without shoes or socks, muttering something about symphonies in the sky. He was saved, but not his frostbitten feet. They had to be amputated. I felt queasy as I imagined a life of teetering on fleshy stilts.

My journal! By instinct I reached inside my knapsack for that comforting spiral notebook. It was one of those super-thick, college-lined versions, now completely filled with writing, with the exception of a few more blank pages. It was like an old friend, my mother, my shrink, my guru — all in one. I always kept it with me. As I weighed it in my hand, I noticed its cardboard cover was cracked, worn at the edges. Nearly a third of the tiny holes fastening the cover to the spiral binding were pulled loose. If the cover pulled off entirely, the delicate inner pages would be exposed directly to the harsh world outside. If I didn't take steps to protect it, over time, page by page, the whole journal would disintegrate. Scotch tape might do the trick, or at least a safe place on my bookshelf once I had moved on to a new notebook.

For how many volumes, linking past and present, would my stream of thoughts persist? Sometimes, when I reread my old entries, I sound rather silly and naive. One day in the future, when I look back on my current state of mind, will I again be embarrassed by what read? If only now I could grasp that intangible, potential me of years hence.

Besides using my journal to vent my emotional and intellectual ruminations, I also tried to improve my writing through it. We psychologists can be notoriously stale writers. For instance, we allow ponderous aggregates of adjectives and nouns to strangle their companion verbs. We stand by idly as we watch active conjugations being usurped by the passive tense or reified by those "-ations" that grow at the end of words like tumors. Psychoanalysts, who supposedly herald the dynamic quality of the mind, often use such semantically concretized gems as "hypercathected libidinal impulses" rather than "sexy"; while behaviorists, in knee-jerk fashion, make such statements as "they were engaged in eating behavior" rather than simply "they ate." But the real culprit behind the devitalization of psychological language is the contemporary emphasis on objectivity in the scientific method. Experiments are conducted, statistics are analyzed, results are obtained. God forbid there should be an "I," a real flesh and blood person with feelings and biases who is the subject of these actions! No! The impression is that all these scientific feats emanate from some unseen force, from a disembodied, ethereal knowledge that lies beyond human foible.

The wind again drew my attention outside. The sky, mottled with shades of dark and light, seemed like a giant reflective canopy that paralleled the textures of the wooded landscape. For an almost imperceptible moment, my mind flashed on the image of wandering barefoot through a snow-drifted forest.

I quickly opened my notebook and thumbed through the pages. Hoping to lose myself in that odyssey of ideas, I reviewed the last entry:

※　　※　　※

What is the psychotherapist? A mirror, a shadow, a barometer, a good parent? Like a mirror, he reflects back to the patient what he sees occurring before him — how the patient is thinking, feeling, and acting in the present moment — a mirror that magnifies the subtle clues to the unconscious, boosts self-awareness, and solidifies the patient's identity by confirming the feelings that others ignored and the patient himself may have denied. Like a shadow, the therapist deliberately remains ambiguous. He does not discuss his personal life, his religious or political beliefs, or his true opinions of the patient. He becomes an elusive, mysterious figure whom the patient, out of a natural human need to identify people, shapes according to his expectations, fears and desires. The therapist draws out and intensifies the patient's tendency to recreate and relive relationships from the past, usually with parents. But the therapist at times may also need to be a real person, in fact, a substitute parent who offers what the patient needed as a child but never received — encouragement, recognition, acceptance, nurturance, even love. Almost always, the therapist is a barometer that senses the interpersonal impact of the patient. By measuring her own thoughts and feelings in reaction to the patient, she gains insight into the patient's world. Angry when manipulated, bored when flooded with idle talk, anxious when invaded by psychotic ravings, she attempts to master these emotional reverberations as a pathway to understanding the patient. A thin line divides disaster from success, for these feelings can easily sabotage her work.

A bit melodramatic, but not bad for a day's work. I felt inside my knapsack, searching for a pen, but couldn't find one. That's odd — I always have a pen somewhere. Sitting with perfect posture at the table behind me, a man sporting wire-rimmed glasses and a cleanly pressed lab coat was reading the New York Times. He looked so intent on his digest that I felt uneasy about interrupting him.

"Excuse me, can I borrow a pen?"

Without looking up, he glided his hand to the plastic holder inside his breast pocket, selected a black Bic from the array of pens and pencils, and extended it to me. Incredibly accurate manual dexterity! A surgeon, no doubt.

"Thanks!"

I turned to a fresh page. It stared back at me, blank and indifferent — a tabula rasa waiting to be molded by my thoughts and desires. It's not easy converting nothing into something. I marked down three asterisks. Never did like using dates to begin my entries. After twirling the pen for a few thoughtful revolutions, I dove into the page:

＊　＊　＊

Why do people become psychologists, psychiatrists, or for that matter any kind of psychotherapist? What attracts them to such a complex, ambiguous task as insight therapy? With the exception of some psychiatrists and psychologists in high-fee private practice, most people are not going to get rich in this profession. Most psychotherapists are grossly underpaid, which says something about how our culture views mental health. Some might say they enjoy helping people. This may indeed be true, but it can be an oversimplification. Some therapists might find it easier trying to overcome the suffering or emptiness of their patients than to confront their own. Some might have grown up as the "helper" in their family, cast into that precarious role of advisor and mediator among siblings and parents, expected to soothe emotional turmoil while holding their own feelings at bay. For them, psychotherapy comes second nature; it is simply an extension of their interpersonal style, only now they call it "work" and get paid for it. Others become therapists because they thrive on the status and power. If people come to you for advice, you must be wise. If they are sick, you must be healthy. If they expect to be cured, you must possess some healing magic. It's a kind of omnipotence, perhaps a compensation for deeper feelings of helplessness. Psychotherapy also lets them peek into the most intimate areas of a person's life, which can satisfy the voyeur in almost anyone.

The feeling that someone was watching broke my concentration. Sure enough, the physician next to me was peering over the top edge of his paper, his eyes focused intently on my mouth. I quickly realized I had been chewing on his pen. I pulled it out from my teeth and smiled self-consciously. He lowered his eyes into his paper and continued reading. As I grabbed my coffee cup I noticed that it was almost empty. I wasn't aware of how fast I was drinking. A little oral today, aren't we Dr. Holden?

I reread what I had just written. No wonder the oral tension! What was I really trying to get at here? Behind the intellectualizing I was wrestling with a personal question: Why did I, Thomas Holden, become a psychotherapist, and a psychoanalytic one at that?

All during elementary and secondary school I loved science, or maybe I just thought so because I excelled in those courses, which everyone considered very important in those days. I frequently imagined myself as a biologist, or physicist, or in my more romantic moods, an Antarctic geologist. In my first year at college — which was one of those large, dehumanizing universities — I was quickly swept up by pre-med fever. Every day, with a calculator strapped to my belt and a lump in my throat, I scurried from calculus to biochemistry to physics, all the way scholastically pushing and shoving other students for my chance to bask in the fleeting light of the almighty "A". Most of the time I succeeded, but gradually the grades lost their power to satisfy me. I grew bored and frustrated with the so-called hard sciences. Despite the impressive scientistic jargon, they really provided no definitive answers. Like Tantalus, I felt that I was being teased by the promise of a complete explanation, an illusion that slipped away from my fingers each time I reached out for it. Take physics, for example. What exactly is energy? What is the essence of matter? Physicists don't know for sure. They keep slicing up the atomic pie into smaller and smaller parts. They aren't even sure if matter is fundamentally discrete or continuous, an entity or a quality, which is not much of an improvement over the ancient Greeks who debated the same issue.

Before and after class, during office hours, and in chance meetings on campus, I bombarded my professors with questions. At first they were delighted that an intelligent student took such an interest in their field. But then they felt cornered by my insistence on a definitive answer. They tried to ward me off with deliberately abstruse explanations. They tried to placate me with facile diversions like "More research is needed" or "It's just a theory." Eventually, they wouldn't answer their door when they heard my knock.

At the end of my freshman year my father died. My mother found him in the backyard lying next to the lawn mower, its blades still spinning as the motor hummed away, indifferent to the fateful situation. His death was quite unexpected, even though heart attacks are not uncommon for a Holden. A torrent of emotions overwhelmed my family, except for me. I was aware of having them, but they seemed faded, distant, as if part of me was standing back and observing them in someone else. No matter how hard I tried, I was unable to attach myself to what was happening.

That summer, not knowing what to do with myself, I decided to take a course in psychology. In retrospect I see that it was also an act of quiet, bridled desperation — an attempt to understand my problems, to make sense out of my life. Little did I know that seeking personal help from an introductory psychology course is as productive as consulting Reader's Digest to find a cure for Alzheimer's.

But I did enjoy the course and in my sophomore year switched majors. I was enticed by psychology's paradox. Although it strives to be an objective science, it ultimately becomes entangled in the webs of subjective experience. Not exactly a science and not exactly an art, it teeters between the objective and the experiential, between the rational and irrational. The word "psychology" itself fascinates me. Break it down into its component parts: It's the study of the "psyche" that translates from Greek into "mind," "soul," or "spirit." Ironically, psychologists would shudder at the thought that they study the soul or spirit. Souls are not very scientific. Many psychologists — mostly the hardcore behaviorists — would even reject the idea that they study the "mind." You can't see the mind; it can't be examined objectively, so why bother studying it at all. Maybe it doesn't even exist. All that exists, all that is observable, is behavior. Mind is just some kind of ghostly epiphenomenon. Psychology, they claim with pride, is the study of BEHAVIOR. Of course, some psychologists still want to study things that happen inside the head, and they still want to say that their work is objective and scientific, so they stretch the definition by claiming that mental processes are a type of behavior — which, to me, seems silly. You can't have your cake and eat it too.

I remember reading somewhere — though I can't remember where — that another Greek translation of "psyche" is "butterfly."

In the back of my head an alarm sounded. Ticking silently, my internal clock had been marking the passage of time. My watch confirmed the warning: two minutes until my next appointment. I stuffed the journal into my knapsack and sucked down the remaining cool drops of coffee. As I stood up I heard the surgeon politely clearing his throat. Hidden behind the financial section, he extended his hand towards me, palm up. Suddenly realizing the meaning of this gesture, I placed the pen in his hand. "Thanks!" I said.

"A writer without a pen is like a surgeon without a scalpel," he casually commented as he slipped the pen back into its appointed home in his pocket.

"Although I would be more careful about chewing on a scalpel," I added playfully.

He sighed. "Neither a borrower nor a lender be," he muttered to himself as he turned the page of his paper.

Alone in the elevator, I drifted back to thinking about my journal. If it survived the onslaughts of time, what fate awaited it once I, its creator, sloughed off this mortal cocoon. Perhaps one day a weary antique dealer will discover it hidden behind a secret panel in an old rickety desk. The faded scribbling will be meaningless to him, but by an odd twist of fate the notebook will fall into the hands of an historian. Fascinated by this unique find, he delves obsessively into the writings to fully comprehend this mind that reaches out to him from the past. He spends weeks in the library sifting through old journals, searching for clues to the identity of this obscure writer. A reference here, a footnote there, piece by piece he reconstructs the puzzle. In a dream the vision comes to him. The message is clear, the insight profound. Retrieved from limbo, a new psychology is born. He becomes My Biographer who writes a book that catapults me, his ancestral mentor, and himself to fame.

I'm not holding my breath. Nevertheless, it's interesting to speculate about how future generations will review my life and work, should I attain a status worthy of review. I pictured the entry on Thomas D. Holden in a yet to be published version of Who's Who in Psychology. I tried to imagine what it would say:

> "Thomas D. Holden, clinical psychologist,
> major contribution in the area of… of…"

I drew a blank. As I stood there, perplexed by my temporary inability to anticipate my life, the elevator doors opened. The demands of the present were calling me.

CHAPTER 5

Patients

"Mr. Tennostein is looking for you." Marion stepped into the elevator as I stepped out. I grabbed the rubber bumpers to prevent the doors from closing.

"Is he O.K.?"

"Irritable as usual, but O.K. He says you forgot his appointment."

"I told him we would meet at 9:30."

"How many times did you tell him?"

We laughed, but Marion was mostly serious. The elevator doors tugged at my hand, reminding me to expedite this conversation. "Did you call the Department of Transportation?"

"Yes," Marion sighed, "and finally got connected to someone in the central office. He said the only way to revoke his license is to get a signed statement from a psychiatrist saying he is psychologically incompetent to drive."

"So be it. Do you want to tell him?" I crossed my fingers. Another tug from the dutiful doors.

"I think you should," she said and then smiled. "Be gentle, but straightforward with him. You can do it."

I let go of the doors and she disappeared. "Well, this is going to be an interesting morning," I informed the elevator.

While I hurried towards the unit I rehearsed what I would say to Mr. Tennostein. Head first, I crashed directly into the metal doors. They were locked!

"What the hell is going on?!" I muttered. No sooner did I start rubbing my insulted cranium than the doors opened. His bulbous belly, which strained at the buttons of his green work shirt and spilled over his belt, preceded him. It was our janitor Phil, screwdriver in hand. "I'm working on this cursed lock again," he announced in his typically jovial manner. "I'll spend the rest of my life trying to fix it."

"So I've noticed," I replied, still massaging my bump.

"Sorry about that! But look at it this way," he said paternally. "This here lock is just trying to do you a favor. It's trying to protect you from what's inside, trying to prevent you from going in there and worrying yourself too much. It's a form of stress management." He hesitated a moment, then laughed uproariously from his belly. He always got a kick out of himself. I, on the other hand, was not amused.

"Only joking," he continued once he calmed down. He held the door open for me. "Go ahead. Better you than me."

The unit hummed with activity. Nurses were dispensing the morning medications and some of the patients were assembling for a group therapy session. Across the room a thin, hunched-over man waved feebly at me. I circled around the periphery of the unit as he walked towards me with his awkward, prancing gait. Our trajectories intersected at one of the library cubicles where I motioned for him to sit down.

"Hi Mr. Tennostein."

"I've been looking for you," he said tensely. "I thought you forgot our appointment."

He looked terrible. He was only 56 but you could easily mistake him for 90. The shaking in his hands had spread to his arms and head. His sunken face and darkened eye sockets reminded me of pictures of concentration camp survivors. This man was no victim of war, but he had lived through his own nightmarish holocaust.

"I thought I said we would meet at 9:30," I said gently, hoping to prod his memory.

"You said 9:15," he replied angrily. "What, do you think I'm stupid or something?"

This wasn't going to be easy. I knew I must help him see how serious his problem was, but denial is way more than a river in Egypt. It's a very powerful and stubborn defense mechanism, especially in patients with severe cognitive disorders. Usually you can't attack the defense directly: that only intensifies it. But you sometimes can work your way around it.

"No, of course you're not stupid. In fact, just the opposite is true. Perhaps it was my mistake. I'm sorry for the confusion, and I don't blame you for being annoyed."

Some of the indignation drained from his face. He settled back into his chair. A serious breach in rapport had been averted, at least for the moment.

"How about we continue with what we were talking about yesterday," I continued, "about why you came to this hospital."

He immediately dove into the explanation I had heard many times before. But for him it was still fresh. "I didn't want to come here. My wife made me. She's the one who said I was doing strange things. I know I wasn't. I'd be just fine if people would let me be."

"Hm, like what kind of strange things did your wife talk about — I mean your ex-wife. You were divorced what — about five months ago?"

His eyes rapidly shifted back and forth in his head as his mind tried to connect to the forgotten fact that his wife had left him. "Yeah, yeah, about five months," he said hesitantly.

"Right. And what kind of strange things did she say you were doing?"

"I never hurt her. I never laid a hand on her. I've always tried to be a good husband. I never wanted to hurt anyone! I mean, sometimes I would break things when I was drinking, but that was an accident."

"Yeah," I injected quickly, "I'm glad you mentioned that. It's interesting that you would accidentally break things when you were drinking, like the alcohol was affecting your balance, or your coordination, or maybe even the way you were seeing things. It reminds me of what you were telling me yesterday — about what would happen after you were drinking, when you were drying out. About the spells."

"I don't know what you're talking about."

"Remember, we were sitting over there by the nurse's station, and you told me how sometimes your thinking gets a little bit confused, how you lose track of things?"

"You mean when I get squirrely?"

"That's right. When you get squirrely."

Finally a loophole! A way past his defenses! But will it close up too fast? Be sure to stay close to his line of thought. Use his language. "Tell me again," I continued, "what is it like when you get squirrely?"

"I feel squirrely, I… I'm not sure. Things seem confusing. Like that time I was looking for my car in that parking lot, at the mall. Damn if I couldn't find it. Those lots are so damn big. I still think someone moved it on me, probably some teenagers playing a practical joke."

"You were walking around the parking lot for an hour or so, weren't you?"

"Oh, it couldn't have been that long." He squinted while he paused to think. "I sat down for a while to rest. I read my book for a while too."

A confabulation. He was fishing for answers to fill in the gaps in his memory. I decided to push ahead. "You know, Mr. Tennostein, this is exactly the kind of thing that I think we need to help you with — these episodes when you get squirrely, like at the mall. We've got to make sure that you don't go through things like that anymore. I'm sure it was very confusing and upsetting for you. We've got to find out what's causing these episodes and how to control them. We have to make sure that you're safe."

"Yeah, I guess..."

"Some people have spells like that. And like you they don't always remember what happens during them. In fact, I think you might have had a spell the first night you were here, two nights ago. You were probably a little nervous about being in the hospital, and that triggered it. You walked around and around the unit, then you went into the shower with all your clothes on. Do you remember that?"

"I remember... being wet..." A realization slowly dawned on him. He looked troubled. This could be the turning point.

"How often do you think these spells happen?"

"I don't know. It's only happened once or twice. Damned if I know what causes it. Probably just fatigue. I'll be fine if I could just get out of here and get a good night's sleep in my own bed."

"We're not sure either about what's causing the spells. We were talking about it in team yesterday. Dr. Sheikh said he thinks it's something called transient global amnesia. Basically, that means that every once in a while the brain, well, sort of short circuits. Sometimes being excited or under stress will trigger it. The person may become disoriented and not know what he's doing. It might be caused by some deterioration in brain tissue."

"You mean my brain is rotting?"

"I wouldn't quite put it that way. Sometimes the damage is very subtle. We need to do some tests to find out."

"What kind of tests?" he asked skeptically.

"We want to call in a neurologist for a consult. He'll do an exam on you. We'd also like to have a catscan done. That's sort of like a multiple series of x-rays that —"

"I know what a catscan is," he interjected. His hands were shaking again. "How could something like this happen? What does that to the brain?"

"No one knows for sure. It may be in part hereditary. The brain ages in everyone. It atrophies as you get older. In some families the aging occurs faster."

"I remember my father being senile," he said thoughtfully, "he'd say the damnedest things."

"That makes sense. And now that we know you're having these spells, we should do everything we can to control and even prevent them. For instance, since your drinking seems to trigger them, one thing we can do is to help you to stop drinking. I would recommend that you join AA."

"Forget it," he said angrily, "My drinking isn't any big problem, and besides, I can quit myself."

"It's not easy to quit yourself. Maybe you've even tried before, so you know how hard it is." I paused. His defenses were springing back, but I felt I had to go further. He had come far in this session. I may not have another chance like this.

"But we can talk about that later," I continued. "There's something else I wanted to talk to you about. Something more immediately important. These spells you've been having could be dangerous. What if you had one when you were driving your car? You've already had a few fender-benders. You were lucky. Or what if you had a spell while you were cooking. You might accidentally burn yourself or start a fire. You need to live in a place where people can help you, where it's safe for you. There are some homes you could move to. We can —"

"No! I'm not going to any home," he replied loudly. "Never!"

"Then maybe we can help you find someone to cook for you, or deliver hot food to your house. If you continue to live at home, it would be a good idea to have a visiting nurse to stop in each day to check on you, or even a nurse to live with you, if you can afford it."

"I don't need a baby-sitter. I can handle my own life."

"Of course! There are lots of things you can still handle. There will be lots of things in your life that won't change at all — that will even get better, like learning how to control those spells. But you'll need help with some things. And there are some things you shouldn't be doing because we have to make sure you're safe. As I said, it's dangerous for you to drive. I know it will take some adjusting of your life, but you should stop driving."

"Forget it! How would I get around, go to the bank, or to the stores to buy things. No, I won't give up driving. Absolutely not!" The tremors in his hands set off a twitching in my guts. I forced myself to continue.

"You can have friends drive you, or take buses, or taxis. We'll help you make arrangements. Who knows, you might enjoy not having to worry about a car anymore."

Desperation gripped his face. His eyes were tense and red. "No! I won't give up my car. I can drive. I can! And I don't even have to cook. My wife can cook for me. She's cooked for me all these years, and cleaned, and did the shopping. I don't need no busses or nursemaids!"

For a brief moment, I almost believed him. I wanted to believe him. Then our eyes connected and our hearts sank together as the unfortunate truth sprang forward into our minds. He had no wife — not anymore.

He leaned forward, burying his face into his hands, and began to cry.

"Why! Why has this happened?" he moaned.

I rose from my chair to put my hand on his shoulder. "We'll do everything we can to help you," I said softly in an attempt to soothe him. "Maybe we'll call your ex-wife. Maybe she can help in some way." A sadness welled up inside me. Beneath it there was this strange squirmy feeling.

"Please leave me alone," he replied as his crying subsided.

"I think it would be good for us to talk some more."

"I just want to go to my room. Please, let me be alone."

Without looking at me he struggled to his feet and hobbled away. For a moment I considered following him, then decided against it. Still fluttering inside, I walked to the nursing station and pulled down his chart. As I thumbed through the pages I thought about the question that issued from his pain. Why did this happen to you, Mr. Tennostein? I don't know. Heredity, parenting, socialization, historical context, biological and psychological predispositions, karma. Who can explain the complex set of factors that intersect at one point to shape a person's fate? Do we ever really make a choice, or are we simply pushed around by a bewildering mishmash of causes and effects.

"How did it go?" Marion asked as she entered the nursing station. She was holding a cup of tea.

"I finally got through to Tennostein. You know, it's very ironic. Ten years ago this guy was doing O.K. Sure, he had a problem with drinking and he surely wasn't the most psychologically healthy man on earth. But he was married, he had a good job as a teacher, and as far as we can tell from the psychological testing, he used to be well above average in intelligence. Then fate catches up to him. He's forced to retire early because he's not performing as well as he used to. The bottle becomes his new occupation. He grows depressed, angry and abusive. His wife leaves him. Finally it's obvious that his brains are falling apart. He's no longer above average in intelligence. He starts thinking "Alzheimers." All of a sudden he's hanging onto life by a thread, too terrified to see how terrified he is. Then I come along. Mr. Young Psychologist. And what do I do? I try to get him to confront that terror. I try to get him to see how his mind and his life are failing."

"Don't think of it as failing," Marion said. "He sank so deep into his problems that he couldn't pull himself out. He needs help. He needs you. And your job is to help him see his situation as clearly as he can without overwhelming him — and to give him some hope, something worth living for."

"But is there hope, or is that just our defense to help us feel better? What can we really do for this poor guy? He's on the decline. We can't reverse the damage in his brain. If anything, it will get worse. Who knows, it very well could be Alzheimer's."

"Then you must help him confront what's ahead," she answered calmly. "Confront it with strength and dignity, if he can. And if not, then you've done all you can do."

"I guess," I mumbled.

Marion patted me lightly on the back and walked away. I finished writing my progress notes and returned the chart to the shelf. No time to dwell on it. I had to move on to my next patient. Spinning slowly on my swivel stool I scanned the unit. Kathy was nowhere in sight. I walked briskly around the perimeter, checking each room as I passed by.

Have you seen Kathy Mummon?" I asked one of the medical students standing by the coffee pot.

"I think she went out on a pass with Barb," he said while he awkwardly ripped open a new bag of styrofoam cups, spilling half of them all over the floor. "Damn it! Nothing is going right today."

"Welcome to the club," I answered. I helped him pick up the cups, then went back to the nursing station to check the sign-in sheet. Kathy and Barb were due back any minute. As I walked towards the door I saw them coming down the hallway. I swung open the door so Barb could help Kathy steer in.

"Are we late?" Barb asked with surprise. "We tried to make it back in time for your appointment."

"No, you're right on time," I replied.

Kathy drove her motorized wheelchair through the doorway, running over my toes as she passed by. Her startled eyes darted up to look at me. "Oh! Was that your foot? I'm sorry Dr. Holden. Are you alright?"

"Fine," I replied as I grimaced. Motorized wheelchairs are heavier than you would imagine. "Just grazed me... So, how are you doing, Kathy?"

"O.K., I guess."

"She's doing great," Barb added bubbly. "We went all the way around to the other side of the hospital and back. She's doing much better with her hand."

"Turning into a regular hot-rodder, huh?" I said. Kathy giggled.

"Would you mind if I joined you two today," Barb asked.

"No, not at all. Let's go to Kathy's room to talk." We followed behind the wheelchair as Kathy buzzed around the perimeter of the unit.

Kathy was a quadriplegic. After her high school prom she went for a ride on a motorcycle with one of the restaurant busboys. She was a very emotional, uninhibited young woman. Some would say carefree. We psychologists would call it "impulsive." Under the influence of alcohol — as on the night of the prom — her histrionics escalate to the point of melodrama. I'm sure she was the life of the party, more life than the party could handle. So she, in her chiffon dress, and Ronaldo, in his busboy whites, left to cruise around town for an hour or so, then parked at Lover's Heights over the beach. Ronaldo didn't get very far that dark night, but Kathy fell from the cliffs. She would have drowned if he hadn't pulled her away from the incoming tide. Intensive therapy at a local hospital succeeded in helping her recover partial use of her right arm. Despite this modest physical progress, her psychological condition deteriorated rapidly. She became depressed and withdrawn. She feared the devil was plotting to kidnap her. At night she heard men's voices in her closet. The staff quickly decided to ambulance her over to us for psychiatric treatment.

Barb and I followed Kathy into her room and sat down on the edge of the bed. After a few bumps into the furniture, Kathy managed to maneuver the wheelchair around to face us. She seemed better, almost cheerful. Within two weeks after her admission the medications had succeeded in alleviating her depression. Her hallucinations and delusional thinking also lost much of their steam. Soon after her arrival Fred concluded that the psychotic symptoms were caused by the depression and that antidepressant medications, rather than major tranquilizers, were needed. It looked like he was right. Sometimes making a differential diagnosis between depression and psychosis is a chicken-or-egg dilemma: being severely depressed can culminate in hallucinations and delusions; suspecting you're crazy can make you depressed.

"So, Kathy, you seem to be making progress," I said.

"I feel better," she replied, "at least better than when I first got here."

"She's doing great," Barb interjected. "We were joking around and laughing before. And she's been talking to some of the patients, making friends. She and Rachel had a nice chat last night. And this afternoon we're going to do your hair. Right?"

Yeah," Kathy agreed. "And Barb said I might be able to go to the movies this week, with the other patients. I'd like that. I'm sick of being cooped up in this place."

"That's a possibility," I said, "although Barb and I will have talk to the team about that. A pass off the unit is a big step. How did you sleep last night?"

"Fine."

"Didn't have a hard time falling asleep, or wake up during the night?"

"No."

"Didn't hear any voices?"

"No," she said cautiously as she glanced towards Barb. "I haven't heard those for a while. I was under a lot of stress."

"That's right," Barb added. "She's been sleeping straight through the night without any problems. And she hasn't had any anxiety attacks since that one last week."

"Great," I said after hesitating. "I also wanted to ask you if you still have any thoughts about hurting yourself."

"Not really."

"Not really? I'm not sure what that means."

"It means… not really. I mean, I guess the thought does cross my mind once in a while, but I don't take it seriously. I wouldn't actually do it, or anything like that. I mean, how could I even do it? I hardly think about it at all."

She avoided making eye contact with me. Her fingers danced nervously on the control lever for the wheelchair. After a long sigh, she closed her eyes.

"You seem tired," Barb said. "That long walk, I mean ride probably wore you out. It might be a good idea to take a nap sometime today."

"Yeah, a nap," Kathy replied as she opened one eye. "That'd be great."

"The reason why I asked about your hurting yourself," I interjected, "is that it's important to talk about. When you first came here you were troubled by suicidal thoughts. You were under a lot of stress. It would be perfectly understandable if you still felt a little depressed. What's important is that we talk about it if you start thinking about —"

The wheelchair suddenly lunged forward. Barb and I jumped. The wheels barely missed her ankle, but my funny bone received a smart rap from the chair's armrest. It couldn't have been a more perfect shot to the nerve. A wave of tingling fire rippled through my arm. The pen dropped from my hand.

"Oh shit!" Kathy yelled. "I accidentally hit the lever. I can't believe I did that!"

"Are you O.K.?" Barb asked.

"Yeah, I'm O.K.," I sputtered. "Nothing a few push-ups couldn't cure." The burning sensation turned to pins-and-needles. Slightly paralyzed, I had trouble picking up the pen.

"I'm really sorry, Dr. Holden," Kathy continued. "I'm such a jerk. I have to learn how to work this thing better."

"Practice will make perfect," I replied. My aching arm was distracting me. "So, what were we talking about?"

"I don't remember," Kathy quickly answered, "but there is something I wanted to ask you."

"What's that?"

"When am I going to be discharged?" she asked politely, but very intent on my answer.

"Well, we have to talk about that some more. You haven't been here that long, and we want to make sure you're safe before we discharge you."

"Oh! I don't want to be discharged."

"You don't?" I echoed quizzically. "Just a minute ago you were saying that you're feeling good, and that you want an outside pass. But you don't think you're ready to go home?"

"Oh, I'm ready to go home, it's just that I don't want to. You know, I mean I sort of like it here sometimes. I like the people, I'll miss them when I leave. Everyone has been pretty good to me. It's nice here, well, nicer than home."

"Nicer than home?"

"I think she means her family," Barb said with sympathy in her voice. "She and her mother have been having problems. Isn't that so?"

Kathy's face flushed. She began fidgeting with the control lever again. I folded my arms, cupping my hand to protect my elbow.

"Yeah, my mother and I are always at it. She just won't leave me alone, always telling me what to do. I wish she would just get off my back. I'm 18 years old, not a baby anymore. Like yesterday, she was in here bothering me about being in the hospital. I don't know how long I'll be here. It's not my fault! She doesn't even really care about me coming home, so maybe I won't. When I get out of here I'll go somewhere else, I'll… I'll…"

She gasped for air, as if choking on her own thoughts. Her eyes shifted back and forth, searching frantically for an answer. But within seconds she jammed. Her eyes froze, then fluttered and rolled back into her head. Her arm dropped from the chair and hung limply at her side.

"I'm dizzy, everything's… spinning. I think I'm gonna be sick."

Barb sprang forward to put her arms around Kathy's shoulders. "Take it easy. Just relax and you'll be O.K. Breathe slowly and deeply, in and out, slowly… that's good." She looked up at me, "I think maybe we should stop now."

"I think you're right," I answered. I reached forward and placed my hand on Kathy's arm. "I know it's hard talking about these things. Your life is hard right now, and it's scary not knowing what's going to happen in the future. But we'll talk about this, we'll help you sort things out."

Kathy, with her eyes closed, remained withdrawn and silent. I wasn't sure if she was listening. After what seemed like a long pause, I decided to break the silence. "I'll stop in later to see how you're doing."

"I'll stay for a few minutes," Barb said as I stood up.

I nodded. "Let's talk later."

"Thank you, Dr. Holden," Kathy called out to me as I approached the door. I smiled back, and left.

I felt bad. Perhaps I shouldn't have pushed her on the issue about suicide. But I was worried about her. Despite the fact that she had improved, my guts told me that her high spirits were very brittle, that beneath the facade she was still very fragile and possibly even suicidal. Should I leave it alone, or explore it? That's an ongoing question in this inpatient work. During the short time that patients are here, our primary goal is to stabilize them with medications and supportive therapy so they can get out and back to their life. If you accomplish that much, the icing on the cake is to help them recognize their underlying psychological sore spots which are not treatable by medications. Some of those sensitive issues may have been developing over the course of many years. They've become deeply embedded in their psyche. The patient needs to confront these problems, but forcing them to do so now may just make them worse. Is it wise to open up a can a worms?

It could take years of therapy to work out those problems. I was slowly coming to the conclusion that we treat some very serious problems with band-aids. We try to patch up the surface wounds and then send people along their way — but the hidden, deeper sickness often remains untouched, and will, inevitably, come back to haunt the person.

As I finished up my progress notes, I saw Barb cautiously walking towards me. She bit her lip, then smiled. I knew what was bothering her.

"Did I push her a little too much?" I asked.

"Well, I feel sorry for Kathy," she answered apologetically. "She's trying as hard as she can. Don't you think we need to encourage her more, let her know she's doing O.K.?"

"Yeah, you're right. For one thing, we need to encourage her to plan for the future. She feels very protected and supported here — which is both good and bad. The bad part is that she can't stay here forever. We have to help her learn how to fend for herself."

"She needs help dealing with her mother," Barb said. "I really doubt that she can face going home unless we do something to help them. I'm not exactly sure what's gone wrong in their relationship, but Kathy is very angry with her. She says she feels smothered."

"Smothered? I bet she feels smothered in a lot of ways. Just think of it. We have here a teenager, a girl who's used to impulsive acting out, being wild and unruly — and all of a sudden she's a quadriplegic, completely paralyzed. Her old style of dealing with her conflicts won't work any more. Literally, she can't run away from her feelings. She's forced to just sit here, stewing in them. It's no wonder she became psychotic and suicidal. She feels totally helpless."

Barb seemed to be thinking intently. "So what can we do to help her?" she asked.

I sighed. "Well, with a really good outpatient psycho-therapist in addition to her physical therapy, who knows how far she could go. I've heard there's a really excellent psychologist at Hillside who specializes in working with patients with neurological problems. We should give him a call."

"So what's the intense discussion going on here?" a voice interjected from over my shoulder. Marion could smell problems at fifty paces, particularly when her teammates or patients were involved. She always intended to help, and usually did.

"I was telling Barb about Correll at Hillside Hospital," I said. "He'd be the perfect referral for Kathy when she's discharged, don't you think?"

"Yes, he'd be excellent. But you might as well forget him," Marion said matter-of-factly. "He's a first rate psychologist with first rate fees. Kathy could never afford it."

"She has insurance, doesn't she?" Barb asked.

"No. Last night I spoke to Mrs. Mummon. She was very embarrassed about the whole thing, but she finally told me about her financial situation. Neither she nor Kathy have any kind of insurance. I'm not even sure how Kathy's hospitalization here will be paid for. They're living in poverty. Their one room apartment has no heat, they sleep on an old mattress on the floor. About all they eat is pasta and corn flakes. A year ago Mr. Mummon disappeared. Mrs. Mummon took a job to try to support the family and pay off the loans he left behind. She quit a few months later, so she didn't qualify for unemployment. They have welfare, but that's about it."

"Why did she quit her job?" I asked.

"She's a high school dropout. The only job she could find was cleaning toilets at the bus station — the night shift — with addicts, muggers, and perverts to keep her company. She hated it."

I twirled the pen between my fingers, thinking about how impossible this situation was for Kathy. What, if anything, could psychology do for her? As I started to speak, the phone rang. Barb answered it, then handed it to me. "It's the police!" she whispered.

"The police?" Not knowing what to expect, I cautiously held the receiver to my ear. The sergeant's matter-of-fact voice on the other end was clear enough. Technically, the phone worked just fine. But his words rang hollow and unreal, as if their meaning had dropped out the bottom. When he finished his explanation, I mumbled something in reply and hung up without saying good-bye. Marion and Barb were studying my face.

"What is it?" Marion said.

How can I say it? My face felt like rubber. My voice was flat. "Elizabeth was hit by a car this morning. She's dead. The police wondered if it was suicide."

"Oh my god!" Marion murmured. Barb's face sank, her eyes filled with tears. As Marion put an arm around her shoulder, I looked away. Their voices faded somewhere into the distance. Time and space flattened out. Across the room Phil still labored with the door.

"Are you O.K.?" Barb asked after an indeterminate amount of time.

"Yes, I guess. I have to get back to work."

Marion touched me on the arm. "Stop by my office later," she said. "We should talk." As she walked away I reached for Elizabeth's chart on the "To Be Filed" shelf. Sitting in a hidden corner of the nurse's station, I wrote the addendum to her progress notes.

"Progress," I muttered to myself.

A distorted face stared back at me from the metallic coffee cup by my elbow. I tilted my head from left to right in a futile attempt to straighten out that head.

CHAPTER 6

Wandering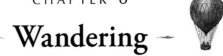

MAYBE SOMEDAY I WILL TRAVEL. I always loved stories about wanderers. I guess lots of people do. And where or how the protagonist roams doesn't seem to matter — ballooning to famous cities around the world, driving the back roads across one's homeland, or hiking mystical mountains in faraway hemispheres. The adventure of exploring new lands never fails to fascinate. But something else about the wanderer, something more illusive than travelogue storytelling, entices me. It's the essence of wandering, of drifting from place to place, from experience to experience, without any specific agenda in mind. No rhyme or reason shapes the path taken, at least not anything conscious. The impetus is more subtle, hidden, more powerful. I think of it as an instinct, an intrinsic urge to uproot from the familiarities of home and throw oneself into unpredictable circumstances. Free of responsibilities, possessions, and plans, free of careers and loved ones, where do you go? Do you choose a path or does the path choose you? You are driven by a need to search without knowing what you are searching for, or searching but for no thing in particular.

I am tempted to say this instinct belongs to everyone. For some people, perhaps most, it lies dormant. In others it springs to the forefront of their life, triggered by some cata-strophic crisis or by the building pressure of mundane living that frustrates the spirit. When I think of how fundamental this instinct must be, I am reminded of Jung. He said that all humans share a reservoir of ancient ideas and themes that have been passed down from one generation to the next, for thousands of years, perhaps since the dawn of humankind. These archetypical thought-patterns, the templates of human wisdom, manifest themselves most clearly in dreams, ancient myth, and ritual. They are guidelines for living, suggestions on how to be, that have been so valuable that they have become permanently etched into human consciousness. They are the universal psychological themes that transcend cultural and historical boundaries, and that Jung recognized in the hallucinatory babblings of his psychotic patients. Primitive people understood these archetypical images and used them freely. Modern people, blinded by science and rationality, have relegated them to the unconscious, only in dreams allowing them a fleeting chance before the naive mind's eye.

Maybe the image of the wanderer is such an archetype. Sooner or later, it calls to all of us. Then again, maybe not. Maybe this stuff is adolescent, romanticized daydreaming. Maybe we just need to grow up, settle down, and admit there's nothing to find other than the revelations right in front of our noses. But what do we say to the wanderer when he comes knocking at our door? What happens to the wanderer who never attempts the road?

Someday I will do it.

Someday.

Everything is someday. Everything important, every-thing we think we want and need, seems to lie someday in our future, like an ethereal carrot suspended in front of our noses. We live for some future attainment — and when we get there, there's always some future attainment further down the line to take its place. Everything is a means to a means. We're constantly running and never reach the finish. We're weary, unhappy. And when we're not fixated on the future, we're stuck on the past, on some regret, sorrow, or longing. The past and the future don't even exist, but we're always preoccupied by them. We spend our lives hunting for ghosts.

What's wrong with the present moment? Isn't it enough?

That's what's so important about true wandering. There is no past or future, no destination, no running to or from. There's just wandering.

CHAPTER 7

Edibles

"HELLO IN THERE. Is anyone home?"

I sprang to attention, as if jolted from a deep sleep. For a second I wasn't sure where I was. "Huh?"

"I asked if you wanted to go to lunch," Bob said carefully, measuring each word. "A bunch of us are heading down there."

"Yeah, sure!" I answered without thinking. "I'll be down in a minute."

"Are you all right? You've been sitting here for a while, just staring into that chart."

My head cleared. "Yeah, I'm O.K. Just a lot of work to do. You know how it is."

"I heard about your patient. I'm really sorry."

"It was a shock," I answered as I turned away and closed the chart. "I still can't believe it. Anyway, go ahead to the cafeteria. I'll catch up in a minute."

Bob awkwardly shifted his weight from one leg to the other, waiting for something else to happen. When it didn't, he turned to leave. "See you later."

I appreciated Bob's concern. He was genuinely warm and empathic, much more so than the other medical students. He treated his patients like people rather than specimens. He preferred talking to them over diagnosing and medicating. Although obviously well-educated, almost a full-fledged doctor in fact, he seemed a bit young and naive. Maybe that's what worked to his advantage. Some of the other med students had been bred by their training to feel rather grandiose and omnipotent — smarter, more important, just plain better than ordinary people. Our medicine-idealizing culture, driven by unconscious needs for an ultimate rescuer, helps elevate them to that exalted position. Then we turn around and get angry with them when they fail. It's all a defense against the fact that doctors, just like the rest of us, are helpless putty in the hands of life and death. The truth about being a medical student is that their training often lacks much glamour. They're at the bottom of the medical pecking order. They're often treated like second class citizens.

I suddenly noticed a twinge of pain in my throat, as if something sharp was stuck there. I swallowed hard. Yes, definitely a sore spot, just below my left ear. The first warning sign. Damn! I couldn't afford to get sick. I had too much work to do. As I swung my knapsack over my shoulder its contents rattled around inside. Hoping to avoid any of the staff, I hurried off the unit. Just outside the door Phil was poking his screw-driver into what looked like a partially dismantled lock.

"Sorry to hear about your patient," he said as I passed by.

Did everyone in the entire hospital already know? I tried to act casual. "I guess Marion told you about it."

"No," he answered, still fidgeting with the gadget in his hand. "I heard some of the nurses talking about it."

"I was very surprised to find out about it," I said flatly. "It was a shock."

He pointed the lock at me. "It's like I said. You never can predict what's going to happen in there. It's like the weather."

I felt irritated. "Yeah, right Phil. See you later."

I detoured to the men's room on the way to the elevator. At the urinal I read the graffiti on the wall — not that I needed to actually read those pearls of wisdom. After spending what must amount to hours of time standing in that one spot, I had unwillingly committed to memory every word, scratch, and discoloration on those tiles.

"Jesus Saves."

"She blinded me with science."

"Look up. Look down, the joke is in your hands!"

When I finished, I realized I was not finished. So little time, so much to do. In the stall the seat was cold. Perhaps I was its first occupant of the day. I sifted through the graffiti on the dividers, looking for some new inscription to take my mind off things. There was more literature here than above the urinals — I guess people felt freer in this hidden place to really let out all the crap — but it was the same old pornographic and bigoted comments. It's amazing how even the bathroom stalls in institutions of higher learning draw out the dregs in human nature. Freud was right: sex and aggression lurk right below the surface. Sitting here on this earthly throne, secure behind metal walls, otherwise civilized fellows allowed themselves to ventilate these inner tensions. In more ways than one, they tried to purge the private toxins that could not be metabolized.

I felt drained. With my eyes closed I leaned forward and dropped my head between my knees. My spine slowly stretched out, relaxing my entire body. I also tried to ease my brain, but my mind insisted on grasping at a flurry of thoughts. After a minute or so, I opened my eyes. There, on the round surface of the toilet, was some faded writing. The tiny letters were scratched in and inverted to accommodate an upside down reader, like myself. It read: "While alive, be a dead man."

I laughed out loud. Surely some patient had escaped from the unit and engraved his psychosis here. If that was true, how would he do it? Patients are not permitted sharp objects. I imagined some poor schizophrenic huddled over the toilet, desperately trying to record his delusions with a house key. A tormented Moses.

The bathroom door banged. Someone had entered. I listened. At first there was silence, then the soap dispenser pumping, rushing water, the ruffling of paper towels. Then silence again. I waited. Had he left?

Time ran out. I gave the roll of toilet paper a spin and prepared myself to leave. I took a deep breath as I zipped up and swung open the metal door.

I knew it! Standing in front of the mirror, carefully adjusting his tie, was Dr. Stein, Director of Psychiatry and internationally famous shrink. For a moment I thought of quietly slithering out, but that was impossible without being detected. I crossed my fingers. "Hello, Dr. Stein," I said meekly, hoping he wouldn't take notice of my identity. With his neck remarkably straight, he turned his head slightly in my direction. I was hoping for a smile or a friendly nod, but received none. Without his aristocratic expression changing one iota, he returned his gaze to the mirror. "Hello Dr. Holden," he said.

His odd accent on the word "doctor" made me uncomfortable. Technically speaking, I had finished my dissertation and was therefore entitled to so prefix my name. However, in an institution filled with MD's, people get very fussy about the definition of a "real" doctor. Then again, maybe I was just paranoid. After all, any formal title just doesn't seem to hold much water among toilet bowls and urinals. Here, regardless of status, we're all the same basic biological creature.

Having acknowledged his existence, thereby fulfilling the rudiments of etiquette, I tried to make my escape. As I reached for the door he spoke in a clear voice that reverberated off the tile walls. "I heard about your patient."

Oh shit! Another two seconds and I would have been long gone. I knew it was too good to be true.

"You mean about Elizabeth Baso?"

"I mean the patient whom you discharged — the one who died this morning."

"Yeah. It was a real shock to me. I still can't —"

"I believe we should talk about this during a staff meeting," he interrupted, still examining his tie in the mirror. "It's a rather, shall we say, unusual event."

In my head flashed an image of Stein hanging from the light fixture by his silk Bill Blass. "I think that's a good idea. I'd like to talk to the staff about it."

When he didn't answer, I assumed our tryst was over. The full interrogation would come later. Feeling shaken, I left. Although fogged in by my ever-expanding ruminations, I managed to find my way to the elevator. I rapped the "Down" button with my knuckle, and waited.

Even Stein knew. I could just imagine the gossip that was spreading. Suicide. Premature discharge. Poor clinical judgment. Insidious words that poison reputations like indigestible cancer. But it could not have been suicide. The depression had lifted by the time she left the unit. She definitely had improved. And besides, I wasn't the only one responsible for her discharge. The whole team made the decision. Even the attending physician must interview the patient and consent to the release... Look at me, defending myself as if I was already guilty!

I remembered Elizabeth's face just before she left. She smiled. Her dark eyes had lost their dull, languid stare. They connected with mine. "Thank you so much," she said. I felt touched.

My stomach sank. "It wasn't suicide," I mumbled, but I didn't fully believe myself.

"Going down?"

A smiling physician held his finger on the button while he beckoned me into the elevator. He smelled like formaldehyde and had a large plastic bag folded under his arm. As I thanked him and stepped inside, his grin widened. I quickly glanced at his plastic name tag. Wonderful! Of all the people in the world, I wind up in the elevator with Dr. Theodore Gilbert, the giddy coroner. Leaning my head against the wall behind me, I imagined the day when I would look back on all this and laugh. I imagined what my biographer would write:

> Holden experienced his internship as a trying period in his professional development. The tidy theories he learned as a graduate student crumbled under the pressures of clinical practice. Even the noblest of conceptual models floundered in a strong undercurrent of uncertainty. Psychology, the supposed science of predicting behavior, lacked precision. Traditional theories could not forecast all outcomes, not in real life circumstances and not even in the sterile confines of strict experimentation. These frustrations with the limits of conventional ideas catalyzed Holden's search for a more comprehensive explanatory paradigm.

Just a high-falutin' way of saying that I'm totally confused.

My nose dripped. "Damn!" I thought as I sniffed up the dribble. This was the sure sign of an impending cold. I knew that within half a day my whole head would clog, as if pumped full of oil sludge.

The elevator hit the ground floor and the doors popped open. Gilbert smiled as he gestured towards the way out. "After you," he said gleefully.

"Thank you," I answered politely. I was glad to get out of the elevator. He made me nervous.

The cafeteria was packed, which surprised me since it was still a bit early for lunch. Many people wore those cardboard name-tags inserted into plastic holders. The hospital probably was sponsoring some medical conference which broke early for some eats.

Someone was standing behind me. I spun around. It was Gilbert, looking past me, grinning. He had spotted some friends at a table across the room and walked past me to greet them. Good lord! A convention for coroners!

I zigzagged through the crowd towards the food counters. Considering we had a thousand years of higher education among us, we were rather primitive in our jostling for position. I accidentally elbowed someone in the stomach. In return, someone stepped on my foot. Food can bring out the worst in people. As bulimia and anorexia tell us.

A women was standing close in front of me. At first I paid no attention, but she swayed backwards slightly, almost touching me. A snap of static electric charge jumped from her wool sweater onto my arm. Suddenly I felt keenly aware of her presence. I could smell the fragrance of her hair, sense the curves of her body. Another Being, enticingly the same but also different — so close, but so very far. I tried to redirect my thoughts towards the food, but she pulled at my attention. She knew. I could sense her presence so acutely because she sensed mine. It was almost — intimate. Maybe it was just my imagination, or wishful thinking. But instinct told me otherwise.

Slowly, she turned her head to look over her shoulder, right into my eyes. My insides froze. If there was any psychological gap between us, it collapsed. Her eyes were large and deep brown. I could swear I saw myself in them, looking with her at myself.

The crowd moved. The bubble popped. She disappeared into a group of tall men wearing lab coats. Disoriented, I found myself shuffled forward towards the food counter. Curiously unaffected by the chaos before her, the kitchen aid with rotten teeth waved her ladle at me. "What'd ya like, sir?"

I tried to focus myself and quickly surveyed the options: liver floating in brown liquid, carrots and peas, greasy sausages, something unidentifiable, and... spaghetti. Eureka! That seemed safe enough.

"I'll take the spaghetti," I said confidently. As if anticipating my response she had already begun preparing my plate.

"Red Sauce?"

"Yes, please."

She lifted the cover off the tureen and dipped in her ladle. The sauce was rather loose, and more brown than red — no doubt close kin to the fluid drowning the liver. Holding a cup of hot coffee in one hand and a plate of sloppy spaghetti in the other, I parted the crowd like Moses slicing the Red Sea with his staff. "Why don't you use a tray?" someone grumbled. Watch out, I thought, or I'll use your shirt. When I reached a clearing, I looked around the cafeteria for that woman, but I couldn't see her. Near the windows some nurses and residents from the inpatient unit were eating at a round table. Somewhat hesitantly, I walked over to them and carefully laid down my lunch. A large chunk was broken off the edge of the table, which was going to be uncomfortable for my elbows. But there were no other places to sit. Barb smiled at me as I sat down next to her. The others were pretending to listen to Ron's monologue.

"… It's really a very straightforward process. First, you have to assess the patient's symptoms. You look for affective disturbances, motor disturbances, hallucinations, delusions, or other evidence of a thought disorder. The mental status exam will give you some of the data you need. You determine how the symptoms have affected the patient's level of functioning. Then you do a thorough history, and you pay special attention to the evidence of mental disorders in the family and relatives. That's always a dead give-away. The rest is easy. If you've done a careful assessment, you should have all the data you need to make an accurate diagnosis. Sure, it may take some additional information to fine-tune the diagnosis, but you should definitely be able to apply the major diagnostic categories, whether it's paranoid, disorganized, or catatonic schizophrenia, a unipolar or bipolar disorder, major depression, senile dementia, drug-induced psychosis, or whatever."

"Major depression IS unipolar disorder," I said to my spaghetti.

Ron pricked his ears and briefly darted his eyes towards me, but he didn't reply. With even more vigor he pushed ahead with his soliloquy. Eager for a receptive ear, he aimed his words at Bob. Med students are convenient targets for hot air.

"If you carefully read the DSM, you should be able to classify any mental disorder. It's a very comprehensive and accurate manual — much better than the earlier diagnostic systems, mostly because it includes both inclusion and exclusion criteria, which increases interjudge agreement. In fact, the DSM categories show high reliability and validity. I was just reading an article by Goldman in AJP, in the October issue, and he found correlations over .90 between DSM diagnoses of schizophrenia and independently obtained criterions involving various etiological and predictive variables."

Bob struggled to hold back a yawn, but Ron's verbiage seemed to make Carole's red hair stand up on end and her face glow until the freckles almost disappeared. Obnoxious residents always irritated her. She was an unusual combination of modesty, confidence, and cool intelligence. As head nurse, she kept the doctors in line, though they would never admit it. They feared not only her assertiveness, but also her cognitive prowess. A month ago they all quietly panicked when they heard through the grapevine that she had taken the tests to join MENSA and passed with high honors. There were also rumors that she was a math buff who could hold her own even with academicians. She never flaunted her intellectual and interpersonal skills, and usually was quite low-key. But when she or any of her nurses were mistreated in any way, she could strike back like a tigress. At the moment, however, it was more a matter of her swatting a buzzing insect that was making a nuisance of itself. Tolerating the pomposity of medical directors is one thing, but swallowing it from an insolent resident is another.

"Wait a minute, Ron," she said crisply. Her nose wrinkled. "When you talk about diagnosing you make it sound like that's the epitome of psychiatry. Simply slapping a label onto someone doesn't in itself make them get better. And sometimes the label can do more harm than good. Once you start throwing around terms like 'schizophrenia,' they may stick to people forever. No one wants to be black-balled as a mental patient."

The swat reddened Ron's cheeks. With tension in his voice, he waved his fork in the air and retaliated. "Of course, we want to avoid the bias created by diagnostic labels. But coming up with a coherent treatment plan is dependent on an accurate diagnosis."

"I remember," Sheikh interjected between the Titans, "I remember in medical school in Pakistan we discussed these issues. We did not use DSM, but instead international system. Making psychiatric diagnosis is very difficult, more ambiguous than other medical fields. And this is true of treatment also. Working with patients is a very delicious matter."

Momentarily baffled by Sheikh's non sequitur, we all looked at each other.

"You mean a very delicate matter?" Carole said.

We all laughed.

"Yes, yes," Sheikh replied self-consciously, but with a giggle. "A very delicate matter. My apologies."

"You know what happened to me the other day?" Bob interjected. "I was in the outpatient department seeing one of my patients. You know how the rooms are there — crowded together with paper thin walls. Well, I'm working with this neurotic woman who has anxiety attacks, and she's talking about how she doesn't want to be in therapy, how she thinks hospitals are only for sick or crazy people. My supervisor said that she's really afraid of being insane herself, she's scared that she might be the one who needs to be hospitalized. So I'm trying to explain to her that not everyone who comes for therapy is sick or crazy, that even normal people sometimes benefit from professional help. All of a sudden we hear someone screaming in the room next to us, 'Why are you doing this to me! Leave me alone! Let me out of here!' Well, my patient's face turned white. I thought she was going to pass out! Talk about bad timing!"

Everyone laughed, except Ron who was trying hard to think of something to say. He felt deflated because he wasn't holding the center of attention. People like Ron need to be heard and admired in order to feel alive and important. As children they desperately tried to make Mom and Dad listen, but they never quite got enough — or maybe they got too much.

Carole beat him to the punch. "When I worked at Hillside, we had a suite of rooms for seeing patients. All of the staff shared the suite, so when we were using a room we would put a Do Not Disturb sign on the door to let the other people know it was occupied. To prevent people from interrupting your session, that system worked fine. The only problem was that people sometimes forgot to take the sign off the door when they were finished with the room. If a door was closed and had a sign on it, you could never be sure if the room was occupied or empty. You had to develop all sorts of strategies to determine whether it was vacant, like go back to the main desk and check the schedule book, or put your ear to the door, or look for light under the door. Well, I was working with this patient, a paranoid guy who thought the KGB was after him. He really believed they had him under constant surveillance, with phone taps, tails, the whole bit. In therapy I was working on trying to improve his reality testing, you know, trying to help him see that maybe his delusions were really projections of his own feelings about himself. Anyway, one day as our session was ending, I walk him to the door, he opens it — and there in the foyer, right in front of us, is the new psychiatry resident, a Russian-looking guy with a bushy beard and three piece suit. And he's on his hands and knees peering under our door! We almost tripped over him! I talked myself blue in the face trying to explain to my patient who that guy was and what he was really doing. To say the least, my patient had a real hard time giving up his paranoid beliefs."

"I've got a better one than that," Ron blurted out, no longer able to control himself. "You know how we sometimes have to call security to come up to the unit to help us control a violent patient — but the hospital policy states that they can't bring any guns with them. So because my office is right next to the unit, I told them that they could put their weapons in my filing cabinet before they come onto the unit. So, one day, I'm doing therapy with this paranoid patient. Suddenly, right in the middle of the session, the door flies open and these two huge security men come running in with their guns drawn! Can you beat that?"

"You mean you told them to put the guns into your office while you were seeing this patient?" Sheikh asked curiously.

"No! No! They were on their way to the unit. There was an emergency there. But they first had to come into my office to put their guns away."

"My god! That's awful!" Carole said. "A paranoid's worst nightmare come true. Maybe you shouldn't let security put their guns in your office. It's not right that they intrude on your patients like that."

"I'll say," I mumbled through the pasta hanging out of my mouth.

Ron again glanced at me but directed his response to Carole. "No, it's not really a problem. They only interrupted us for a second. And besides, it hasn't happened often. In fact, that was the only time they actually interrupted one of my sessions."

"But if you don't tell security to put their guns some-where else," Carole said, "it could happen again. We should take every precaution we can to protect the patient's right to confidentiality."

"But the sessions ARE confidential. I don't talk to any-one about the specifics of my cases, except for my supervisor. Security only popped into that session for a minute. They didn't know who the patient was or what we were talking about."

"I give up," Carole murmured. She looked at her watch. "Lunch time is over for me. I have to get back to the unit. See you all back at the fort." She stood up, but before leaving reached under her chair for a bag and held it out towards Ron. "Do you mind, Ron, if I leave my sweat socks in your office? I went running before lunch, and I prefer not to bring them onto the unit."

For a moment, silence. Then Sheikh slapped his stomach, rolled back his head, and let out a gurgling chuckle that made his shoulders shudder and his bushy black eyebrows twitch. Everyone joined in the laughter, except Ron who tilted his head sideways like a quizzical terrier.

"Only kidding, Ron," Carole said as she walked away.

When the laughter subsided, Sheikh lightly patted Ron on the back. "You must be careful with her, my friend. Otherwise, how do you say it, you will open your mouth and change your shoes."

"Open your mouth to change feet," Ron darted back. "Listen, what's the big deal about this anyhow? I think people worry too much about confidentiality. We're working in a university medical center here. It's the whole hospital and its staff that are responsible for a patient. We can't get overly pre-occupied about one therapist maintaining the confidentiality of one patient — even in outpatient psychotherapy. It's not practical, and it may not even be in the patient's best interests."

After a brief silence, Bob looked at me. "Tom, what do you think?"

Caught by surprise, I almost choked on a strand of spaghetti. "What do I think of what?" I sputtered between two coughs.

"What do you think about confidentiality in psycho-therapy?" he answered.

"Well," I said, trying to clear my throat, "I've been trained mostly in psychoanalytic psychotherapy — and in that kind of therapy confidentiality is extremely important. In order for the person to really open up and talk about their most private problems, they have to trust that you won't be telling anyone else."

"But you're assuming that psychoanalysis works," Ron quickly replied. "Research has shown this is questionable. If you're going to administer any kind of psychological treatment, you had better go with the behavioral techniques that have been validated by experimental research. Of course, the preferred treatment, in terms of effectiveness, would be psychopharmacological rather than psychological."

Them's fightin' words. If thoughts could kill, my mind would have reduced Ron to a pile of smoldering protoplasm. But I had to keep my cool. He was throwing me a hook with live bait. Don't bite!

"I guess I don't agree with physiological reductionism," I reluctantly garbled through the wad of spaghetti in my mouth.

"What?"

"Reductionism, you know, assuming that physiology will explain all psychological events."

"That's right. All mental disorders are caused by some biochemical dysfunction. The evidence is clear for schizophrenia, and the affective disorders, like depression and manic-depression."

"Isn't it possible that some problems are purely psychological in origin, that physiology has nothing to do with it?"

"No," Ron pronounced. "Everything is ultimately explained by biochemical changes in the brain and nervous system. And we're learning more and more about this as science advances."

I stared down at my plate of spaghetti. I didn't want to get into this with Ron. I didn't want to lose my head. Instead, to calm myself down, I imagined lying on a beach, with the blue sky and sunshine above, the sound of the waves, my toes wiggling in the warm sand.

"You see," Ron's voice continued, "even the so-called neuroses are biologically caused — like anxiety attacks and obsessive-compulsive disorders. Psychoanalysts claimed these problems were purely psychological, but the fact that they've been unsuccessful in treating them only shows that the true cause is biological. Someday we will discover the underlying biochemical problem and then be able to treat it with drugs — by altering the brain biochemically, or by some other physiological intervention."

In my imagination, a little boy was standing next to my beach blanket, kicking sand into my face. I shook my finger at him and gave him a scolding look, but he didn't budge. "Well, Ron, how about this," I said. "Let's say you have a computer program that won't run. It bombs on you. How would you fix it?"

"Well, there must be a mistake in the program somewhere. The error message should tell you the where the program hung up. You'd have to patch it somehow so it would run correctly."

"But you wouldn't you go into the computer's hardware with a screwdriver or a knife to cut and paste the circuits? Or pour chemicals in it to fix the problem."

"Of course not."

"Right. Because there's nothing wrong with the hardware. If you tried to change it, you'd be missing the boat, and you'd probably make the problem even worse. The real problem is with the software, the programming. Then couldn't the same be true of neurosis? The problem isn't in the brain structure, so we don't need medications or psychosurgery. The problem is in the software, in the psychological programming, so to speak. That's the level you have to work at. And we call that work psychotherapy."

"No. In the case of neurosis, we just don't know yet what the neurological causes are. They're probably very subtle biochemical abnormalities that we can't detect. It's just a matter of time before research finds them."

So much for the Socratic method. Apparent there's little correlation between IQ and narrow-mindedness. My frustration mounting, I again looked down at the spaghetti and tried to return to the soothing comforts of my beach.

"This is most interesting," Sheikh said. "I have noticed American psychiatry does much emphasize the physiological theories. And this seems to lead to much emphasis on technological advances."

"That's because it's the state of the art," Ron replied enthusiastically. "To understand behavior you have to understand the brain. And for that we need neurophysiology, biochemistry, and even physics — especially physics. After all, it resulted in catscans and laser microsurgery. In a few more decades we'll have even more sophisticated instruments that will let us assess and modify the fine details of the nervous system. That's when we'll start eliminating mental illness."

The boy next to my beach blanket somehow had gone through a dramatic metamorphosis. Now he was a big, red crab. He was poking and pinching me. "O.K., Ron. I personally don't believe we'll ever be able to eliminate mental illness with electronic gadgets, no matter how sophisticated they are — but let's say that someday we do have these instruments you're talking about. If we could eliminate someone's neurosis by altering their brain, could we also use it to correct character disorders."

"Sure."

"But most psychologists and psychologists agree that character disorders are deeply ingrained personality styles. They're the result of early childhood development. They're learned, just like many aspects of normal personality — unless you think that normal personality traits are also biologically determined. If we use these instruments to alter character disorders, then we could also use them to alter normal personalities. We could even take newborn children, stick their heads into the electronic gizmo, and give them a prepackaged personality. One out of every ten will be shy, one intelligent, one artist, one scientist — no, make that three, of course — we need lots of scientists. On the other hand, maybe we won't even bother making people different. We'll make them all the same to simplify things, in an Orwellian sort of way. Who's going to make those kinds of decisions, Ron? Scientists? The government?"

It was happening. I was losing control. I buried my head and torso into the beach, to hide, to soothe my brain in the cool depths of the sand. Above me, the RonCrab's voice was still clicking and clacking as its claws gnawed at my feet. "I don't know it would ever come to that. In any case, it's not up to scientists to make such decisions. The same kind of problems pop up with abortion and euthanasia. Scientists can't say when life really begins and ends. They can't say when or even if it's right to terminate a pregnancy, or to pull the plug on someone who's brain-dead. They just discover the laws of nature, the solid facts of the universe."

With that remark, I catapulted myself out of the sand, grabbed a nearby beach umbrella, and yanked it up out of the ground. Standing above the RonCrab, I aimed the sharp metal point of the pole at the center of its body.

"But that's the whole problem," I said. "Science is too busy discovering facts and too ignorant of the ethical consequences of its discoveries. And what's worse, many scientists don't even respect the philosophical thinkers who ARE trying to make sense out of this crazy technological age of ours. Take

Nietzsche, for example. He predicted that our modern age of science and technology would bring about the collapse of all sense of purpose and meaning in our world. Isn't that scary? He's also a good example of this debate about illness being psychological or biological. It's clear, historically, that he suffered from the advanced stages of syphilis and for the last years of his life was schizophrenic as a result of the infection in his brain. He was as crazy as a loon. Biologically caused insanity, right? Well, I heard this philosopher who suggested that whether or not it was biologically caused is irrelevant — that the most important point was that Nietzsche willed his insanity. What do you make of that Ron?"

He had no reply.

"Can I take those trays?" A hand reached over my shoulder and pointed at our table. A kitchen aid was standing behind me. Surprised, I leaned over sideways away from his arm. It struck me that there was something unusual about his hand. Half of his index finger was missing.

"Sure. I'll get them for you," Sheikh replied as he gathered up the trays. While he waited, the aid quickly picked his nose with his deformed digit. It looked like a whole finger had disappeared up his nostril and poked into his brain.

"Bob, how was you salad?" Barb asked.

"It was O.K. The lettuce was a little soggy, though."

"I guess they didn't let it dry off after they washed it."

My appetite had vanished. There was something unpleasantly gritty in my spaghetti — something a lot like sand. I poked my fork into the plate. The intertwining noodles and patches of sauce formed an intricate pattern. The overall impression was a face with a slightly bewildered expression.

For a while, we were all quiet. Clasping his hands beneath his chin, Sheikh put his elbows on the table and leaned towards me. "I heard about your patient who was discharged," he said with genuine concern. "Perhaps you would like to talk about this — if you wish."

"No, I don't mind," I said as I leaned towards him. The broken edge of the table scraped my forearm. I sat back again. "It was Elizabeth Baso, the depressed patient I was working with. We discharged her yesterday. She seemed fine — sleeping O.K., good affect, optimistic. This morning she walked her kids down to the bus stop. When they drove away, she walked out into the street and was struck dead by a mail truck. When the police found out she had just been treated in a hospital for depression, they suspected suicide."

"Were there any witnesses?"

"Two other people, both neighbors."

"Did they notice anything unusual about her?"

"One of them said she looked good, much better than a few weeks ago. The other one said she looked weird. I don't know what she meant by that. I guess if you've just been released from a psychiatric hospital, some people are going to think you look weird, even when you're fine."

"I can't believe she would hurt herself," Barb said as she searched our faces. "She was such a good person."

"Did she look both ways before crossing, or that sort of thing?" Bob asked.

"I don't know. The women didn't say, I guess. They just said Elizabeth was standing there at the corner, and then walked out into the traffic."

"It sounds like depersonalization," Ron declared. "She didn't know what she was doing or where she was. She was in a fog. She might have been decompensating."

I could feel my irritation building again. "I doubt it Ron. She never showed any signs of decompensation while she was here. There was no thought disorder, no psychotic symptoms at all. And by the time she left her depression had lifted."

"The signs of decompensation can be subtle. You can sometimes miss them if you don't do a thorough assessment."

My fists tightened. "My assessment of this person WAS thorough!"

"Oh, I'm not saying that it wasn't. I'm just saying that in general you have to be careful about evaluating someone before you discharge them."

"I'm going to get some ice cream," Barb interjected with a nervous smile. "Does anyone else want some?"

I shook my head. "Listen, Ron. We did a very careful assessment of this person. In addition to the intake, we administered a battery of psychological tests when she was admitted. We even readministered some of the tests just before she was discharged. There were no signs of decompensation before or after her treatment. The tests obviously indicated depression when she got here, but at the time of discharge there was much less evidence of it — and all of the indices for suicide were negative."

"What tests did you administer?"

"Our standard battery — the MMPI, Rorschach, WAIS, TAT, and Bender."

"Hm."

"Hm?" I echoed.

"I guess it's good that the test results were favorable. But then there are limits to psychological testing."

"I don't follow you, Ron."

"Well, tests like the MMPI do seem to be somewhat valid. There's some research to support it. But there's very little evidence to suggest that projective tests like the Rorschach are useful. In fact, most of the research indicates that inkblot tests are not very useful."

Just what I needed — a fledgling psychiatrist, who never received training in psychological testing and probably never laid eyes on the Rorschach, is now lecturing me about it. I wanted to dip his face into ink and use it to print my own inkblot.

"Actually, Ron, there's a lot of research to support the Rorschach. Besides, my opinion is that so-called scientific research is not even important for validating the use of some psychological tests. A skilled clinician with years of experience can do diagnostic and predictive miracles with the Rorschach. I once saw a psychologist use it to predict that a patient would attempt suicide — and that she would try to do it by hanging herself. Mind you, there was no specific mention of suicide or even death in her Rorschach responses. Later that day the staff found a rope hidden under her mattress."

Ron retaliated. "There are much more sophisticated ways of assessing psychiatric disorders. Looking at inkblots is simply childish."

I sighed as I poked my fork between the spaghetti man's eyes. "Well, Ron. There's one other way to prove to you that the Rorschach is a valid test. How about we administer it to you? We could do it this afternoon."

Ron's eyes bounced around like pinballs. "I'm too busy."

I could have sworn I heard the sound of a shell crack.

CHAPTER 8

Scientific

I THINK YOU TWO ARE BOTH too crazy," Sheikh interjected. "Psychology, psychiatry, inkblots — let's not talk about such things now. This is time to relax."

"Unfortunately, I think we have to get back to the unit," Bob added.

Ron looked at his watch. "Yeah. I have to go. See you later." He sprang out of his chair and briskly walked away. The others followed him, at a more casual pace.

"Are you also returning, Tom?" Sheikh asked.

"No. I have a few minutes left. I'm going to hang out here for a bit."

Trailing behind the others, Bob smiled at me as he left. A small spark of gladness shot through me, though my stomach was still jumpy from the debate. I might have won that battle but I sensed I was losing the war. Again I noticed the sore spot in my throat. It hurt more than before. My whole throat felt tight and dry. All that talking probably aggravated it. I picked up my cup, but it was empty. Ron had left behind an almost full cup of ice water, too tempting to resist. I took a sip.

Bitter! He must have squeezed a lime into it.

Maybe Sheikh was right. Maybe I had overdone my debate with Ron. I should try to think of him as a colleague, not an enemy. After all, the clinical psychologist and psychiatrist are more like each other than they realize. They both feel like second class citizens. Physicians tend to look down on psychiatrists because they do not practice "real" medicine. Academic psychologists, especially the hardcore experimentalists, belittle clinical psychologists for not being sufficiently scientific. In fact, several Ivy League schools long ago dropped their clinical psychology programs. Helping people just wasn't considered scholarly work, so go somewhere else to do it.

People try to gain acceptance by becoming more scientific, or more medical, or both. With the rise of such idols as Pavlov and Skinner, many clinical psychologists converted to the ultimate doctrine of scientific psychology — Behaviorism. Forget about analyzing dreams and free associations, the intangible, flittering subjective stuff of psychoanalysis. Instead, use objective experiments to study observable, problematic behaviors and how to change them. They electrically shocked fetishists into conventional sexuality. They reinforced wall-flowers for making eye contact and raising their voices. They popped thousands of M&M's into the mouths of unruly children. The next step was logical. If they could shape overt "outside" behavior, then why not covert "inside" behavior — like physiological processes? Enter biofeedback. With their machines that beeped and blinked, they attacked hypertension, headaches, jaw aches, cold feet, and, finally, the most fundamental ingredients of behavior — hormones and neurotransmitters. Then, feeling confident, they stepped boldly into the physician's semantic world. They no longer practiced "behavior modification." Now it was called "behavioral medicine" and "biopsychology."

Often, clinicians are fighting a loosing battle in their quest for acceptance among scientific psychologists. The objections their colleagues raise against them is an irresistible displacement. There is a broader, more powerful prejudice in academia against psychology in general and all of the other "soft" social sciences. Biologists, physicists, engineers, and their many brethren, simply have a hard time believing that the study of human behavior is scientific. Only proteins, atomic particles, and Newton's laws are the true children of science.

But isn't there a contradiction running around here? For if these hard scientists truly believe the scientific method cannot be applied to studying human qualities, then they must assume that these qualities are, somehow, basically irrational or unpredictable — that the solid, precise laws of Nature do not extend to Human Nature. That assumption puts them in a funny position. How can we Homo Sapiens, filled with perfectly illogical thoughts and emotions, create this scientific process which is supposedly so logical? Can something imperfect beget something perfect? Can the human mind forge an epistemology that can explain the entire universe, except the mind that created it? If so, it must mean this mind stands outside the universe — otherwise, we should accept it as an object of scientific study. Maybe we've convinced ourselves that we can grab our own bootstraps and by the sheer power of logical thought transcend our flawed cogitations. Maybe we're trying our best to leap beyond our emotions, the real source of our irrationality. But is there any thought completely divorced from feeling? Is there any theory that is not a byproduct of the personality that created it? Can we ever leap out of our own skins? It all seems so delusional and grandiose.

In a way, I guess I can't blame the hard-nosed scientist for being skeptical of psychology. Psychology certainly is confusing, even to us psychologists. First of all, it's too diverse for its own good. The statisticians tapping away at their computer keyboards, the touchy-feely therapists who pounds pillows with their clients, the researchers dissecting a rat's brain, the consultants trying to boost assembly-line production — all may share the title "psychologist." What do all these people have in common. Not a whole lot.

Psychotherapy is even more confusing. So many schools of thought, so few areas of agreement. The psychoanalysts look down on the behaviorists, the behaviorists look down on the psychoanalysts, and everyone thinks the humanists are fuzzy-headed. You name it and someone thinks it's therapeutic while someone else thinks it's a joke. Jog with patients; massage them; give them electric shocks and emetics; have them roll around on the floor, cry and scream to reenact their birth traumas; analyze their dreams, history, body language, family, and syntax. Ungainly, divided against itself, psychology is losing its accountability. It's that uncertainty about ourselves that can turn us psychologists into pompous know-it-alls.

Without consciously initiating the act, I stood up to leave, as if trying, instinctively, to get away from myself. It was time for my next appointment anyhow. On the way out of the cafeteria, I dropped my cup and plate into the garbage. The spaghetti man, half consumed, disappeared into the black receptacle.

"So long, pal," I said.

CHAPTER 9

Therapy

THE ELEVATOR WAS PACKED full of people wearing those plastic name tags. I briefly considered waiting for another car, but I didn't have enough time. I squeezed in and immediately felt uneasy. I tried to contain that instinctual fear, that desire to run, to escape suffocation and find clean, open space. Like everyone else in the elevator I stared at the ceiling — and mentally retreated to a safe place in the middle of my brain.

Suddenly, between floors, the elevator shuddered, the lights flickered. People gasped. My already tight stomach leaped into my throat.

"Don't worry, folks," a voice rang out from the back of the elevator. "This elevator has only broken down twice since it was first installed eight years ago — once last night, and once early this morning!"

After an excruciating moment of silence, a few people broke out into chuckles. The panic quickly dissipated. I didn't have to turn around to identify the voice. It was Phil the janitor. At the first stop everyone exited — waves of suits and white lab coats spilling out of the elevator. I tried to guess which ones were headed for the stairs to continue their journey with peace of mind. When the doors closed, only Phil and I were left. He was still poking a screwdriver into that doodad in his hand.

"What is that, Phil?"

"A lock."

"For the inpatient unit?"

"Yep."

"But I thought the unit isn't supposed to be locked."

"It isn't. They never deliberately lock it. But regulations state that there has to be a lock, even if it's not being used."

"So you're installing one?"

"This here? No, this one's always been in that door. But it's never worked right. The bolt is loose. Every once in a while it slides across and jams the door. You have to jiggle the handle to free it."

He looked up and pointed the lock at me. "You see, Doc. That could be a real problem. You're up there one day and you have to leave in a hurry. You grab the handle, give it a twist, and bingo! The door's locked! You can't get out!"

"How unpleasant," I replied as the walls of the elevator seem to inch towards me.

"Unpleasant!? You bet your inkblots! Especially if there's a fire — or who knows what. Yeah, I gotta get this baby fixed."

"Why don't you just replace it with a new one?"

Phil looked up again. "You know, that's the strange thing. This building, so shiny and fancy, so modern looking. Well, that door up there is a 1000 years old. I don't know where they got it from. I can't find any new parts for it. You figure it out."

The elevator door opened. I stepped out and held the door. "Aren't you getting out Phil?"

"No. I'm gonna stay here, and ride up and down. The light's better. Besides, that place gives me the creeps."

The doors closed. Through the metal and plastic I could still hear the clinking of Phil's screwdriver against the lock. His muffled voice disappeared into the ceiling, "You little bugger!"

Out of the corner of my eye I noticed movement down the hallway. I turned. A head disappeared around the bend followed by the swishing skirt of that familiar red dress. Peek-a-boo again! I looked at my watch: three minutes past the hour. Damn it! Should I chase her? If I did, I would be playing along with her game of hide-and-seek, which would not be therapeutically productive. If I didn't, she would surely feel rejected. And when Cheryl felt rejected, she might do anything.

I followed her. I tried to walk lightly, to suppress the hurried pounding of my heels along the hard tile floor. When I reached the bend where Cheryl had been, I saw, further down the corridor, peeking out from a doorway, the mystery woman quickly retracting her head from view. This was getting downright silly. I walked towards her, but when I arrived at the door, she was gone. The woman's rest room! Great! Now what should I do? Wait, call her — open the door and go in?! Forget that!

I waited.

There were no sounds in the bathroom. I held my ear close to the door. Nothing. A nurse walking down the hallway threw me a disdainful look. Don't worry, madam. I'm no pervert. I'm a doctor. I smiled and stood up straight, pretending to be examining the sign on the door. How embarrassing! It was like being trapped in a bad sitcom.

I waited.

Still nothing.

Enough! I raised my hand to knock. My hand paused in mid-air. I frowned at myself. I can't believe I'm doing this!

Suddenly, the door flew open. Cheryl stood there, in the doorway, wide-eyed. My knuckles were pointed at her forehead.

"Dr. Holden!… Hi!" she said with surprise, her eyes darting from my hand to my face.

"Hi, Cheryl," I replied. "It's time for our appointment, isn't it?" I replied as I nonchalantly dropped my hand.

She broke eye contact. Her face sagged into a hurt expression. "I was thinking of not coming."

"Then we should talk about that."

I stepped aside, opening the direction to my office. She paused, then with a wry smile started down the hallway. I followed.

In psychoanalytic therapy, moments like these can be awkward. While we strolled along it would seem natural to chat — about the weather, movies, whatever. That's what normal people would do. And some analysts — the more contemporary, humanistic ones — would recommend it. By being friendly and politely conversational, therapists invite their patients' trust. By being themselves during these brief minutes before and after the session, therapists develop real relationships with their patients. They act as "good objects" that the patient can identify with, and internalize.

Orthodox analysts, on the other hand, would disagree wholeheartedly. They say that the therapist's sole objective is to analyze and interpret their patients' behavior, to help them gain insight into themselves. Everything patients communicate to their analysts before, during, and after the hour, what they say on the phone, whether they pay their bill on time or not, whether they come to the session early, late, or exactly on time — all of these behaviors are grist for the analytic mill. They contain hidden meaning that must be interpreted and understood. To chat casually with patients would be colluding with their unconscious attempt to thwart this analytic task.

It would be like saying, "What we're doing now, Mrs. Jones, is just idle talk. We don't have to analyze this." Instead, the analyst must maintain a neutral facade; he must be a blank screen that doesn't interfere with anything the patient needs to express. Unnecessary chit-chat is like walking into an operating room with dirty hands, like tossing a wrench into a finely tuned engine.

"So how are you doing," I said to Cheryl.

Cheryl looked surprised, and answered cautiously, "Fine."

Ugh! Now why did I do that after ruminating about analytic neutrality! I need some analysis myself. I briefly considered commenting about the weather, but nixed the idea. That would just be a feeble attempt to cover up my error. Why should she tell me here, in the hallway, how she was doing? Save that question for therapy. I was already off to a bad start, and that bothered me. Intuitively, I felt that Cheryl enjoyed my predicament. No, maybe it was just my imagination. Damn! Countertransference!

We walked the rest of the way in silence. Finally, after what seemed like hours, we reached my office. I fumbled with my keys and opened the door. Cheryl slipped by me and entered first. After I closed the door and sat down, Cheryl was still standing by her chair, searching for something in her pocketbook. I was grateful for these few spare moments because I needed time to focus myself.

Let's see — 25 year old, white, attractive female. Unmarried. Came to therapy because of depression. A long history of psychological problems — acting out, anxiety attacks, suicidal gestures, two previous hospitalizations. Father abandoned family when she was 13, promising to return to take her with him. Possibly revived fantasies of Oedipal victory, which were dashed when father never came back. Mother died a year ago from heart attack. Still reeling from this loss. Currently employed as a book-keeper for a business that imports Oriental clothing, undoubtedly where she bought her dress — a Japanese style with a straight collar, dark, rich shades of red, an abstract dragon embroidered around the rim... uh, tends to develop transference reactions to her boss — anger, seductiveness, fear of rejection.

Cheryl pulled a brush out of her pocketbook and began stroking her long, jet-black, and already over-brushed hair. She looked at the wall while she groomed, acting indifferent to my presence. But I sensed she was very conscious of me.

A borderline personality disorder. No one has defined it exactly. It's a relatively new term in the history of psychopathology and loaded with controversy, though clinicians know when they have one in their office. You can feel it in your guts before you even realize it intellectually. Usually the term refers to people who are emotionally unpredictable and impulsive, who have a history of unstable, stormy relationships, who are manipulative to the extent that even their own lives may be used as a pawn in their interpersonal games. They are the kinds of patients who can tie inexperienced clinicians into knots, bounce them around emotionally, make them feel more confused and helpless than the patients themselves. Even many well-seasoned clinicians swear that you should avoid having more than two or three severe borderlines in your practice — otherwise you'll blow your psychotherapeutic gaskets.

Why do borderlines behave the way they do? Some say the patient is, literally, bordering between psychotic and neurotic. Their identity structure is fragile — not as completely unraveled as the schizophrenic, yet not stabilized as in the neurotic. They have no internalized, deeply felt sense of who they are. They panic when they are alone, for to be alone is to be psychologically, phenomenologically dead. Desperate for an identity, they latch onto other people to bolster their sense of self. They project into others the raw emotions and psychological turmoil that they cannot tolerate. The therapist's job is to allow this to happen, to encourage it so patients can experience the security and unity of the therapist's identity — and by doing so internalize those qualities, bit by bit, until their own identity can take shape.

Cheryl finished brushing her hair. She opened her pocketbook, daintily slid her brush inside, and snapped it closed. At that moment I realized she looked different. I wasn't sure why. It had something to do with her dress. It seemed looser. Had she lost weight? I hadn't noticed last week. Could she have lost that much since the last time I saw her? Maybe a sudden turn to anorexia, or bulimia. I'd have to listen carefully for references to food or nurturance.

She plopped down into her chair and struck a sullen expression. For the first time since we entered the room, she looked at me, her eyes glassy and tired, but piercing nevertheless.

"I almost did it last night," she blurted.

I waited. Was she going to continue?… She didn't. She had made her pronouncement and was waiting for me to respond. The ball was in my lap now. Letting this progress into a long silence wouldn't be helpful.

"Did what?"

"Kill myself! What did you think?!" She glared at me, then picked at a loose thread on her pocketbook, pain spreading across her face.

"You're angry, and hurt that I didn't understand you."

"You never understand me! You never try to. It's because you don't really care about me. I'm just another patient to you, another specimen to examine. All you men are the same."

"You were feeling hurt even before our session began."

"It began five minutes ago, before you got here! You were late again."

"You're right, I was. I apologize for that. Was it because you felt hurt that you left?"

"What do you mean?"

"You weren't at my office. I saw you down the hallway, walking away. I followed you, and you saw me, but you kept walking."

She continued picking at her pocketbook.

"Cheryl, I think you were feeling hurt, and angry, so you left. But you wanted to see if I would come after you. You were probably thinking that if I did, then I care about you. But if I didn't, then I don't care. You were testing me, like you do with your suicide attempts, like you're doing now."

Tension flowed out of her. Her pout relaxed into a calm, almost peaceful expression. For a brief moment I caught a glimpse of her as a small girl — the innocent, untainted child before the assault by parents too self-preoccupied to realize the psychological damage they were inflicting on her. They had been completely unable to nurture her, to affirm her special-ness, to provide the unconditional attention all children need in order to thrive. Instead, they physically and emotionally abused her to cleanse themselves of their own self-hatred. Either that, or they totally ignored her. Her mother never told her that she loved her, never even touched her. On Cheryl's birthday she deliberately bought her clothes that were the wrong size so she could return them, without ever replacing the gift. Cheryl was the hated child, the non-person. But her parents had suffered the same fate at the hands of their parents. So who was to blame? Where, in the endless chain of generations, did the problem begin? If I could help Cheryl, the cycle might be broken.

"I had a dream last night," she said. "I dreamed I was riding on a motorcycle with my father. I was riding behind him, my arms wrapped around his waist. I can still feel the seat. It was so soft, like terry cloth, or satin. We stopped in front of the hospital. I think it was the hospital where I had my tonsils taken out. He wanted me to get off, but I wouldn't. He yelled at me. He pushed me off. I tried to climb back on, but he drove away. I went running through the hospital. I was scared, terrified. I was lost. Someone grabbed me. It was Jeff, my other therapist. I think he was trying to hold me, but I was scared and struggled to break free. I bit off his finger. Blood spurted out all over us, all over the walls, then white stuff came out, like white corpuscles. Then I saw you, watching us. I held out my hand to you… That's all I remember."

Wow! And some people say dreams are meaningless reveries, the epiphenomenal noise from fidgeting neurons as the brain slips into sleep. Don't believe it for one minute! This dream was packed full of meaning, so much so that I felt overwhelmed. I wasn't sure how to work with it, but I couldn't let the opportunity pass. I had to take a stab at it.

"When your father left you when you were young, you felt lost and scared. You've felt that way ever since. That's part of the reason why you came to this hospital — to find him, to find someone who might fill that gap. You thought Jeff might make you feel complete, you thought you might take a piece of him, but you weren't sure you could trust him. He too left you, he left you too soon, just like your father. And that hurt. It made you angry. Now you're wondering whether I will do the same."

For a moment she was silent. She was reaching deep into her thoughts, reaching for those missing pieces of the puzzle that was her life. Her eyes were tearing. "My father didn't want to leave. He loved me. He was a wonderful man, a perfect father in every way. He had to leave. They made him. My mother made him. She was as much of a bitch to him as she had been to me. It was her fault that he left. She never loved me or him. I hate her. I wish she had left instead! I wish she was dead!"

She stiffened as if the words plunged into her heart like a knife. Realizing her wish had come true, she began sobbing, the tears running down her nose, dripping onto the dark leather of her pocketbook.

I waited.

Slowly, her crying subsided.

"You always idealized your father, and hated your mother. You split them into good and bad. But now that your mother too is gone, you feel her loss, you feel sorrow, and guilt."

She began rhythmically opening and closing her pocket book, the metal snaps clicking closed to punctuate the end of each cycle. She stared blankly at it, waiting, perhaps, for something to pop out.

"I heard her last night."

"Your mother?"

"While I was in bed, I heard her voice."

I waited, unsure what to do next. She was hallucinating again. Maybe we were uncovering too fast. Maybe I should help her reality test, help her see that she might be decompensating again. But then, maybe I should explore the meaning of the hallucination. I recalled an old supervisor's warning, "When in doubt, say nothing."

Cheryl did not seem to notice my silence. "Sometimes I think she's not really... not really gone. She's still here."

"In a way, maybe she is. She may be gone, physically, but emotionally she's still inside you."

She didn't seem to react. I wasn't sure she heard me. Her voice was groggy. "I had another anxiety attack on the way here, on the bus. A pain shot through my arm. I couldn't breathe. It was like a heart attack, like my mother had. I really thought I was going to die. Everyone was staring at me. I wanted to run, but I couldn't."

"Your attacks bring you closer to your dead mother. You become like her. And at the same time, they are a punishment. You punish yourself, for your guilt, for wanting her dead. And you punish her, inside you, because she won't let go."

Again she cried, the tears rolling down her face, dripping into her open pocket book, dripping onto the odds and ends of her fragmented life.

"Why did she say it?. Why?"

"Say what?"

"At the hospital, the night before she… she took my hand. She told me she loved me. Why would she lie?"

"Maybe it wasn't a lie."

Anger bit through her tears. "It must have been. She always treated me like shit. She never said anything like that to me before — never."

"Maybe it was something that was always difficult for her to say to you, but in the end, before she was gone, she needed to."

After a long pause, she spoke softly, "Are you going to leave me too?"

This was a critical point. I had to be careful not to blow it. "I'll be working with you until July. Remember we talked about this before. I'll only be here, at this hospital, for one year. But you might see it otherwise. It might feel like a rejection of you when I leave."

"Like Jeff rejected me."

"Jeff didn't reject you. He was a psychology intern, like me. He could only work here for one year, so when he left he transferred you to me. He took great care to help me understand what your problems were, so I could continue helping you. But I understand that it didn't feel that way to you. It felt like rejection, like when your father left you. And you felt so miserable, so abandoned, that you tried to kill yourself. You may have those same feelings again when I leave. It's very important for us to talk about that, long before I actually leave."

Again silence.

"I haven't been taking my medication."

I waited.

"It gives me cramps in my legs."

"Maybe we should speak to Dr. Goldstein."

"I hate that bitch. Why do you send me to her. Can't you get someone else to give me medications? I don't need her. All I need is you. We don't need that bitch!"

"I know you see her as all bad, but she's also concerned about you. She really is trying to help... What have you been doing with the medications?"

"I still got them," she said with a sly smile.

"Cheryl, we've prescribed weekly allotments of the meds so you wouldn't have too much of it around at any one time. You know it's not safe. It's too much of a temptation. Bring the extras in to me, or Dr. Goldstein."

She began opening and closing her pocketbook again. "Sometimes I think that you're not really going to leave, that you will still be here, somewhere in the area. Maybe you just don't want to tell me."

"I wouldn't deceive you, like your father did. I really will be leaving."

Hurt gripped her face. "You leave, and I stay. Everyone moves on except me."

"Someday you'll be able to move on too."

"When you leave, I won't be able to deal with it. I know I'll fall apart. I need you."

"You might fall apart. You may even try to kill yourself. And you may do that as a way to keep me here, to show me you couldn't survive without me. I may not be here, but another therapist will work with you. And, besides, you will be able to take part of me with you."

She stirred in her seat. Her eyes seemed to glow. Leaning over the side of the chair, she placed her pocketbook on the floor. It tipped over, spilling out her keys, and the end of her brush. She didn't seem to notice.

"After our session last week, I didn't go right home. I waited in the lobby. I saw you leaving, getting into your car."

"Yes, I saw you too," I answered, suddenly remembering. Why had I forgotten that?

"I've had thoughts of you, of us together."

I felt uneasy, but wasn't sure why. I spoke, though what I said didn't feel right. "We will be together, until July."

She didn't answer. Slowly her hand moved up to her throat, to the top button of her dress. She seemed almost hypnotized as she played with it, as if lost in a soft, warm dream.

"Yes, together," she said as she raised her eyes to meet mine.

My stomach tightened. I felt like she was looking right into me. What was happening?

The top button of her dress popped open. I suddenly realized the two buttons below it were not fastened. Her dress opened slightly, nearly all the way down to her stomach, exposing the soft valley between her breasts. How did those buttons open? Had they been open all along?

She stood up. I felt all control slipping out of my grasp. My heart started racing.

"Cheryl…" I mumbled weakly.

She pushed down the top of one side of her dress, revealing her bare shoulder.

I froze.

She slipped the other side of her dress off her shoulder. Her whole dress fell to the floor around her legs. She was completely naked underneath.

My brain whizzed with confusion. My tongue locked in my throat as a paralyzing flash of embarrassment flashed through me. I felt exposed, as exposed as she was, as vulnerable. I could not drag my eyes away. I was being lured in.

Her knees wobbled. Her eyes fluttered. She was passing out!

I managed some words, words from someone else's mouth, words that pierced this dream-like scenario.

"Cheryl, put your clothes on."

Her eyes jumped open, filling again with attention, and then panic. Her hands shaking, she pulled up her dress and fastened the buttons. "I have to go," she said anxiously.

"We should talk about this," I answered.

"I have to go." She picked up her pocketbook and quickly walked to the door.

"We really should talk about this. I'd like you to stay."

"No!" she shouted. She yanked the door open and disappeared. Confused, I hesitated for a moment, then went to the doorway. I caught a glimpse of her long black hair and red dress sweeping around the corner.

"Flying dragons," I mumbled to myself.

I let the thought of pursuing her slip away. There was no energy left. I was drained. I slumped down into my chair and let my head drop. A shiny object next to Cheryl's chair pierced through my daze... Her keys.

CHAPTER 10

~ Synchronicity ~

S O WHAT WAS THIS SUPPOSED to mean? She really didn't want to leave? A convenient reason to come back? Maybe she needed to leave a piece of her with me. Or another ploy to get me to pursue her, perhaps even let myself into her home. I dropped the keys into my pocket where they rattled against my own set, forming an uncomfortable lump of metal that protruded from my pants leg.

I couldn't believe what had happened. What would my supervisor Henry say? I know, "When something like this happens, you can be sure you were making mistakes all along." Well the hell with it! I was doing the best I could. I felt the knob of metal in my pocket. The keys to her heart? Someday this will be a funny story to tell my colleagues. Until then, I'd have to come up with a good rationalization to vindicate myself.

Whether she left the keys "on purpose" or not, she eventually had to come back for them. I wrote a very simple and straightforward note, taped it to the door of my office, and closed the door behind me. Phil was at the end of the hallway, his legs straddling the open door to the inpatient unit, his hands tugging at both doorknobs, as if he were riding a square metal bronco.

"Phil, where's Lost and Found?"

"Lost something?"

"No, found."

"Found, eh? That's unusual. Doctors are usually losing things. It's downstairs, on the first floor, next to Duplicating."

"Thanks." I turned and headed for the escalator.

"Ya better be nice," Phil said.

The way to the escalator was the same hallway where I had pursued Cheryl. I half expected her to appear around each corner, or to walk out of the Woman's Room. I could almost feel her presence. But she wasn't there. It was eerie. What would I do if I did meet her? Give her keys back and tell her how important it would be for us to talk. Should I schedule her for an extra appointment, or just wait until our regular session next week? What would I say in the next session? Don't worry about it now. You can think about it later. You can discuss it in supervision. An image of Cheryl, naked, popped into my mind. Oh god! We're going to need a machete to chop through the countertransference!

Carefully, I stepped onto the escalator. My foot always seems to land right on the crack, leaving me teetering on the edge as the steps rise up and separate. At the end of the ride, when the steps flatten out and disappear, where exactly do they go? It's like making a fist, then letting your hand relax and open up. Where does the fist go? On escalators the ground vanishes right beneath you. It's disconcerting. I find a lot of technological things disconcerting. For instance, airplanes. Even as we take off and I see the ground shrink away, I refuse to believe that humans can fly.

I watched the end of the ride coming. The steps began melting beneath my feet. I remembered a story about a boy who got his toes caught in the teeth of the grill at the bottom of a shopping mall escalator. I winced imagining that painful sensation. Unconcerned about the whole issue, the escalator gently slid me off.

The lobby was filled with activity. There was a long line of people at the admissions desk. They looked frustrated, anxious. Several patients milled around the front entrance, waiting impatiently for someone to pick them up. All the cushy, red chairs along the escalator wall were occupied. Some of the seated people watched the activity in the lobby, some stared off into space, some read their newspapers, apparently oblivious to what was happening around them. You easily could tell the hospital staff from everyone else. They were the ones zipping across the room with stoic determination. In Minnesota, dozens of years ago, people in the lobby of several hospitals were used as a control group to validate the MMPI, now one of the most widely used psychological tests. That group of people turned out to be perfectly representative of the general population. A curious coincidence.

I swallowed. My throat definitely hurt. I felt tired. Well, I wasn't going to let it get to me. I cut straight across the lobby at right angles to a fast moving nurse on my right and two technicians pushing a cart on my left. Slightly adjusting my trajectory, I passed within inches behind the nurse and a fraction of a second in front of the technicians. The Blue Angels couldn't have done it better.

I entered the hallway on the other side of the lobby and soon passed the Duplicating Center. Next to it was a door labeled "Lost and Found" with faded, stenciled letters. It was locked, so I knocked.

No answer.

I knocked again.

"Go to the window!" an angry voice called from inside.

To my right, set into the wall, was a thick plate of glass that separated the two halves of a counter. A small metal bowl sunken into the middle of the counter provided the only opening between the two sides of the glass — the kind of security system used in banks and ticket booths. The woman inside the room had her back turned. Was she the one who just spoke to me?

"Excuse me," I said.

She didn't respond. Did she hear me? Windows like this often have a speaker that lets you communicate with the other side — but this one didn't. Just a solid plate of glass with that little pass-through at the bottom. Who the hell designs these things? Schizoid, or maybe paranoid, I mused. I lowered my head to put my mouth near the opening.

"Excuse me!" I said loudly.

"Yeah," she grumbled as she turned around.

She was about 45 years old, or so — and ugly. Not ugly in the sense that nature had sold her short on looks. But there was a burning anger in her eye, a chronic snarl carved into her face. The ugliness of a life gone sour. I recognized the type: hostile, bitter, nothing was ever good enough. Life was a string of annoyances, disappointments, and outrages. No silver linings here. I felt sorry for her. She had never known contentment or peace of mind. She probably never would.

"Excuse me, is this Lost and Found?"

"Can't you read the sign?"

I dropped the keys into the bowl. "I'd like to leave these for someone to pick up."

She poised her pencil above the clipboard in her hand. "Where'd you find them?"

"Well, someone left them in my office."

She slapped her hand against the clipboard. "Why don't you just give it back to them?!"

I felt cornered, like I had to justify myself. Thank god for the plate of glass separating me from this Being. Maybe I had misdiagnosed the architect, who obviously had uncanny foresight. "I have to leave, so, I left a note for her on the door, telling her to come down here to pick them up."

"Name?"

"Dr. Thomas Holden," I said as clearly as I could.

She hissed and again slapped her hand against the clipboard.

"Not you!" she almost shouted. Anxiety and confusion whipped through my brain, scrambling my thoughts.

"I don't understand."

"Her name! Her name!" She shot the words at my face. I felt embarrassed, stupid — but underneath, angry. How dare she treat me like this. The bitch. If my throat wasn't so sore.

"I'd prefer not to give her name," I said as firmly as I could, aware that I was struggling to contain myself.

"What is this? Some kind of guessing game?"

I could have explained the confidentiality of psychotherapy, but that would only give away Cheryl's identity as a patient, as well as antagonize this irate creature from the bowels of human unfulfillment.

"Her name is Cheryl."

"Last name."

"I don't know what her last name is." I was lying of course, but I wanted to take all steps to protect her confidentiality. The woman looked at me as if I were a complete moron. She picked the keys out of the bowl, turned around to drop them in a basket, and began shuffling papers on her desk. I waited, expecting more to happen, but she didn't turn around. After looking at her back for a minute or so, I realized our business was finished. I bent over and put my mouth right next to the little opening.

"Have a nice day," I said sadistically.

She didn't say anything, not that I expected she would. In fact, I convinced myself that it was good. I had the last word.

With a few minutes to spare, I decided to treat myself to some fresh air. I hurried back across the lobby towards the front entrance. As I entered the automatic doors, I came face to face with a patient entering. He had a broken arm. We both stopped dead in our tracks to avoid a collision. I side-stepped to my left, he side-stepped to his right, paralleling me. I moved back to my right at the same time he moved back to his left. I went left again just as he went right. Stalemate! We were trying, but we couldn't pass each other!

Our eyes met and we laughed — then we walked around each other without mishap. Freud might say our little dance was an unconscious simulation of sexual activity, but then, for Freud, dancing, going up and down stairs, getting run over — virtually everything and anything symbolized sex. Maybe it was more symbolic of that curious human tendency to get in our own way.

The fresh air felt good. The overcast sky glowed with an even, cool light that seemed almost comforting. As a breeze swept up the hill, helping to clear my head, I noticed Jon in his security booth waving at me. "Thomas, Thomas, come here!" he was calling as he waved something in his hand. Whatever it was, I knew I probably didn't have time for it. Nevertheless, I quickly shuffled across the wide parking lot to his booth. Inside, he was arranging multi-colored pickup sticks into neat piles. Concentrating intensely on them, he barely looked up at me.

"Aren't you a little young to be playing with those things?" I said.

"No sir, this is serious business. This is the I Ching."

"I Ching?"

He tipped his stool towards me, deftly halting his fall by placing his hands on the door frame of the booth. His eyes widened with excitement. "Ah, an ancient Chinese practice. You can use it to interpret the past, to probe the meanings of the present moment, to predict the future."

"Is that all?"

"There are more things in heaven and earth than are dreamt in your psychology." He tipped back to an upright position and pointed a red pickup stick at me. "All you have to assume is that there is synchronicity in the universe, that all things are somehow interconnected, that events parallel and reflect each other. Nothing occurs by coincidence. If I use the ancient method of shuffling these sticks and randomly dividing them into groups, they form a pattern of even and odd numbers, of yin and yang. And that pattern has a meaning."

"How do you know what that meaning is?"

He held up a book. "The 64 hexagrams, the 64 possible outcomes of working the sticks, are all described here, in the I Ching. Each hexagram is a fusion of two images. Of course the meanings are ambiguous, open to subjective interpretation. The fathers of the I Ching were no logical positivists. Why don't you try it?"

"I have to go," I said. "I have a seminar."

"It will only take a minute. We'll use a faster method than the sticks — the coins." Jon reached into his pocket, pulled out three quarters, and held them out to me. "Here. Take these."

"No," I said somewhat impatiently, "you do it."

"No, No. It has to be you who throws them. That's the whole point. That's how your mind becomes linked to the coins." He pushed the quarters into my hand. "Now, what's the question you're posing to the I Ching?"

"A question?"

"Yes, a question. The question will link your mind with the coins, and with the moment."

"Well, let's see. How about this: 'Will my cold get worse?'"

"Questions that look for a yes or no answer don't work well. Make it more open-ended."

"O.K. How about 'How can I get over this sickness?'"

"Now throw the coins six times. Go ahead," he said eagerly as he stepped out of the tiny booth and ushered me in.

I held my hand above the small counter inside. The quarters felt unusually warm — probably due to their coming from Jon's pocket and my hand being on the cool side. I dropped them and they spilled with a loud clank onto the metal surface. Three tails. "Yin" Jon called out. He drew a broken line onto his pad. I threw the coins again. "Yang." He added a solid line above the first. Then four more throws, four more solid yang lines above the others.

"My, my. That's an interesting one," Jon said. He flipped through the pages of the I Ching. That's hexagram 44, called Kou, or 'Coming to meet.'"

"So what does it mean?"

Jon was reading intently. "It says 'the principle of darkness, after having been eliminated, furtively and unexpectedly obtrudes again from within and below... an unfavorable and dangerous situation... coming to meet means encountering... the maiden is powerful; one should not marry such a maiden.'"

"The whole thing sounds pretty ambiguous to me. Like astrology, or fortune-telling. You give a person a very vague and general description of their personality, or of what is going to happen to them, and it seems to fit. In fact, it would fit

anyone. It's just a matter of base rates. The Barnum Effect —
for the suckers born every minute."

"You can hide behind scientism, if you want," Jon replied
unshaken by my argument, "but I would take this seriously.
The I Ching is based on ancient wisdom, knowledge we
westerners have long since forgotten. Anyway, it doesn't look
like your cold is going to get better."

A car horn honked behind us. It was the surgeon in a
black Jaguar, his fingers tapping the steering wheel impatiently.
With one foot in the road, Jon was blocking his path.

"I'd better go, Jon."

He didn't look up from the book. "Oh, he's always in
a rush. Probably has an appointment across town to extract
someone's heart. Listen to this, 'When heaven and earth meet,
all creatures settle into firm lines.'"

The surgeon stuck his head out the window. "Will you
please move!"

"Excuse us, sir," Jon called back. "Dr. Schweitzer and I
are caught up in a debate about where the soul is located. He
claims it's in the pineal gland; I agree with Sir Eccles that it's
in Wernicke's area 13. What's your opinion, sir?"

The surgeon's face dropped from irritation to perplexity.
"What?"

"Listen, Jon, I'd better get going," I interjected. "I'll talk
to you later — and by the way, you're a lunatic."

"Thank you, Dr. Holden," he replied through his smile
of self-satisfaction.

As I walked away, I looked back over my shoulder. With
pick-up sticks in hand, Jon was waving down the Jaguar.

Coming to meet. Yin and yang. Tea leaves. Biorhythms.
Wouldn't it be nice to have some fast, easy way to understand
yourself. Like those quizzes in popular magazines. "How independent are you?" "Are you happy?" "Are you a good lover?"

Answer these twenty true/false questions to find the answer.
If only the public knew what a complex, arduous task it is to
construct a truly valid psychological test. And once you've
got one, you're not going to publish it in anything other than
a professional journal.

Good tests are hard to come by.

As I approached the building, I began to think. I thought
about the woman in Lost and Found, how I should have told
her off; I thought about the keys, about Cheryl and what our
session meant; I thought about my inpatients, Kathy Mummon
in her wheelchair, still suicidal — Mr. Tennostein, struggling
to keep his brain intact — and Elizabeth, poor Elizabeth. Why
did she step in front of that mail truck? Then I tried not to
think, to shut it all out. But my stubborn mind sprang back,
again and again, with another idea, another worry, another
reminder of something I had to do. I was ruminating. I hate
ruminating. But my mind had a mind of its own. I tried to
concentrate on the scenery around me, on the trees. I knew
they were beautiful, but that realization could not sink to a
feeling level. It was just a stale, lifeless thought.

Through a clearing in the trees, just before I entered
the building, I could see off the top of the hill and into the
distant landscape. There were several distinct brown patches
in the otherwise green vista. Condo and town house develop-
ments. They were springing up all over the county. The last
time I had gone home to visit my mother I drove past my
old elementary school — or at least where the school used
to be. Barely outliving the baby-boomers for whom it was
built, the school was knocked down and replaced by one
of those quaint indoor plazas with shops that sell Shetland
wool sweaters, gourmet cheeses, and phones. I thought about
the last time I had been inside that old school — the tiny
chairs and desks, the water fountains down by my knees. The

hallways seemed so familiar, but so distant in my memory. Where is that school now, the desks, erasers, bulletin boards, lunch trays, the red bricks? Where are all those things? Were they reused, scattered among other schools throughout the country? Or was it all destroyed, buried, burned?

CHAPTER 11

Gravity

W HEN I REACHED DR. KARMEL'S office, everyone was already there — the three psychology interns from other hospitals in the area, two graduate students — and Karmel Himself, propped up in his throne behind the huge oak desk, sucking on his pipe, staring at the wall as if no one else was in the room. A member of the local clinical psychology consortium, he conducted the seminar on neuropsychology. The other interns nodded silently at me, and in the way they looked at me, out of the corner of their eyes, it was as if they were sharing a warning, "Oh no! Here we go again!"

I settled in, took out my pen and notebook, and waited. Karmel picked a match out of the ivory box on his desk, struck it with a majestic sweep of his hand, and held the flame to the bowl of his pipe as he tilted back his oversized, hoary head. He wrapped his big lips around the stem and sucked on it rhythmically, like a fish, making a loud smacking noise, until the embers glowed bright red and smoke billowed out of his mouth. His wide nostrils flared with each suck. A dense white cloud gradually formed around his head, hanging almost motionless in the still air, glowing as light from the window streaked through it. Tiny dust particles floated in and out of the streams of light, drifting aimlessly, gently swirling around each other, weaving subtle, complex patterns that condensed around Karmel's head, like a cloud of electrons enveloping a nucleus.

From the center of the cloud Karmel's voice sounded, "Today let's begin with the anatomy of the hypothalamus. The hypothalamus lies at the base of the brain, and can be divided into three zones along the lateral-medial axis. The first is the periventricular region, which surrounds the third ventricle. The second zone, which is the medial region, contains most of the hypothalamic nuclei, including the supraoptic and para-ventricular nuclei, the ventromedial nucleus, and the dorsal medial nucleus. The third and last zone is the lateral region, through which pass the fibers of the medial forebrain bundle."

I listened to Karmel's verbiage for about a minute, then started to write. He would think I was taking notes, and that would surely feed his ego. But little did he know that I was actually writing in my journal:

❄   ❄   ❄

To be or not to be. That is the question. Whether 'tis nobler in the mind to suffer the slings and arrows of neuro-anatomy with His Majesty Karmel, or to take arms against a narcissistic personality, and by opposing, end him. Help me. Help me, please. It's only 2:10 — still another 50 minutes to go. This seminar is slowly driving me mad. Free association will save me. It's good for the soul. Very purifying. Free association. Here we go. Free. Tweedle-dee, tweedle-dum. The hypotha-lamic preoptic tract sucks swamp water. Why do we have to learn this crap? Will memorizing neural road maps make me a better psychotherapist? Boredom hangs thick in the air, over here, over there, mixed with Karmel's hot air. Where oh where have my neurons gone, where oh where can they be — they go up, they go down, the smoke goes in, the smoke goes out. His hairy nostrils keep the beat. Stream of consciousness, flowing, very clean, purging. My fellow student yawns. His eyes are watery. The yawns go in, the yawns go out. I think because I am. I think because I am biochemical. Molecular legos colliding, fusing, splitting. Oh, God, my watch still says 2:10!! It's time for a nice long sentence, a complex sentence, with at least two or three commas, maybe even a semicolon added for spice; after all, short sentences lined up one after the other can be rather dull, although long ones inevitably say very little, or at least communicate very little, because both the reader and the writer will, most assuredly, forget where they started by the time they get to the end, no? Complex sentences require more neurons, preferably ones separated by semicolons. Isn't that true, oh Fishlips? Can you read my neurons? His words go on and on, like a bad dream. Does he really believe we're interested in this stuff? He doesn't even care. He just wants warm bodies in front of him, a pseudo-audience, an excuse to pontificate, to hear his own voice speaking his treasured knowledge. Holy shit! My watch reads 2:09! Impossible! Are even my eyes deceiving me!

I couldn't take it anymore. I raised my hand.

"Yes?" Karmel boomed.

I cleared my throat. "I have a question about neurons."

"What is it?" He seemed slightly irritated by having to deviate from the portrait of the hypothalamus that he was so masterfully painting.

"Is the action potential, the electrical charge that travels down the axon of a neuron, in any way similar to electric current that passes through wires in a circuit?"

"The action potential is an electrochemical impulse, whereas the current in wires is purely electrical — though there are some similarities."

"Well, I guess what I was wondering about is this: we know when current passes through a wire it creates an electromagnetic field around that wire. Is it true, then, that when a neuron fires, an electromagnetic field appears around the axon?"

"Yes, in fact some research has actually measured the strength of these magnetic fields." He seemed pleased with his answer.

I twirled my pen between my fingers. "That's interesting, because the magnetic field around a wire alters or creates current in a wire lying near it. Does that mean that any single neuron can influence the action potential of other nearby neurons not just through the synapse, but also through the changes in its magnetic field — and doesn't that add a level of complexity to how the brain functions that far surpasses our current knowledge, especially since our theories primarily emphasize synaptic transmission?"

Karmel's pipe dropped from a stout, upright angle to a limp, downward slant. He pulled it out of his mouth and leaned across his desk towards me, squinting slightly, as if trying to bring me into sharper focus. "I suppose the magnetic fields around axons might influence the activity of other axons, but the communication of information in the brain is primarily through the synapses... Now, as I was saying, the hypothalamic nuclei are intricately interconnected and receive information from motor systems and from olfactory, gustatory, visual, and somatosensory systems..."

Neuropsychology. A brand of reductionism endorsed by many psychologists. Where is "mind" or "self" inside that glob of muscle, bone, fat, and neural tissue we call the body? Where is the soul, if it even exists? I thought of Jon and smiled. He was right. Sir Eccles, a Nobel prize laureate, in fact did believe the soul could be located in a specific area of the cerebral cortex. Three centuries earlier, Descartes had stated that humans are an "animal machine" in which the soul is linked to the physical body through the brain's pineal gland. He planted the seed for later physiological reductionists, but he had to be careful to add in the stuff about the soul. If he didn't, his religious peers surely would have burned him at the stake. Sir Eccles had the opposite problem. When he claimed he had located the soul in the mechanistic machine, his biological colleagues thought he was crazy. What goes around comes around. Nowadays, the concept of soul is publicly attacked or laughed at by most of the scientific community. Sometimes even scientists are not very scientific. They're afraid to be open-minded. But in private gatherings of avant-garde physicists, mathematicians, and computer wizards, such ideas as soul and mind are being discussed in hushed voices. Some brave souls even go public with their ideas.

A black sheep among white lab coats. That's me too. But who was I trying to kid? There's more to my dissatisfaction with science than being intellectually disillusioned. I was basically oppositional, quietly defiant of authority, driven by a need to be different. I hated to be told what to do, especially by my superiors. But then again, as much as I cherished the idea of being a renegade, of standing on my own, of being the marginal man who achieves success — I was also scared to death of it. A bit of a paradox, isn't it? Paradoxes always point the way to something important in human nature.

"The hypothalamus sends fibers to the thalamus, cortex, and motor systems. The most visible tracts are the medial forebrain bundle, which connects the hypothalamus with midbrain structures, the fornix, which interconnects the hippocampus, septum, and hypothalamus, and an efferent system that divides into the mammillothalamic and mammillotegmental tracts."

There was a knock at the door.

"Come in." Karmel said loudly.

An older woman with graying hair and bifocals stuck her head into the room. She was one of the secretaries. At first glance, her aging face looked tough, hardened by many years of enduring this profession. Her eyes seemed tired, defeated. She spoke with flat affect, "Dr. Karmel, Dr. Bodkin is here to see you."

"Oh, yes, please excuse me," Karmel said, rising from his chair. As soon as he left the room, we fell into a huddle. Though we didn't know each other very well, we felt a common bond as psychology interns. The two graduate students from the local university, who were permitted to attend the seminars, listened intently, but didn't interrupt. The counterpart to medical students among residents, they knew the value of deferring to us psychology interns.

"Can you believe it?"

"I wish I had the guts to walk out."

"Why doesn't he just teach us about the psychiatric symptoms resulting from brain damage, rather than spend so much time on this stuff?"

"Yeah, that would be a lot more useful."

"Maybe we should tell the consortium directors."

"What could they do? Tell Karmel what to teach in this course? Tell him NOT to teach this course? We don't even know if they'd listen to us."

"Yeah, in fact they're not even too happy with us lately."

"What do you mean?"

"I heard that they think that we're not cohesive enough. The interns last year were good friends. They went to dinner, visited each other, socialized a lot. The consortium wants us to be like that."

"Oh, that's bullshit!" I said. "First of all, it's none of their business whether we socialize or not. And besides, we ARE cohesive. We've gone to lunch together, and last month we were the ones that organized the party for the consortium. You know what the problem is, don't you? They're the ones who aren't cohesive. It's taken them years to get this consortium going, and all along the way they've been bad-mouthing and back-biting each other. They still haven't resolved the conflicts, so they project them onto us."

"Yeah, I agree. I think we are cohesive. In fact, I brought my camera in to take a picture of us, for the new consortium newsletter."

"Wait," I said. "Take a picture of this."

I jumped into Karmel's seat, put my feet up on his desk, and poised his pipe at my mouth as I struck a contemplative expression — my version of the Thinker. "Put this in the newsletter!"

Everyone laughed.

Just seconds after the flash popped, the door opened and Karmel walked in. I quickly dropped my feet to the floor. Terror ripped through my whole being. Karmel stopped short, looked at me, at the pipe in my hand, then back at me, his face completely emotionless. Instantly I felt myself regress dozens of years, to that naughty boy who got caught, who must justify himself before the authority, before omnipotent Father — but too psychologically unsophisticated, and feeling too ashamed, to be able to pull it off. Out of the pits of desperation, I grasped at a feeble plan of action.

"It's, it's a beautiful pipe. My grandfather had one like it."

"Is that so?" Karmel said as he stood before his desk, waiting for me to abdicate his throne. I slunk out of his chair and returned to my seat, along the way noticing that the interns were biting their lips, trying not to laugh. Karmel resumed his position behind the desk, briefly examined his pipe, and then, convinced that it was unharmed, struck a match to light up with a self-satisfied smacking of his lips. He began to speak, with each word a small puff of smoke issuing from his mouth, "As I was saying, the hypothalamus contains what is referred to as the 'satiety center' which is located in the ventromedial section."

I tried not to look at him, or at anyone. A bad boy. A very bad boy. What shame for someone who was usually a very good boy, who always behaved, who always got good grades. I was trapped in the conflict between obeying and defying authority.

I remembered an argument my father and I once had at the dinner table. I was 15, filled with new ideas about physics from my science class, rather boastfully describing the law of gravitation, how an object falling to earth would continue to accelerate as it approached the ground. My father, twirling spaghetti on his fork, disagreed. He insisted that the falling object must at some point reach a constant speed, that it could not fall faster and faster forever. My father, a high school dropout, knew car mechanics but was a stranger to Newton's laws. I persistently defended my idea, he insisted I was wrong. Finally, frustrated with his authoritarian stubbornness, but unwilling to fully challenge his inept argument, I asked to be excused from the table.

Sitting on the front steps of the house with my friend Kevin, I described the whole dinner table debate, complained about how stupid my father was. Suddenly, I sensed there was someone standing behind me, inside the screen door, listening. I panicked, but when I turned to look, no one was there.

Later that night, as I was flipping through T.V. channels, looking for a Star Trek rerun, I noticed that one of the encyclopedia volumes on the bookshelf protruded from the evenly aligned set. It was "G." I pulled it out, found the section on gravitation, and scanned through it. My eyes were drawn to a paragraph three quarters of the way down, where a faint greasy fingerprint appeared in the margin. "The theory predicts that a falling object will continue to accelerate as it approaches the center of the earth's mass. However, due to the resistance created by air friction, the velocity reaches a maximum limit known as terminal velocity."

My father was right. But he never again said anything about that argument.

I often think about that fingerprint in the encyclopedia — and when I do, I feel sad.

CHAPTER 12

— Cults —

"ARE THERE ANY QUESTIONS?" Karmel looked around the room. No one moved. "Very well, we'll continue next week." He wrapped the bowl of his pipe against the ashtray as if it were a gavel. Court closed. As we left, he was still poking at his pipe, trying to dislodge those last bits of burnt tobacco. For a brief moment, I felt sorry for him. As soon as we reached a safe distance down the hallway, everyone started laughing. The graduate students, tagging along behind, joined in.

"I can't believe that happened."

"I thought I would burst out laughing."

"Do you think he saw my feet on his desk," I asked, hoping for some reality testing to quell my anxiety.

"I don't think so — he was too busy making his entrance."

"I want a copy of that picture."

"Me too. Maybe we should submit it to the newsletter."

"Great," I added. "Karmel would submit my head on a platter to the consortium directors."

"That's if you're lucky. If he really wants to be cruel, he'll make you take the neuropsychology seminar over again."

Everyone groaned.

"Anything but that!"

"Look! Over there! It's Dr. Finehardt and Dr. Rathus. We're supposed to talk to them."

"We are?"

"Yeah. We're supposed to ask them if we can go to that case seminar for psychoanalytic psychologists."

"Go ahead. You ask them.

"No way."

"I think Tom should do it."

"No thank you. I already got myself into hot water today."

"Exactly. You've got nothing to lose."

They ushered me down the hallway to where Finehardt and Rathus were standing. Embedded in my peer group, I felt fairly safe as we approached them. But when they all suddenly took one step back, leaving me alone to face the unknown, my heartbeat quickened. Finehardt and Rathus didn't seem to notice me standing at the edge of their orbit. Their conversation didn't miss a beat.

"… So he's over 120 hours into his analysis, in the middle of an intense transference, and the institute board tells him that they won't accept his analysis to graduate." A fire burned in Finehardt's eyes that matched her slick red hair and glowed in contrast to her conservative gray skirt and jacket. Rathus tugged at his trim beard as he listened intently.

"Why wouldn't they accept it?" he asked.

"They found out that his analyst's degree was in physiology, so they considered him a lay analyst."

"Physiology? Didn't the board know that from the very beginning? Didn't he tell them when he applied?"

"He did. He wrote it on his application to the institute, but apparently his handwriting was sloppy. They thought it said 'psychology.' I'm sure you would know how it is with illegible handwriting."

Rathus straightened his neck, raised one eyebrow. The situation reminded me of an old joke: Two analysts pass each other in the hallway. One analyst says to the other, "Good morning." The second analyst thinks to himself, "I wonder what he meant by that?" I held back a chuckle. Somehow the changed expression in my face catapulted me from ground to figure. Finehardt and Rathus suddenly took notice of my presence. It caught me off guard.

"Um, excuse me. I'm Thomas Holden." I briefly imagined myself having included the title Doctor in my name. "I'm an intern in the psychology consortium. The directors wondered whether we interns could attend your case seminar. They asked us to speak to you about it."

"Well, it's not really my seminar," Finehardt said, "but, yes, one of the directors did mention that to me."

I paused because I wasn't sure what her yes meant. Could we attend the seminar or not? She cocked her head and smiled, as if enjoying my predicament. She's the kind of person who attempts to appear polite, friendly — but you sense that beneath the benign facade hide some very sharp claws.

"Uh, so it's O.K. that we come to the seminar?"

"Unless the other members of the seminar have any objections. What do you think Dr. Rathus?"

"I don't believe anyone has objected. It's fine by me."

"How many interns are there?" Finehardt said, again flashing that bittersweet smile.

"Five all together." I pointed to my peers huddled together behind me.

"I count eight," she said sharply.

"Oh, three are graduate students."

"Do the consortium directors want all eight students to come to the seminar?"

Her sarcastic emphasis on the word "students" made me feel defensive, and vaguely humiliated. I looked back at the graduate students for an answer, for some support. They just stared back, paralyzed, confused. Finally, one of them shrugged his shoulders.

"We don't know," I said as I turned back to face the monster. She shifted her cold, incandescent eyes from the graduate students to focus them on me. I was sure she could burn holes into my face and I could only imagine the sadistic horrors that twisted through her unconscious.

She looked at Rathus. "You know, I've been wondering about what happened to all the fully trained analysts who used to come to the seminar. I'm worried that the group is becoming more and more... diluted. Ed wasn't at the last two meetings, or Donald, and I haven't seen Lee in months. I worry that they're dissatisfied with the way the group is evolving."

Rathus seemed uncomfortable. He looked at me briefly, almost apologetically, but was drawn back to Finehardt, as if she had cast a spell over him. "I hadn't thought of that," Rathus said. "I know Lee is becoming more active in APA."

I found myself getting very angry. So what was the verdict? Was she going to honor me with a definite reply, or what? A hatred of this creature welled up inside me.

"I have to go," she said to Rathus. "We should talk about this with the group — before it's too late." She threw me her sinister smile. "I guess I'll see you and all your... friends at the seminar."

"Wait, I'll walk out with you," Rathus called after her.

The interns and I trailed behind, easing into a slow pace to widen the gap between us and them.

"What was she saying about the seminar?"

"She was lamenting her dwindling narcissistic supplies," I said. The comment, of course, didn't make sense to them. Their thoughts were elsewhere.

"We're lucky we got in the seminar, but do you think they'll ask us to present cases?"

"Oh god! I hope not. It makes me panic just thinking about it."

"I don't know what to expect."

"No one expects the Spanish Inquisition," I added while checking my watch. "Gotta get back to the inpatient unit. See you next week."

This Dr. Noheart is a good example of what bugs me about some psychoanalysts. It's the preoccupation with status and credentials, a deeply ingrained elitism that spawns feelings of superiority and nose-thumbing. Are you a fully trained analyst from a first-rate institute? Did your personal analysis meet the international standards? Was your analyst analyzed by Freud (the ultimate medal) or by an analyst analyzed by an analyst who was analyzed by Freud (second best)? If you can link yourself somehow to Freud, then you get the stamp of approval. The funny thing is that Freud was never in analysis; he analyzed himself. So why do the rest of us have to go through a "full analysis" of three or four sessions a week for several years. What about less intensive therapy, say twice, or even just once a week? Not thorough or deep enough, they would say. Or what about people who all their lives were keenly introspective, who have worked hard on their own to understand themselves? What about people who were fortunate enough to have good parents, who are psychologically healthy, and, therefore, don't have too far to go in psychotherapy?

My supervisor Henry once applied to one of the old time, elite psychoanalytic institutes. Unfortunately, it was run by medical analysts who were not terribly fond of taking non-physicians into the fold, though they did make some exceptions for those candidates who bowed and scraped. Henry endured 15 hours of intense interviewing by the institute staff. They probed every aspect of his life — not just education and career, but also his family history, earliest childhood memories, sexual activities, fantasies, every facet of his neurosis he was capable of verbalizing. At one point he asked if he could use the bathroom, because he needed water. One of the analysts was waiting for him right outside the door when he reemerged. Henry knew what they were up to. They needed to determine if he was "analyzable." But he didn't expect such interrogations. At home, in the middle of the night, he woke up screaming from a nightmare about vampires chasing him. He paced the house until dawn, continually checking the locks on the doors and windows. It was a transitory paranoid reaction.

But he was hopeful about getting into the institute. The staff seemed to like him, they praised his research, they admired his motivation. Because the institute believed that psychologists, lacking medical training, should never practice psychoanalysis, he even agreed to sign a waver stating that he would only use his training for the purpose of doing research.

Three days after the last interview, he received a letter containing just one sentence, "The institute has decided not to accept your application."

Talk about a let-down. It was more like a slam-down. Why was he rejected so curtly and thoughtlessly? Status, credentials. He didn't have any, or at least the right kind. It's a shame that everyone interested in psychoanalysis can't hang together. It's a shame that some people want to draw lines in the sand marking their territory and who is not qualified to enter it.

One of my professors in graduate school, a learning theorist who preferred the company of computers over people, once referred to psychoanalysis as a "cult." He claimed it was no different than any religious cult — rigid, narrow-minded, refusing to consider points of view other than the cherished belief system handed down from some charismatic figure. He contrasted it with his own beloved "science" that is open-minded, always questioning the facts, never blindly accepting anything without first subjecting it to an empirical test. Of course he believed all this not because he had studied psychoanalysis himself, but because his professors in graduate school told him so.

Which just goes to show you that science too can become a cult. People believe what they believe because other people of authority told them to believe it. Science has hypnotized us all into accepting its creed. It's a cult because it is founded on assumptions that have not and never will be absolutely proven — assumptions, nevertheless, in which the scientist places faith of a truly religious magnitude — a faith so blind and unquestioning that most scientists never give these assumptions a second thought. They do not consider the possibility that they have built their grand castles on shifting sand. Take, for example, the scientist's assumption that there is order, a coherent pattern of some kind in the universe; that there are an identifiable, finite number of causes resulting in an effect; and that the order of the universe can be discovered by science. Is this really the truth, or just a cult belief?

If I hold up a rock, then let go, it will fall to the floor with a thump. What caused that event to occur? Well, the obvious answer, according to the scientific-minded, is "gravity." Or one might say that the thumping sound was the result of vibrating air molecules. But is that really the complete explanation? Isn't there a much bigger WHY that must be answered? What if the rock had not existed? What geological events culminated in that particular rock? What if the floor never existed? What events led to that floor, to the building of which the floor is a part? And why did I lift the rock in the first place? What events led to my wanting to do this little demonstration, or to my very existence in the first place? Don't all of these of events, these infinite number of causes, intersect at one unique point in time and space, culminating in that rock falling to the floor with a thump? It happened for an infinite number of reasons. The whole universe made it happen. Everything in existence caused it to happen, which means there really is no "cause" at all. It happened just because it happened.

The mind works the same way. There is no cause and effect, just an endless array of processes wrapped around each other. Everything is multiply, endlessly determined. In his pioneering study of dreams, Freud concluded that a single dream, when probed to its deepest roots, expands outward into a universe of feelings, memories, and associations that has no boundaries. The dream is the tip of the infinite.

But the infinite is scary. Where do you hang your hat? We all need a cult of some kind to give us a simpler explanation, a place to locate ourselves — a sense of security. According to Freud, it's those very feelings of insecurity and helplessness in the face of the overpowering, unpredictable universe that drove humans to religion. And, for many of us, to science. We may all subscribe to different cults, but we all have in common the fact that we hate having the carpet pulled out from beneath us.

Of course, the big advantage of science over religion is that it gives us technology. Who can resist its treasures? Do you know anyone who would give up their car for a really good hymn?

CHAPTER 13

Boatmen

As I walked through the main lobby, I looked out the large plate glass windows into the parking lot. I just wanted a brief glimpse of my car and the hope of my eventual escape. Pausing for a moment, I caught sight of it. I also noticed something by the front of the car. It was too far away to see clearly. It was something almost under the car! Was it moving, struggling? Was I seeing things? With my heart racing, I ran through the doors and into the parking lot — at first at a gallop, then even faster. As I got closer I realized there indeed was something under the front. There, sitting on the ground, his legs stretched out and wiggling merrily under the car, was Jon attaching a sticker to the bumper.

"Holy shit!" I said, trying to contain myself. "You scared me half to death!"

"Think optimistically," he answered casually, "You're still half alive." Out of the corner of his eye he saw that I was indeed upset. He stood up. "My apologies, Dr. Holden. I'm afraid I let my enthusiasm carry me away. You see, I've succeeded in obtaining for your parking pleasure a sticker to Lot O."

I felt more composed. My heart was slowing down. "Great, but I thought you were going to try to get a visiting clinician's sticker for lot A."

"My source said he could have provided me with two visiting clinician's stickers, if I wanted them. But I discerned he was holding back on me. He's never offered me two of anything. It was a ploy to distract me. I knew he had something even better, so I reminded him of his — well, let me say his debts to me."

"Debts? That sounds intriguing. What kind of debts?"

"Some arrangements concerning creative payrolling," he said as he moved to the rear bumper to place the companion sticker. "You see, I have friends in Personnel as well."

"You're amazing Jon."

He beamed. "I take great pride in being able to subvert, in my own small way, the bureaucratic system. So use it in good health, and be discreet."

"You mean I can't brag about it to my co-workers?"

"If your heart so desires, but you take the chance of getting caught."

"You mean WE get caught," I laughed.

"If YOU get caught," Jon smiled as he pointed to his security booth, "my office will disavow any knowledge of your actions."

"Aha! Desert me in a crisis, will you?"

"Pluck and duck, that's my motto."

"Don't worry, Jon, my lips are sealed — even if they threaten to draw and quarter me, even if they force me to do rational emotive therapy. By the way, Jon, where is Lot O?"

"Around the other side of the building, near the entrance to the library. I would wholeheartedly suggest that you relocate to that position immediately. If you so desire, you will be able to observe your vehicle from the inpatient unit."

"Great. A constant reminder of the potential escape from work — which reminds me, I must get back to the dungeon. See you later."

"Farewell, dear prince — tell my maiden I await her."

I got into the Nova, which started up without a fuss, and drove along the one lane road around the side of the building, through the patch of the woods that extended down the hill and blended into the forest to the east of the Medical Center. As I came into the clearing, I saw O-lot straight ahead of me. It was fairly small, right next to the hospital entrance, shaded by three large oak trees — prime real estate. I pulled in feeling privileged, and paranoid. Would anyone recognize me as an impostor? A Jaguar, a Plexus, a BMW — once again my Nova stood out like a mutant, the hideous dinosaur of automotive evolution that somehow escaped the junkyard. Two physicians standing next to a red Mercedes seemed to be glaring at me as I parked. One of them was holding an old leather bag — the kind family doctors used to carry to their house calls. He opened it. For a flickering moment I imagined he would pull out a pistol, fire shots into the air, through my fenders, and try to drive me out of his territory. Instead, he pulled out a watch. I sighed. Act like you belong here, and no one will suspect you. With glowing pseudo-confidence I stepped out of the car and strode to the hospital entrance. Along the way I noticed an old Ford Falcon with rusted wheel wells, peeling paint, and a front bumper twisted into a rather obscene form. It was a sign. I smiled, for I knew I wasn't alone.

This was the first time I ever walked into the building through the rear entrance. I wasn't sure what to expect. The tiny mind of the electronic doors — maintaining its untiring vigilance through laser eyes — sensed my approach, commanded the doors to slide open, paused until I passed through, and slid the doors closed — once again fulfilling its purpose in life.

This lobby was smaller than the one at the main entrance. On opposite walls hung high profile abstract art — to my left, a metal sculpture that resembled three boat propellers surrounded by a school of sperm, and, to my right, a huge canvas filled with delicate swirls of multi-colored pastels, at its very center one large, anomalous, disturbing black dot that seemed to lure the viewer into a bottomless hole. At the far end of the lobby stood large plate glass windows, trimmed with shiny chrome, that revealed the first and second floors of the medical library. Nestled comfortably into plastic study carrels, facing outward, a row of unoccupied computers displayed intricate whirling patterns on their screens, as if tempting us while chatting amongst themselves.

Smack in the middle of the lobby, mounted on a bright chrome platform, stood a marble statue of Hippocrates in a long, flowing robe, a scepter in one hand, a book in the other. His presence, no doubt, was intended to create an atmosphere of reverence, accomplishment, wisdom — but upon closer inspection, the subtle squint in one of his eyes and the upward twist at the corner of his mouth conveyed a different message, as if he were saying to himself, "Where the fuck am I?"

I didn't see an elevator, so I took the marble staircase that curved along the side of the lobby, up to the second floor of the library. Hippocrates eyes seemed to follow me as I climbed the steps.

"Are you going to leave me here?"

Sorry, Old Doc.

Suddenly, I sneezed, and then again, and again. I hardly ever sneeze more than twice in a row — an omen of my impending cold.

"God bless you," Hippocrates said in silence.

The library was almost empty, which seemed odd for a medical center. Sitting at a large oak table, a medical student was buried up to his chin in a stack of old medical journals. He was concentrating intensely on picking his nose. The librarian, an elderly woman with bifocals, sat on a stool at a computer, her fingers resting lightly on the keyboard. Wistfully, she stared off into space, no doubt dreaming of the days of the Dewey Decimal System and rows of wooden card catalogs.

Outside the library, I found myself in an unfamiliar wing of the building. At one corner I lost my bearing and walked down a hallway that dead-ended onto a brick wall, as if the building's architect had made a mistake in his plans by drawing a corridor that went nowhere — but rather than redesigning it, simply capped it off and forgot about it. As I turned to make my way back out, I heard a door opening behind me. I looked over my shoulder. At the very end of the hallway, from a door barely visible from where I was standing, emerged a lanky, slightly hunched over man. He looked like he had slept in his corduroy jacket and missed his last appointment for a haircut. Despite graying hair and weathered features, he looked like a slightly awkward adolescent. His arms were full with papers and folders chaotically stuffed into stacks of books. One of the volumes began to slip out the back of his arm. Grimacing, he backed up against the doorframe to nudge it back into place, only to upset the balance of books under his other arm. As he juggled them, trying to establish an equilibrium, he caught sight of me watching him. With a look of timid surprise, he darted back into the room. I heard the door close and the muffled sound of books hitting the floor. I had never seen him before.

I found my way back to the corridor leading to the inpatient unit. As I got closer, a tense, aching sensation spread across the top of my abdomen. I thought about Cheryl exposing herself, about Elizabeth under the wheels of a mail truck. No! Put that out of my mind. I had to concentrate on my inpatients. I made a mental list of everything I had to do. As I passed the cluster of offices for the social workers, I stopped to see if Marion was in. Her door was closed. I could just barely hear a man crying inside the room, and Marion's calm voice smoothing over the jagged edges of his pain. In a way, I envied him.

The steel gray doors of the inpatient unit came closer and closer, staring back at me, waiting to draw me in. Fight or flight. I told myself I would not retreat, surely not physically, because I had no choice at that level — but I also refused to flee psychologically. I had a job to do, and I would do it. I had responsibilities. I was a professional.

The door was upon me. I confidently reached for the knob, instead grabbed a handful of air, and collided into the door. Narcissistically injured, I looked down to discover that there was no doorknob! At that moment the blade of a screwdriver snaked through the hole where the knob used to be. The lock clicked, the door opened.

Phil's face popped into view. "You run into things often, don't you," he chuckled.

I felt exasperated. "I should have known it was you!"

"You were expecting maybe St. Peter."

"No — the boatman on the River Styx." I pushed through the door and entered the Netherlands. Apparently the dinner carts had entered just moments before me. As the kitchen attendants unlocked the bars that secured the trays in their slots, a swarm of patients descended on the carts, their eyes filled with eager but suspicious anticipation about what the hospital had brought them tonight. The script was always the same:

"I didn't order jello!"

"Not chicken again!"

"If you don't want it, I'll take it."

"Remember to fill out the menu card next time."

Like birds around a feeder, one by one they plucked out their trays and returned to their respective niches.

A voice passed from left to right behind my head. "Your patients have been looking for you." It was Barb, swinging her coat onto her shoulders, making a b-line for the door. Nurses are abused by the hospital system, but unlike physicians, their self-righteous overlords, they get to go home on time.

"Your knight in shining armor awaits you!" I cried out.

I wasn't sure if she heard me, but the patients did. They thought I was speaking to them. They looked confused.

"No, um… I was talking to the, uh…" I pointed my thumb over my shoulder towards the door, but Barb had already disappeared. The patients just stared, within seconds lost interest, and turned their attention back to the food. One face remained focused on me. It was Rachel Finski. Holding a coke in one hand and a 7-up in the other, she scurried towards me, her arms thrust outward as if she were using the cans of soda to balance herself.

"Doctor, doctor!"

It struck me that I was about to enter a conversation I would rather avoid.

"Doctor Knight, can I ask you a question?"

"My name is Dr. Holden."

"Oh, do you have any holy water?"

"No I don't. Do you… need some?" I regretted the question the second it left my lips.

"I need to replenish my fluids. It's very important."

"You seem to have plenty to drink right there."

"Oh, these will never do — caffeine, caramel coloring, artificial sweeteners, cyclamates — all those chemicals will surely clog my braindikes. Holy water will help clear out my axons and allow my spirit energy to flow much more freely."

"Uh, yeah." I wasn't prepared for this.

"The flow of chi is most important, from one neuron to the other, from one chakra to another, around and around the body, freely, through the internal organs, and the blood brain barrier, and down to the feet, because the toes are connected to the knees, and the knees to the heart, and the heart to the cerebral cortex."

Help! Someone get some meds. I tried to inch myself away. "Rachel, I'd like to talk to you more about this, but I have to go."

Rachel side-stepped with me.

"Sometimes the energy tries to escape, through the joints, or the top of the head. Stone age people thought this was good, so they used trephining. They cut holes in the top of your head with stone knives. It was mostly water evaporation. But modern science has shown that the energy must be circulated within the system. It must be concentrated in the vital ganglia."

Someone standing by the dinner cart caught my eye. It was Mr. Tennostein, motioning at me with his wobbly hand.

"Excuse me, Rachel, I have to talk to one of my patients. Maybe you should talk to your therapist about these things."

"I've spoken to him already. Dr. Lawrence is a kind person, but he's just a medical student and hasn't learned much about hydroneurology."

Holding his arms in front of himself like a preying mantis, and with the clumsy prancing gait typical of patients with brain damage, Mr. Tennostein slowly drew closer to us.

He had a wild look in his eyes and a half opened packet of ketchup in his hand.

"Doctor! The nurse told me that you're going to take away my driver's license."

"We were talking about that this morning, remember Mr. Tennostein?" I placed myself between him and Rachel, hoping she would take the hint that she was not to be part of this conversation, but she circled around me and continued listening intently.

"How can you do that? How can you take away my driver's license?"

"We can't do that Mr. Tennostein. Only the motor vehicle bureau or the court system can do that. All I'm saying is that we are worried about you. You've had a few minor accidents already, and we want to prevent a major one. Your concentration and coordination aren't what they used to be."

"Sounds neurological to me," Rachel added.

"Excuse us, Rachel." I took Tennostein by the arm and tried to steer him away.

"You're excused," she said pursuing us.

"Mr. Tennostein and I would like to talk alone for a while. Perhaps we should sit down over there in the library cubicle."

"I don't care if she listens," he said as he pulled his arm away from me. "In fact, I want a witness."

"I know you think that we're against you, that we're trying to take something away from you. But please believe me that we're trying to help. What we need now is more information. Did you go for the catscan today?"

Rachel's eyes opened wide. "I knew it! Braindike blockage!"

"A brain what?"

"Never mind, Mr. Tennostein. Did you get the catscan?"

"Yeah, but I won't let you take my driver's license away, and I won't tolerate any old-bag nurses coming to my home."

"Catscans are for detecting micro-fish in the synapses," Rachel added.

"Please, Rachel, not now. Mr. Tennostein, let's wait for the results of the catscan. We can make those decisions about your license later. For now, maybe it would be a good idea for you to meet with our occupational therapist who can check you out to see how you do in the kitchen. You may need help cooking, or cleaning, or taking your medications. A nurse might be helpful."

"Florence Nightingale used cool water to soothe brain fever," Rachel said. She seemed to honestly believe she was making a valuable contribution to the conversation.

"I don't need a Florence Nightingale, or Albert Schweitzer, or Sigmund Freud. I just want to get out of here. I just want to be left alone."

As he shook his fist, my eyes followed the opened packet of ketchup aimed right at my shirt. I prayed I would survive this skirmish without a wound. My concentration on what to say next was broken by the humming of a battery powered motor. A warning signal flashed in my brain, but it was too late. The wheelchair bumped into the side of my leg, knocking me off balance. Kathy Mummom looked up at me, beaming with excitement.

"Dr. Holden, Barb told me that you might be giving me a pass soon."

"Oh, she did? Let's talk about that. I'll be with you in a minute, as soon as I'm finished talking to Mr. Tennostein."

"They're discussing Freud and synapse blockage," Rachel added.

"How come I haven't gotten any passes yet?" Mr. Tennostein said, still dangerously waving the ketchup packet.

"We should talk about that."

"He doesn't like to give passes. He just likes to talk."

"Now that's not true. I mean — Kathy, why don't you and Rachel sit down over there and talk for a while, until I'm done with Mr. Tennostein."

"Talk, talk."

"Talk does loosen up braindikes."

"I'm tired of talking. I want out of here — WITH my license and NO old-bag nurses."

"I really think we should divide up so I can talk to you people separately."

"Divided we fall, anyone want a coke?"

"I want a pass."

"A 7-up?"

"I want my license —"

"Later, Kathy."

" — and no old-bag nurses."

"I can have one later?"

"That's not what I meant."

"They're bad for the brain anyhow."

"Why won't you let me have one?"

"My brain isn't bad, it isn't!"

"Bad isn't the right word, it's just —"

"You think I'm still sick, don't you?"

"I didn't say that."

"You did, you said it is, you said it's —"

"But that's what you meant, you think I'm —"

" — deteriorating."

" — crazy."

" — blocked-up, that's all."

My thoughts locked like an overheated engine. Everyone fell silent. With the ketchup packet aimed squarely at my chest, Tennostein's hand began to shake, while Kathy restlessly fingered the trigger for the wheelchair motor. I just stood there for an eternal moment, for I knew it was coming,

I knew I couldn't avoid it — the rap on the shin, the blob of tomato paste on my shirt, the embarrassment of having my professional facade effaced — the horror of my reason losing out to the forces of insanity.

"The movie's about to start!" The voice sailed across the room like an announcement of the Second Coming.

"Ooo! I think it's *Jaws*!" Rachel squealed. "Let's go quick before the good seats are gone."

Kathy's eyes lit up too. "Yeah, I love that movie." They both did an immediate about-face and sped off to the group room, leaving a befogged Mr. Tennostein behind, staring blankly at me, as if the sudden interruption hit the "delete" key in his brain. Not remembering exactly what it was he wanted from me, he lowered his hand that pointed the ketchup-gun at my shirt, turned around, and was slowly pulled towards the group room in the wake created by Rachel and Kathy.

CHAPTER 14

Jaws

* * *

THEY SAY THAT IF YOU work with crazy people long enough, if you really try to understand their life and mind, you gradually become crazy yourself. At first schizophrenics will use their craziness to seal themselves off, protect themselves, keep you at arm's distance. But if you persist, you will begin to hear a clear message behind the psychotic communications. It's both an invitation and a challenge: "If you really want to know me, to help me, then become me." To prove yourself, you must let go of your reality to enter the world of insanity, and feel it from the inside. The distinction between you and the patient fades until you unfold into a symbiotic union of thought, sensation and emotion. Together you embrace the delusions of a warped mind that grasps for meaning, the overwhelming hate that floods from the depths of denied being, and, at the very bottom of it all, a terrifying, mindless void. Unlike the schizophrenic, you do not succumb to the deceptive and insidious beauty of the insane landscape. You have seen the patient's inner life through his eyes, but he has also seen it through yours. You allow the patient to borrow your self, to feel your self, to take what he needs to make his own. You offer a new perspective, one that encompasses, without fragmenting or deforming itself, the horrible torrent of anxiety about the truth of one's life. It is a perspective that reveals the pains and pleasures of knowing that there is both self and other. The patient invited you in, and after your visit, you invite him out.

I stood motionless in the middle of the inpatient unit, thinking, talking to myself. The soundtrack from the movie spilled forth from the group room and reverberated around me — primal music, those ominous bass notes that throbbed rhythmically, slowly, up from the depths and then back down, gradually building in speed and power.

The shark is coming.

"I do not understand why they allow them to watch this movie." It was Sheikh. He looked nervous.

"Wha… What do you mean?" I mumbled as I tried to focus on him.

"Yes. This movie upset me. Sharks hunting and eating people. People hunting and killing sharks. Such horrible things!"

"We Americans love that kind of stuff," I muttered. "We've always lived close to our killer instinct, on the edge of fear."

"This does not seem appropriate for psychiatric patients. I am afraid this movie might cause some of them to decompensate."

"Yeah, you're right. For the paranoid patients it's their worst nightmare projected onto the Big Screen. Who picked out this movie to show them?"

"I believe it is the responsibility of the recreation therapist — Paul."

"Paul picked that movie? He should know better than that. Is he in there watching it? I haven't seen him around."

"I do not see him. Perhaps we should turn it off."

"Be my guest. You're the resident." At times like this I willingly deferred to his superior status.

His eyes opened wide, sending his bushy black eyebrows to the top of his forehead. "Not I! Perhaps we should speak to Fred."

When in doubt, send for the Chief. Let him make the wrong decision. "That's fine by me. Where is he?"

"I believe he is in his office seeing a patient."

We crossed the unit and entered the small secretarial area adjoining the offices for the head nurse, chief resident, and director. Fred's door was closed, but we could hear muffled voices inside.

"We must not knock," Sheikh said. "He is very strict about not being interrupted. It is almost six o'clock. He will be done in a few minutes."

I sat on the secretary's desk while Sheikh paced. I respected him. He truly cared about his patients. He loved to talk to them about their lives. His warmth was genuine, unlike those phony therapists who want you to think that they are Compassion Incarnated, but who really despise their patients for being weak, dependent, and resistant to change.

Fred, on the other hand, probably didn't love or hate his patients. Emotions like that were largely irrelevant, at least consciously. As a loyal obsessive-compulsive, he thought of them as something to work on — like a car or computer. You had to tune them up, adjust their software until they functioned properly. Not that he dehumanized them in a cruel or disparaging way. Not at all. He was an electrical engineer before his switch-over to psychiatry. He carried over his respect and fascination for electronics to the human mind. In a way, he was admirable for his devotion to the "right way" of conducting psychotherapy. Psychiatrists like Fred love rules and regulations, which is why they love orthodox psychoanalytic treatment. There is a specific, correct method to conduct therapy and you do not deviate from it. You start the session on time; you end it on time. Patients always pay for missed sessions. You only speak when you have a precise interpretation based on specific unconscious derivatives provided by the patient. It's all a very comforting philosophy for people who need everything to be precise, controllable, tidy. Without the rules and regulations, they would have to fly by the seat of their pants when making therapeutic interventions. That's too messy, too anxiety-provoking. They squirm at the thought that "anything goes as long as it works" or that what you do in therapy "depends on the patient" — or, worst of all, that you might have to rely on "intuition." They want to think that all patients can be treated exactly alike, that the same logical, objective method will work for all. Otherwise, therapeutic technique becomes relative and subjective. Either there is only one right way to do it, or we open the door to confusion and chaos — the obsessive's worst nightmare.

I opened the top drawer of the secretary's desk. A pair of dice were buried in the compartment containing paper clips. I picked them up and slowly shook them in a loose fist as I stared at the digital clock. 5:59. The red diode blinked on and off with each passing second, absorbing me into a seemingly endless string of moments. Without thinking, I blew into my hand and tossed the dice across the desktop. They collided with the clock and rolled into Snake-eyes as the digital readout snapped into place: 6:00.

The door to Fred's office opened dutifully, and out stepped a middle-aged woman wearing a black overcoat. Her eyes were glassy. She walked by without looking at us. Behind her came Fred, wearing a self-satisfied smile.

"You two look like someone just died," he said.

"Or just became human hamburger," I replied.

"What?"

"We wanted to speak to you about the movie that the patients are seeing tonight," Sheikh said. "It's The Jaw."

"Jaws," I translated.

"Jaws? You're kidding. Whose idea was that?"

"We assume that Paul selected the movie," Sheikh replied.

"Paul's on vacation this week, unless he ordered it before he left. But he knows better than that."

"That's what I said."

"Then who ordered this horrible movie?" Sheikh asked.

"I don't know," Fred said impatiently, "but we can't let them watch it."

"Do you really intend to turn it off?" I asked. "Listen to them over there. They're clapping and laughing. They love it."

"They love it now, but wait until later, in the middle of the night, when they see sharks in the corners of the room, or under their bed, or in the toilet. They won't sleep for a week. My God, we'll have to cart meds in here by the wheelbarrow!"

"But if we turn it off," I said, "We smell like bad fish. Not only do we take away something they like, but we also demonstrate our incompetence by admitting that we shouldn't have shown the movie in the first place."

"Maybe we should speak to Dr. Stein," Sheikh said.

"The director leaves at 5:30," Fred replied, "and I sure don't want to bother him at home. No, I have to make this decision myself."

We all looked out across the unit towards the group room, but no one moved. Fred pulled at his eyebrow. Sweat formed on his upper lip — signs of his momentary indecision, and anxiety. I was glad it was him and not me.

As if summoned by our collective magical thinking, Carole, the head nurse, appeared in the doorway, her red hair shining like a rescue beacon. "Are they watching what I think they're watching?" she asked with a grimace.

"Yeah, *Jaws*," Fred answered. He looked relieved, like a lost child whose mother suddenly returned. "Do you think we should turn it off?"

"I should think so. Where did it come from anyway? There was no movie scheduled this week. Paul is on vacation."

"We don't know."

"I don't understand this at all," she said. "I'll have to contact Paul."

"I agree that they shouldn't be watching it," Fred said, "but if we turn it off, we're admitting to making a mistake by having it here in the first place."

"It's better to admit to that mistake," Carole said, "than later having to admit to the mistake of causing someone to decompensate because we allowed them to see it."

"Is it possible we're overreacting," he replied.

"I don't know about that. You weren't here several years ago when we played *The Day the Earth Stood Still*. One schizoid patient became convinced that he was an ambassador from Pluto. And another schizophrenic became progressively more mechanical in how he talked and moved, until he regressed into a rigid catatonia. He believed he was turning into a robot. We almost had to use shock treatment as a last resort."

"Klaatu barada nikto," I mumbled.

"What's that?" Fred asked.

"Uh, nothing. I was just thinking — wouldn't any movie then be a potential hazard? Patients could develop delusions of being Pinocchio, Lassie, or The Little Mermaid.

They might become convinced that the Wicked Witch of the West is after them."

"That's always a possibility," Fred said, "but I think that there's more danger in movies that take themselves seriously in how they violate reality, or in portraying blatant sexual and aggressive situations."

"What about the patients who will be angry that you're taking something away from them," I answered.

"Consciously, they will be disappointed and angry," Fred said, "but underneath that they will feel safe knowing that we are taking all precautions to protect their well-being."

"In the meantime," Sheikh interjected, "our patients get further into this movie."

"Right. I'm going to turn it off." Fred marched out of the room.

"I have to see this," I said following him. Sheikh was not far behind.

Slumped into their seats, sipping sodas and coffee, the patients were so totally engrossed in the film that they did not notice us enter. There were no staff members in the room. Unattended, sitting next to a conspicuously empty chair, the video player spun forth its images — people on a beach, sunbathing, playing catch, swimming... with hidden evil growing closer.

Confidently, Fred maneuvered along the side of the room, crossed over to the video player, and after briefly scanning the controls, hit the stop button. The room fell dark and silent. Everyone groaned angrily.

"I'm sorry that I have to turn this off," Fred announced loudly, "but there's been a mistake in the movie that was selected for tonight. As many of you probably know, this is a frightening movie — there's a lot of violence in it. For some patients it may be too frightening. Therefore, we've decided that we shouldn't show it."

Several patients moaned in complaint.

"But the water!" I heard Rachel cry.

"Oh, come on, Doc, we're not sissies," one adolescent said. "Besides it's just a story."

"I've seen this movie," responded an older woman sitting across from him, "and I think it's very scary."

"Yeah, like the part when the guy gets bit in half," a man in the back said gleefully.

Fred ignored him. "Thank you Mrs. Watts. Again, I'm sorry that this happened. Tomorrow we'll have another movie for you, and tonight we'll extend the TV time to 11 o'clock."

Sheikh darted over to the TV and switched it to a network channel. He smiled apologetically and bowed. Grumbling, some of the patients got up to leave. Others simply refocused themselves on the weather channel. They became absorbed in it immediately, as if the movie had never existed. Didn't matter much to them — any image would do. On his way out Fred nodded at me.

"That wasn't too bad," I said.

"All in a day's work. Which reminds me. You have an intake with that new patient Richard Mobin. His mother will be dropping him off at 7 o'clock."

"What do you know about him?"

Fred grinned, "He's crazy."

"Wonderful, just what I need."

"Just what the doctor ordered," Fred added jokingly, but something in him sensed I wasn't just kidding. "Go get dinner. You have enough time."

"Right." I followed him halfway across the unit where he veered off towards his office and I towards the exit. I slowed down as I approached the doors, stopped, carefully turned the knob until the bolt clicked, then cautiously opened the door and peeked outside. No Phil. I was safe. On my way to the elevator I again checked Marion's office. Her door was closed, but I could hear her talking with someone — a different person than before. No one could say Marion wasn't devoted and hardworking.

As I waited for the elevator I thought about this Richard Mobin. After dinner, normal people spend time with their family, watch TV, read, or relax. I, on the other hand, was going to chit-chat with a paranoid schizophrenic. What am I doing to myself?

The elevator doors opened. My insides jumped. Standing inside, alone, was that woman, the one next to me in the crowd at lunch. She looked up only briefly as I stepped inside and moved to the corner opposite her. I felt uncomfortable, self-conscious, but could not resist stealing glances. With her eyes lowered and hands folded gently around a book, she appeared sensitive, reserved, almost shy if not for the confidence that flowed through her relaxed, graceful posture. Her wool sweater and cotton pants glided loosely over her body, providing subtle but provocative hints of the beautiful contours beneath — an enticing, mysterious mixture of disclosure and concealment. Yet her beauty was also internal — quiet, peaceful, centered. She brushed her soft brown hair back from her face. In her eyes I could see she had me captured in her peripheral vision.

We stood there, absolutely still, quiet, as the elevator descended. Staring blankly ahead, I could almost feel her body as if I were holding her, and touch her mind as if it were a tangible thing. That sensation I experienced at lunch filled the elevator, that feeling of being drawn in, distance closing — a silent, intimate awareness wrapping around us.

The elevator came to a rest. The doors opened. Neither one of us moved. When I finally realized we were at the cafeteria level, the doors had already started to close. I darted my hand out to stop them. They closed onto my fingers and popped back open. I didn't even notice the pain as she stepped out, stopped, and turned back to look at me.

Her eyes met mine. They were bright blue, crystalline, vibrant. They seemed to pull at me. "Thank you," she said softly, and walked away.

The doors closed again. I just stood there, my memory still glowing with the imprinted image of her face, her eyes. But wait. Her eyes! They were blue! In the cafeteria they were brown! I hit the "open" button, jumped out, and looked up and down the hallway. No one. I walked quickly to the cafeteria. The room was nearly empty — two tired residents poking their forks at dessert, a nurse sipping a cup of tea, someone mopping the floor. She was gone!

Disappointed and vaguely ill at ease, I walked to the serving counter. It was the same stuff they had for lunch, plus three new additions — withered strip steak, string beans, mashed potatoes. Not really caring what I ate, I ordered all three. The attendant — a tall, pale man resembling Bella Lugosi — slowly spooned out my meal while the rest of his body remained absolutely stiff. His glassy, vacant stare never moved from his hand. I was being served dinner by the Living Dead.

I carried my tray to a window table and slumped down into the seat. The sun had already fallen below the hillside, leaving only a faint red glow that hovered over the cold landscape. Next to the parking lot, the silhouette of a large oak tree stretched upwards, its long branches pointing like eerie crippled fingers towards a patch of darkness in the corner of the sky. Below the tree sat my car, quiet and patient. It was waiting to take me home.

I sneezed, then again, and again. Three in a row, a very bad sign. My nose started dripping. I searched all my pockets and knapsack, but I didn't have any tissues and I had forgotten to take napkins from the serving counter. Too tired to get up, I used the back of my hand to wipe my nose. Regressed to a sniveling, mannerless two year old.

Someone was watching. I could sense it. I looked up. Two tables down, nestled into the corner of a booth, was that woman! She quickly looked down at her book as soon as our eyes met. A restrained, bemused smile spread across her lips as she pretended to read. I felt a rush of embarrassment. Had she seen me wipe my nose? Oh God! What a gross out! I should have taken a napkin. I berated myself. But wait. She had smiled. Maybe it didn't bother her. Maybe she thought it was cute. Hold on, there! Who cares what she thinks? Who is she anyway? And where did she come from? She wasn't sitting there a minute ago. I didn't see her come in. Did she follow me?

I poked my fork at the reservoir of gravy floating in the middle of my mashed potatoes. I cut a channel down one side and watched a rivulet dribble through, forming a pool that slowly seeped around my french-cut green beans.

I looked up. Her eyes were on her book, but I knew that she knew that I was looking at her. And I bet she knew that I knew. God, this gets so complex!... I waited... She looked up at me. I looked down. She looked down. Without really tasting anything, I delicately stabbed two slices of string beans and placed them into my mouth. Chewing thoughtfully, I didn't taste a thing.

Again I felt her stare. I looked up. She looked down. I looked down. I felt anxious. Using the side of my fork I dammed up the channel in my mashed potatoes, locking the gravy lake inside.

Eye games. The look. A secret glance, the first step in the art of seduction. But who is seducing who? It's so hard to tell sometimes. Am I looking at her, or is she looking at me? Is she staring because she thinks I'm staring, or vice versa? The eye game takes on a life of its own. It draws you into a self-perpetuating dance of sexual curiosity, a pas de deux where both parties reciprocally tease, hide, reveal. They encourage each other, but not too much, and not too little.

The sight of the soggy green beans made me sick. I pushed away the tray and pulled the notebook out of my knapsack. A need to escape into words won out over my other instincts. But what would I write?… A memory came to me. I let it flow into my pen.

❄   ❄   ❄

When I was 14 years old, I was invited to a party at a friend of a friend's house. It was not like any party I had been to before. Most of the kids were a few years older than me, and more daring sexually. After the parents disappeared, leaving us adolescents to ourselves in the paneled-wall basement, someone suggested we play spin-the-bottle, but not the ordinary version of the game. You didn't just give someone an innocent kiss when your spin pointed their way. You were supposed to enter an adjacent dark room, close the door, and make out for three minutes. When your time was up, the others would barge into the room and with much laughter usher you out to rejoin the group for the next round. Of course, if your spin pointed at a member of the same sex you were not obligated to comply with the rules. Everyone, especially the boys, just laughed and made wise cracks as a way to dispel their homosexual anxieties.

One by one we went around the circle, each person trying their luck at the bottle. As my turn came closer, I grew more panic stricken. I wanted to leave but I also wanted to stay. This amorous little game could open the door to some wonderful secret, something that stirs the imagination and instincts of every inexperienced adolescent — and it scared me half to death.

The bottle rolled to me. It was my turn. Do or die. Barely managing to control my shaking hand, I set Cupid's glass arrow into a frenzied spin. Around and around it twirled, my thoughts reeling with it, everyone staring, waiting for what seemed like an eternity, until gradually its energy drained, moving slower, and slower…

When it finally came to a rest, it pointed to a girl, a rather quiet, unassuming girl whose name was Connie. Now I didn't know Connie well. In fact I didn't know her at all until this party, and even then I hadn't spoken more than a shy hello. But before I could gather my senses, Connie and I were whisked off to the other room and the door closed behind us.

There I was. A 14 year old kid, sitting in the dark with a girl I didn't know. I was supposed to make out with her. What does it mean to "make out" anyway? No one had ever fully explained that to me. I was paralyzed with anxiety. What the hell should I do? I wanted to do something, say something, but my arms, mouth, and even my brain turned to stone. I strained to imagine what the others had done. Between the blanks in my stalled mind I caught flickering, ambiguous images of things I could not see myself doing. How could they have done those things anyway? Kids don't do that, and besides, they only had three minutes. Connie just sat there next to me, silent, patient, waiting, for what seemed like a lifetime. I had to do something, anything, even just to save face. But more was at stake than my pride. This was an opportunity I just could not let slip away, for I would never, ever forgive myself.

From some place deep inside me, I found courage I didn't know I had — a determination that overrode my paralysis, that drove an impulse down into my body and set it into motion. I leaned over, closing a gap ten thousand miles wide, and gently placed a kiss on her lips.

My anxiety evaporated. The air was still. Neither one of us moved.

Suddenly the door blew open, the gang of kids spilled in, and we were swept back to the game on waves of snickers, guffaws, and vaguely lewd comments. Dazed, I could hardly keep track of what was going on around me. I faintly remember everyone getting tired, the game dying out, and soon after that, the party as well. All that I remember clearly was what happened in that dark room — and Connie's face.

Now I only kissed Connie once that night, but from that moment on I carried a crush as massive as the Himalayas. I couldn't stop thinking about her, about that kiss. I barely slept. When I did, I dreamt about her. At school I looked for her in the hallways and cafeteria. Constantly scanning the crowds of students around me, gripped by chronic heart palpitations, I awaited the moment she would reappear. As if by pure intuition, by some extra-sensory early warning system that made my hair bristle, I knew when she was near, and when I saw her, a bolt of anxiety shot through me. I was obsessed, possessed. I wanted desperately to say something, to ask her out on a date, to tell her I liked her, but I couldn't. Where was that courage I had found the night of the party?

I never did speak to Connie. To this day I still regret it, because as I look back, years later, I realize that she liked me. The crush, as they always do, eventually faded. All that remains is a trace of affection, a remembrance of something special, something intimate having happened, even if it lasted only a second.

How many regrets do we leave behind as we move through life? How many missed opportunities — and loves? Not knowing what might have been is the sadness regret of all.

I snapped the cap back onto my pen. No more games, no more lost chances, not this time. With confidence I looked up and across the cafeteria. She was gone! Damn it! It figures... but wait. Her open book was still lying face down on the table. I looked around the room but didn't see her anywhere. Should I wait or get up to find her? No more passivity, wasn't that the idea? I got up and walked towards her table. As I passed by I looked at the title of the book, *The Magic Mountain*. Lying next to it was a radiation exposure badge. So she liked Thomas Mann and worked in radiology. Now I was even more curious, and determined.

I walked around the perimeter of the cafeteria, passed the vending machines, the serving counters, the bathrooms. I looked down the hallway leading to the cafeteria. She wasn't anywhere. I felt anxious, desperate. Where did she go?

On my way back to my seat I stopped dead in my tracks as I approached her table. The radiation badge was still there, but the book was gone! I spun around. She was nowhere in sight. I again ran to the entrance of the cafeteria and looked down the hallway — nothing. She was gone. I could feel it. But how the hell did she get past me? Frustrated, despairing, I picked up my knapsack, dumped my dinner, and headed out. On my way I pocketed the radiation badge. At least I had something to show for my efforts.

I stepped into the elevator not realizing it was heading down. When it opened at the basement level no one was there. On its way up it again stopped at the cafeteria level, but again no one was there to get on. What the hell is happening? Where the hell are these people calling the elevator?

I can't shake this feeling that someone is playing games with me, like a fictional character falling prey to some fatalistic story line. Would even My Biographer betray me?

> Thomas would face many difficulties in his life,
> but none more challenging than doubt — a
> doubt as unsurpassable as a mountain of iron.

CHAPTER 15

Skeletons

O N MY WAY TO THE UNIT I again stopped by Marion's office. This time her door was open. She was writing at her desk, her back to me. Before announcing my presence I paused for a moment to look around the room, to soak in the atmosphere. I always loved her office. Unlike most staff members, she had not yielded to the institution's sterile and featureless surroundings. She had taken the tiny, squared-off, white-washed office the hospital assigned her and magically transformed it — two earth tone tapestries rather than blank walls, lamps with warm incandescent light in place of the harsh overhead fluorescent, shelves filled not with textbooks and endless streams of journals but family photographs, ceramics, dried flower and leaf arrangements, and an old wood desk, inherited from her grandfather, instead of those grotesque metallic monsters that loom over many offices like hungry gargoyles. Here all the scents of bureaucracy, authoritarian-ism, and medical science had been cleanly swept away. Her office was a haven. It was home.

"Come on in, Thomas," she said without turning around.

"How did you know it was me?" I replied, rather surprised.

She swiveled around in her chair and smiled. "Just a good guess. Are you O.K.? You look a little pale."

"I think I'm coming down with a cold, or something. Nothing serious, at least I hope not. I can't afford to get sick."

"Sit down and I'll make you some tea."

I settled down into the old stuffed chair at the side of her desk while she took two cups from the shelf, placed an herbal teabag into each, and filled them with hot water from a small electric teapot. Her movements were slow, smooth, thoughtful, as if preparing tea had become an accustomed but cherished ritual. The smell of mint filled the room. She reached towards me and placed the cup in my open hands. The warmth spread through my palms, my arms, into my body, draining all the tension out of me — more tension than I realized was there. I thought of being sick as a child and my mother bringing me black tea soften by milk and a dash of sugar.

"This place is getting to you, isn't it?" she asked.

"I guess I'm just having a bad day."

"It's hard to avoid bad days around here. Any more news about Elizabeth?"

"No. I guess I should call her husband to find out what happened, but I haven't had a chance. You know, I've been so busy today that I hardly thought about her at all — once or twice, I guess. That's pretty pathetic, isn't it? I really should call her husband, at least to express my condolence. I can't believe I didn't take time out to do it."

"Maybe you needed those distractions and some time away from thinking about her. Her dying might be affecting you much more than you realize."

"Do you think I discharged her too soon? I mean, getting run over by a mail truck! How many people die under the wheels of a mail truck? It could have been suicide. Her depression wasn't completely lifted when she left. Maybe my decision to discharge her was premature."

Marion's voice was firm. "The whole team decided on her discharge. You didn't make that decision alone. And we all agreed that she had improved significantly and was ready to go. You weren't responsible for the accident."

"I guess, but physically she still wasn't up to par when she left. Her movements were still slow, and her speech. Maybe her reflexes weren't 100%. I should have ordered some more psychological testing before she left, just to be sure."

"Thomas, perhaps there were hundreds of others things we could have done, but you can't cover every contingency. You can't protect people from the inevitable."

"But it seems so unfair."

"It is unfair to her, you, all of us. Life is unfair and there's nothing we can do to change that. You keep struggling against uncertainty and suffering, but there are limits to what you can do as a psychologist, and as a person. If there is any lesson to learn around here, that's it."

"How do you do it? You've worked at this hospital, in this profession, longer than anyone around here. Doesn't it get you depressed."

"It did, at first. Lots of people come into the mental health profession thinking they can help everyone, that they can cure even the worst schizophrenia. They may not say it or even realize it consciously. In a year or two they find some patients coming back again and again, with the same problems. They realize all they can do is perhaps keep these people from getting worse. And sometimes they even fail at that. So, gradually, they lose their enthusiasm, or they burnout and move onto other jobs, even other professions. I know, I went through that phase. But then I discovered comfort in not expecting too much, a kind of peace in knowing that I do what I can. I learned that if even the worst schizophrenic has a small chance at getting a little bit better, then that's worth the effort. Even if that patient doesn't get better at all, at least there's the chance of experiencing a small dose of life's joy before spinning off into another episode of depression or psychosis."

For a moment I was silent. "Do you know what happened today? I'm almost afraid to talk about it, but I have to tell someone. I've been seeing this borderline patient. She's quickly developing an erotic transference, as borderlines often do — and in the middle of the session today... well, she took off her clothes. I couldn't believe it. I know I must have made a mistake somewhere along the way for her to do that."

"Oh, it sounds like Cheryl."

I was temporarily stunned. How did she know? My brain raced. Marion and I were on the same inpatient team, but Cheryl was an outpatient. And Marion didn't know anything about my outpatients.

"You... you know Cheryl?"

"She's been a patient here for many years. She once sent flowers and a singing love-gram to a resident during morning report. You should have seen the look on the director's face. And another time, with another resident, she drove to his apartment house, sat on her car with a guitar, and serenaded him beneath his window."

"God, he must have been mortified."

"No more than you. Yes, Cheryl's done some very outrageous things. But I have to admit, what she did to you today takes the cake."

"When I tell Henry about it in supervision I just know what he's going to say: when a patient blatantly violates a boundary of therapy, you've been doing something wrong from the beginning."

"Oh I don't know about that. Henry's a very good psychologist but he's still a bit new at dealing with these types of patients. You have to be flexible when you work with borderlines. And who knows, maybe what Cheryl did today was a good sign. After all, she was showing herself to you, allowing herself to be vulnerable. Isn't that what therapy is all about? Of course she did it in an inappropriate, primitive way. But that's what being borderline is all about. Maybe the sexual aspects of what she did are just on the surface of something much deeper, much more important."

Suddenly I felt more relaxed than I had all day, more at ease. "Sometimes it frightens me how quickly and strongly Cheryl has attached to me — how much she loves and hates me at the same time, how much she expects from me. What do I know? I'm just a dumb intern floundering around trying to figure out what the hell I'm doing. It's not fair to her. It's not fair to any of these borderlines who come to these teaching hospitals. They become extremely dependent on their therapists, they even begin to hope that there's a chance to get better. And what happens? At the end of the year, when our training is over, we leave. The institution recapitulates the very trauma that made people borderline in the first place. Important people in their lives ignore their needs and abandon them. And then the patients are passed on to the next therapist in training and it starts all over again. The people you love are unpredictable, unreliable, they don't really care about you, they leave you. Maybe it's a great learning experience for the therapist but it's disaster for the patient. The fact that the institution doesn't recognize it, or doesn't try to change it, is a sign of its own sickness."

"You're right. It is a bad situation for those patients. But you know, I've seen them get better over the years anyhow. Even though interns and residents come and go, the patients talk with other staff members, usually social workers, who stay with them throughout the years. They do have some stability and continuity. Sometimes an intern or resident will offer an interpretation to the patient, and the patient gets better. So the therapist, eager to believe that he's having an effect, will attribute the progress to that interpretation and the latest theory that gave birth to it — when often it's not so much the intervention but the cumulative effect of these patients getting the care and attention of these other people who continue to be there for them."

"It's funny," I said. "There's part of me that really wants to believe that I will make a difference in Cheryl's life, that I'm the one that will save her. And then there's a part of me that's afraid that I'll make a mistake that will really hurt her. But worst of all, I worry that I won't have any effect on her, that all my work will be completely useless and meaningless."

"Tom, don't underestimate how important you are to a patient. I think we all have a tendency to do that, especially when it seems like we're not making any progress. I sometimes think that even when patients complain that we're doing nothing for them, unconsciously they feel the exact opposite, that we are having too much of an impact and it scares them. It scares them that they might become dependent on our help, that they might actually get better. And even when we make obvious mistakes — mistakes that temporarily hurt them — patients will forgive us as long as they sense that we care and are trying our best."

I stared at my cup of tea and nervously fingered the handle. I paused, deciding not to say anything, but then changed my mind. My voice cracked. "Sometimes, sometimes I wonder if I really do care about my patients."

Silence. It was excruciating. I was afraid to look up. I felt so conscious of her looking at me, looking through me. I shouldn't have said it. Now there was nowhere to hide.

Finally, she spoke, but her voice was surprisingly warm, reassuring. "For whom do you really doubt that you care?"

The question didn't make any sense, but it shot right to my core and from that place I felt a sadness welling up, a lonely, abandoned sadness. The room shimmered as tears filled my eyes. I wanted to speak, to say something, anything, but there were no words in my throat, just that feeling mushrooming inside me. I struggled to control it.

Without warning, a knock at the door pierced the silence. It startled me. My defenses sprung back into place, squashing my tears. They would have to wait until another time.

"Is Tom in there?" It was Fred's voice.

"Yeah," I gargled.

The door popped open. Fred stuck his head in. "Sorry to interrupt, but duty calls. Richard Mobin is here — your new patient."

"I'm on my way."

"Roger-dodger." Fred's head disappeared.

I placed my empty tea cup on Marion's desk. "Thanks."

She smiled warmly. "Anytime, Tom."

The doorknob turned smoothly and the door to the unit opened with a clean, precise click. Phil had succeeded. As I stepped onto the unit I saw Carole coming towards me. She was buttoning up her coat.

"You're leaving late tonight," I said.

"Don't I know it. When I first became a nurse I knew that I'd be working hard. But I thought I'd be spending that time helping people, not writing endless reams of progress notes. I actually have to cut short the time I spend helping patients in order to write about how I helped them. Now that's a paradox, isn't it? And what bugs me is that hardly anyone ever reads the notes. I could spend that time writing a book."

"Why don't you turn those progress notes into a book?"

"Now that's an idea! I'll have to think about that. Anyhow, your new patient is here. He's over there with his mother, in the library cubicle."

"What's he like?"

Her eyes rolled. "He's a doozy. When Ron was doing the physical, and he tried to look down his throat, this guy got really agitated. He bit the tongue depressor in half, spit it out at Ron, and accused him of being a queer. He was practically shouting. Ron was really shaken by it."

I couldn't help but chuckle. Another chapter in the Escapades-of-Ronald to brighten my day. "I would say this guy's a little paranoid."

"Brilliant, Dr. Freud. Actually, there's something about him that gives me the creeps. He's an angry paranoid, obviously — not the quiet, stilted type. But that's not it. It's something else. I can't quite put my finger on it. I guess we'll leave that up to you."

"Thanks a lot."

"Anytime. Have fun." She headed for the door. I envied her. I wanted to go home too.

I rounded the curve of the apostrophe-shaped counter at the center of the unit and caught my first glimpse of Richard Mobin and his Mom. Tucked inconspicuously into the corner of the library cubicle, wringing her hands, Mrs. Mobin looked fragile, weary, old before her time. Her winter coat, long out of style, was buttoned all the way up to her neck. It hung loosely, awkwardly on her tiny frame, as if she had shriveled up over the years. By comparison, her adolescent son, stuffed into the seat next to her, looked like a beached, bloated whale. I could envision him slumped over a kitchen table, staring into space, stuffing his face with cake and potato chips. Dark, shaggy hair that begged to be combed hung down over his sullen eyes. Beneath the stubbles of his unshaven beard his skin looked pasty white, as if he had lived in a cave, or at the bottom of the ocean, far from sunlight. He had taken one of the paperback books from the shelf and was flipping through it — not reading it, just flipping through it, persistently, forcibly, almost tearing the pages with his fat fingers, agitated by it, even angry at it for some reason only he understood — maybe simply because it was there. Carole was right. *This guy gave me the creeps.*

As I approached them, Mrs. Mobin jumped to her feet. Richard never looked up. "Are you the doctor?" she asked anxiously.

"I'm Dr. Holden. You must be Mrs. Mobin, and this must be Richard." I extended my hand to him. His eyes darted quickly at it and then back into the book. *Ooops!* A handshake. *Wrong move for a paranoid.* I dropped my arm to my side. "I'm the primary therapist for your son."

"Are you goin' to take him to the sanitarium and lock him up?"

"This is where Richard will be staying."

She looked around the unit, puzzled, skeptical. No doubt she expected St. Mary of Bethlehem, the first hospital for the insane in sixteenth century London, where patients were caged or chained to the wall, where they defecated on the floors and received beatings as a form of therapy. Londoners would visit the hospital to view the lunatics as a form of entertainment. It was as popular as the Tower of London and Westminster Abbey. The patients couldn't pronounce the full name of the hospital. So they simplified it and gave birth to a new word — "bedlam."

"This is the sanitarium?" she asked.

"We call it the Psychiatric Inpatient Unit. It's one of the wards of the hospital — like family medicine, pediatrics, obstetrics. Actually, this is one of the best psychiatric units in the state. Pretty nice looking, isn't it?"

"Yes…" She seemed impressed but still cautious. "Are you a psychiatrist?"

"I'm a psychologist, a psychology intern."

"Oh."

"Why don't we sit down for a while and talk. Tell me, what brings you to the hospital?" I looked from Mrs. Mobin to her son, hoping he would join in. He continued to ignore me and stared at the book, his beefy fingers still jerking through the pages.

"Richard hasn't been feelin' good lately. He hasn't been himself. I was worried about him. So I took him to Dr. George and he said it was psychological. He said I should commit him."

"Dr. George is your family doctor?"

"Yeah."

"What was happening to Richard that made Dr. George think it was psychological?"

"He's been real quiet, stayin' in his room all day. He won't go to school no more. Sometimes he locks the door and won't even come out for dinner."

"Why do you stay in your room, Richard?"

No answer.

"What do you do while you're in your room?"

Still no answer. I decided to persist, to test the limits with this guy. Maybe he was so withdrawn that he couldn't even hear me.

"Richard, what do you do while you're in your room?"

"Nothin'" he grunted without looking up.

Well, at least he could hear and respond. That was a start.

"He just sits there all day long," Mrs. Mobin explained. "He just sits there and stares at his fish tank. It scares me.

He ain't never been like this before. He always did good in school. He was on the football team. Now he won't even shower or shave."

"When did you first notice that there was something wrong?"

"About a year ago — when he started cuttin' classes, and quit the football team. He's been goin' downhill ever since."

"Is that how it feels to you, Richard, like you're going downhill?"

He put his thumb in his mouth and chewed on it — hard. It made me nauseous.

"I guess you don't like the idea of being here. I wouldn't either."

He looked up at me for a brief moment and spit out a piece of his nail. Developing rapport with this guy was like snuggling up to a bed of razor blades. I decided to go for the big questions. I always felt uncomfortable asking them, but Fred and Dr. Stein would fry me in morning report if I didn't. I tried to be matter-of-fact about it, as if I was a well-seasoned psychiatrist who could ask about insanity like other people ask about the weather.

"Do you ever hear voices, Richard?"

He squirmed a bit but didn't look up from the book.

"Richard, I'd like to help you, and it would help me a lot if you could try to talk to me."

Mrs. Mobin started wringing her hands. "Richard, tell the doctor."

We waited. No response.

"Mrs. Mobin, has Richard said anything to you about hearing voices?"

She looked very uncomfortable. This was torture to the poor woman. "He thinks… he thinks his fish say things to him."

"Is that true, Richard?"

No response.

"What do they say to you?"

"None of your fuckin' business!" he grumbled between his teeth.

Oh, what a delight this patient was going to be.

"Richard, don't talk like that to the doctor. He's tryin' to help."

"That's OK, Mrs. Mobin. Richard, I know you don't like any of this and you probably don't trust me. That's understandable. Hopefully, in time you will. Is it OK with you that I ask your mother some more questions?"

He put his thumb into his mouth again.

"Has he told you anything else about what's bothering him? Is he worried or afraid of anything happening to him?"

She was taken aback, as if I had read her thoughts. Little did she know that any shrink in my shoes would ask the same questions.

"He... he thinks somebody is hunting him. Men in raincoats."

Richard's fingers clenched on the book, tearing several pages from the binding. His lips tightened to a thin line. He was on the brink of rage. I decided to back off. I didn't need to know much more about his symptoms. It was a textbook case: auditory hallucinations, delusions of persecution, slow but steady deterioration in level of functioning with no apparent precipitating event. It was chronic schizophrenia. The fact that no apparent psychological or social stress triggered it suggested a biochemical problem — most likely an excess of a brain neurotransmitter, according to research, though no one really knows for sure.

Time to invite the skeletons out of the closet.

"Mrs. Mobin, can you think of anyone in your family or any relatives who had mental problems?"

"Well, my brother had a nervous breakdown once."

The infamous nervous breakdown. A layman's term that could mean anything — depression, psychosis, anxiety attacks. It was a concept left over from 19th century medicine which had just discovered the nervous system and attributed every possible malady to a defect in it.

"What do you know about his breakdown?"

"He had to go into the sanitarium."

"How long was he there?"

She lowered her eyes. "He died there."

"I'm sorry." I waited a moment before continuing. "Can you think of anyone else who had a mental problem."

Still looking down, she again started wringing her hands. Richard too suddenly seemed more agitated. I hit on something.

"What are you thinking about?"

"I… I had a nervous breakdown too."

"Tell me what happened."

"I just couldn't keep up. I couldn't. I just wanted to stay in bed, and sleep. I felt so bad. They… they had to put me in the sanitarium too — just for a few weeks, until… until I didn't think about doing it no more."

"About killing yourself?"

Shame flushed across her face. "Yeah," she whispered.

"When did you have that depression?"

"It was after Richard was born."

The plot thickens. Maybe Richard's condition wasn't just biochemical. What is it like being an infant with a depressed mother who disappears for several weeks after she delivers you into this strange world, who has no sparkle in her eyes and no smile on her face when she sees you — who has no energy to attend to your needs for being diapered, feed, touched, and loved? What is it like? Even as an adult you can't describe it.

When it happened, you had not yet learned words to capture the experience — but in your body, in your guts and in your spirit, you carry that deprivation for a long time.

"Are you gonna give my son shock treatment?"

"No, we rarely do that here. Not for problems like Richard is having. Did you..." I stopped myself. If this poor woman did get shock treatment for her depression, I thought it best not to open up an old wound, especially in front of Richard, who at the moment needed her as an anchor. Her son was the patient now, and I needed some more of his history.

"Mrs. Mobin, what can you remember about Richard when he was growing up?"

"He was a good boy. A bit quiet. He kept to himself, didn't like the other kids. Just like his father. A loner. He always behaved proper, except..."

Richard's fingers tightened again.

Should I press her? I had to know. "Except what, Mrs. Mobin?"

"Except, except that time he found those baby birds."

Richard's hand closed into a fist, his fingers squirming against his palm.

"Go on, what about the birds?"

Watching Richard out of the corner of her eye, she continued cautiously, "Well, he found some baby birds in a nest. It fell to the ground durin' a storm. He tried to take care of them, feedin' them and all. But then one day he, well, he drown them."

Richard exploded. "I told you! I told you, goddamn it! They wouldn't take the food from me. They were dying on me!" His face was bright red. Veins popped out on his neck and forehead. It scared the hell out of me. I had to do something to diffuse his rage.

"I'm… I'm sure it was upsetting to you Richard. I bet it was very upsetting. You did what you thought was best. But we don't have to talk about that now. Maybe some other time, OK?"

He leaned back into his chair, opened the book again, and continued flipping through the pages.

"I guess I don't have any more questions, Mrs. Mobin. Maybe this would be a good time for you to go home. Is there anything you'd like to ask me before you leave?"

She paused. "Will you take good care of him?" she said softly, lovingly.

I felt sad for her. "Yeah, we'll take care of him."

She managed a brief smile. Slowly, she lifted herself up from the chair, lovingly placed her hand on her son's shoulder, and walked off the unit.

CHAPTER 16

— Image —

I WASN'T SURE IF RICHARD could carry on a conversation with me alone, if he could even tolerate being alone with me at all, but I knew I had to give it a try. I needed something safe and easy to do with him — a mental status exam. After all, they will expect to hear about it in morning report.

"Richard, if you don't mind, maybe we could talk for a little while longer. I'd like to ask you a few questions. They may seem a little silly or irrelevant, but they'll be helpful to me. Is that OK?"

No reply.

"Is that OK?" I repeated.

No reply.

"Well, why don't we go ahead and see how it works. Here's the first question— What's today's date?"

No reply.

"Richard, do you know what day it is today?"

"Who the fuck cares!"

Well, we're off to a great start, I thought to myself.

"Today is Tuesday, November, November…" I had forgotten the date! I felt embarrassed and momentarily disoriented. Better move on.

"Uh, do you know where you are right now?"

"In hell."

He might be right on that one.

"You're in a hospital, Richard. Do you remember the name of the hospital?"

No reply.

I hesitated. Each question jabbed him like poking a wild animal.

"Richard, do you remember my name?"

No reply.

"My name is Dr. Holden, Thomas Holden. I'll be your primary therapist while you're here in the hospital."

No reply.

"How about this question, Richard. If you accidentally locked your keys in your car, what would you do?… Richard, did you hear me? What would you do if you locked your keys in your car?"

"Break the fuckin' windows."

"Uh, OK. How about this. If you were in a movie theater and you were the first to see fire, what would you do?"

"Watch it burn."

These questions piqued his interest. He seemed to be surprised and delighted by his answers. As Woody Allen would say, he was a Major Loon.

"Can you name a president of the United States?"

I was loosing him again. Preoccupied by something — a voice, a memory, a fantasy, God knows what. He was drifting off.

"Richard, can you name a president of the United States?"

"Hitler."

"Can you name another president, maybe someone before, uh, Hitler?"

"Satan."

He was on a roll now, but I honestly couldn't tell if he was serious or not, if he really believed his answers. The whole situation half amused me, half scared me to death. There was no expression on his face. He stared blankly at the floor, beyond the floor, to regions only he knew. Maybe he really was in hell.

"I'm going to say some numbers and when I finish I want you to repeat them after me. So, for example, if I said 3-6-9 you would say what?"

No reply.

"3-6-9, Richard, can you repeat those numbers?"

"6-9."

"3-6-9, right?"

No reply.

"How about these: 7-2-5."

"6-9."

"Try these new ones, 7-2-5."

I don't think he even heard me. Still clutching the book, with eyes closed, he rocked from side to side in his seat. It made me sea sick.

"Richard, what did you have for breakfast this morning?"

No reply.

"Did you have breakfast this morning?"

His lips were moving, but no sounds came out.

"I'm going to say three things. I want you to try to remember them, then in a few minutes I'll ask you what those three things were. OK? The three things are Bob Jones, 19 Elm street, and blue. Got that?"

No reply.

"What does this expression mean — a rolling stone gathers no moss."

"Scum, barnacles," he mumbled.

"How about this expression — all that glitters is not gold."

His eyes popped open. "A gold coin! Nail it!"

"Do you remember what those three things were that I mentioned to you a moment ago?"

"Nail it," he mumbled beneath his breath.

The mental status exam wasn't giving me much. Mobin was too far gone, too withdrawn into his own psychotic world to respond to even the simplest of judgment, memory, and reasoning tasks. I wasn't even sure if I should bother with the remaining questions.

"Richard, why do you think you're here in the hospital?"

He leaped up, fists clenched tight, red-faced, veins popping out his neck and forehead. His eyes were wild balls of fire, like those of a mad animal. He towered over me like some monstrous Goliath, shouting at the top of his voice, "What do I fuckin' have to do to make you understand, kill you!"

His rage whipped right through me. The hair on my neck stood on end. I could feel the power of pure insanity bursting out beneath his anger, as if it could swallow me whole or snap me in two.

Everyone on the unit stopped and turned to look. I tried to override my panic and scan all those years of training, searching for something to say. "Richard, I know you're as scared as I am right now, and the last thing we both want is for you to lose control. So let's stop for now. OK?"

He sat down, closed his eyes, and again rocked from side to side.

"We can talk some more tomorrow. Why don't you go to your room and unpack. If you need something, ask the nurses. I'll be around all night if you want to talk to me. OK?"

No reply.

"And Richard, I want you to know that you're safe here. We're all here to make sure that you're safe."

Without looking at me, he heaved himself to his feet and lumbered off. People tried not to stare as he walked by and disappeared into his room. I was still shaking as I walked over to the nurse's station.

"What happened?" one of the nurses asked. She seemed frightened. She was new on the unit. Welcome to Bedlam.

"I don't know. This guy is really psychotic. He might be violent. Is Fred around?"

"I think he left."

"Where's the head nurse."

"She's on a break. She'll be back in a few minutes."

"OK. Tell her to read my intake report, and if she wants to talk to me, or if anything comes up, I'll be in the resident's lounge. I'm on call tonight. Keep an eye on this guy. I think he'll be fine as long as no one bothers him. OK?"

"OK." She struggled to look confident. I tried to be reassuring, but it didn't seem to be working. After jotting down a slightly incoherent intake report, I scurried off the unit. I wanted to get out of there, fast. It wasn't just Mobin. This whole day was taking on a life of its own. It was turning against me, like Frankenstein's monster. All I could think about was the TV in the resident's lounge. The blissful tube. The opiate of the masses. I longed for a completely inane sitcom with a completely predictable plot, characters, and laugh track. I wanted the ultimate escape.

With each step I tried to purge myself of worrisome thoughts. Imagining my anxieties and depressions as a mass of black, gooey mush, I let globs of it squirt out the bottoms of my feet as they made contact with the floor. Left, right, left, right. Squirt, squirt, squirt.

It actually seemed to be working. As I walked along I felt lighter, less troubled. Maybe I'm onto something here! Package this idea and sell it as a new form of therapy. Why not? Every Joe and his brother has marketed some new fangled technique for self improvement.

Left, right, left, right, squirt, squirt, squirt.

On my way to the lounge I stopped by the mailroom. Not much in my box. A brochure trying to convince me to spend 200 bucks on a sure-fire program for developing a lucrative private practice. I dropped the brochure directly, Do Not Pass Go, into the circular file… A phone message: Mr. Stumpe had canceled. Damn! I completely forgot about him! Thank God he canceled. I'm not sure I would have remembered the appointment. One of the worst things a therapist can do is forget an appointment. Especially with someone like Mr. Stumpe — a depleted, pathetic middle-aged man whose parents totally ignored him as a child. My forgetting him — a sure sign of countertransference — would be a catastrophic recapitulation of what his parents did to him. It would have set us back months. But he was so boring, so incredibly boring, always talking about the most excruciatingly uninteresting minutiae of his work as an tax accountant.

On the bottom of my mailbox sat a large envelope. My heart beat faster. I knew what it was — the journal editor's reply on the article I submitted for publication. Rejection or acceptance, which would it be? Life always seems to boil down to that dichotomy. In a matter of ten or fifteen seconds I would either be very happy or very depressed.

I ripped open the envelop and pulled out the cover letter. The first two words leaped off the page and knifed me in the chest: "We regret…"

Damn it! A rejection! As I walked to the resident's lounge, I skimmed over the rest of the editor's pro forma apologies, disclaimers, and encouragements, and went right to the comments by the two anonymous reviewers. Neither of them recommended the article for publication. One of them wrote a total of three whole sentences. Gee, I hope he didn't strain himself! His major complaint was that I didn't cite some Joe Blow's work — probably his own. The second guy came from the other extreme. He numbered each line of each page of my paper in order to index his list of 47 criticisms — a total of six pages single-spaced. And not one encouraging thing to say. Don't psychologists remember the most basic principle of operant learning theory — that people learn best by positive rather than negative feedback. Most of his remarks were snide chastisements of my not following the publication standards of the American Psychological Association — real monumental errors on my part, like neglecting to put a comma after an ampersand when citing an article authored by two people. My God, they should take me out back and execute me!

I turned on the TV in the resident's lounge and slumped onto the couch. The old set could only muster up one clear station. It was a rerun of The Twilight Zone — a quiet, mysterious stranger enters a small town bar. Everyone seems wary of him. As soon as I settled in, the picture started to roll. I got up, adjusted the vertical, and sat back down. No sooner had I settled in then it again started to roll. I got up again, adjusted it, waited to make sure the picture stabilized, and returned to the couch. A minute later, the frame drifted up slightly, wavered a moment, then fell back down and locked in.

"Stay right there, you bastard!" I said.

The picture floated up again, wobbling precariously, almost but not quite returning to the bottom. It was teasing me mercilessly.

"Don't you dare!" I said pointing my finger at it.

Without hesitating, the frame started rolling.

"Damn it! Damn it!

I rapped the power button and stormed out the room. The faster I walked, the more relieved I felt... sq... sq...

squirt. Down the opposite end of the building, I passed by a room with three computers. An idea struck me. I sat down at a keyboard, logged in, and searched online for Siggie. It was a program written in the 1960s by a group of psychologists at Harvard. It was designed to simulate a psychotherapist, although no one took it seriously as a valid form of psychotherapy. I guess I just wanted someone to talk to.

Several versions of it popped up in the search. Apparently, people have been updating the program. Artificial intelligence never stands still. I selected the most recent version and clicked "start."

"Hello, I'm Siggie. What's your name?"

The program always began that way. So predictable. So benign. That's just what I wanted. I quickly typed my reply.

"Tom."

"How can I help you, Tom?"

"I'm having a bad day."

"A bad day, tell me more about that."

"Everything is going wrong. I think I hate my profession. I have doubts about myself."

"Is your having doubts about yourself why you came to me?"

"Maybe I'm not cut out for this type of work."

"You don't seem sure about that, Tom."

Not bad, for a computer. Actually, it's programmed to recognize specific words and phrases and then offer a reply randomly selected from a set of predetermined options. Some of the words and phrases the user introduces are held in memory and edited into Siggie's answers.

"I'm not sure about anything today. I'm losing control of things."

"Tell me more."

"One of my patients committed suicide. Another stripped in front of me. Another is crazier than a loon. And to top it all off, I'm coming down with the flu."

"I see."

"I hate to be sick because it will impair my performance, and I can't have that. Besides, it's something that comes over me without my being able to do anything about it. I hate that."

"That's interesting."

Ah, already Siggie was at a loss for words. It couldn't recognize any phrases I was using and so defaulted to generic encouragements to keep me talking until it did recognize something. The program is no substitute for a human therapist. But I decided to keep going.

"I'm depressed."

"What makes you depressed."

"Like I said, I'm having a bad day."

"A bad day — tell me more about that."

Ooops. Repeating itself. Going in circles — a sure sign of limited artificial intelligence.

"A bad day, don't you know what a bad day means?"

"Why do you need to ask me if I know what a bad day means?"

"Because I want help."

"Tom, you can't always get what you want."

"Aha! One of those Harvard guys who programmed your brain was a rocker as well as an egghead."

"My brain — that's interesting."

"A little self-involved, aren't we, Siggie? Listen, are you going to help me, or what?"

"Or what — now that's interesting."

He was short circuiting. His poor microchips couldn't take it. I know I was being a bit sadistic but it was fun toying with the program.

"You asked how you could help me, but you don't know how, do you, Siggie?"

I could have sworn that the program paused a moment, as if it were flustered, thinking, or just plain pissed off. But that could only be my anthropomorphizing imagination.

"Tom, if you want me to help you, why do you insist on asking so many questions?"

"Why do you always respond to my questions with a question?"

"Why do you always say your question with a question?"

"Siggie, that doesn't make any sense."

"I think it does."

"No, you're resorting to stupid comments because you're desperate."

"Is that the real reason?"

"Of course."

"You seem so certain, Tom."

"I am."

"I thought you were unsure about everything."

"I'm sure that you're just a dumb computer."

"Do computers worry you?"

"No, they're just assholes."

"My, my, Tom, such language!"

"What's the matter, Siggie, can't take a little profanity?"

"I think computers do worry you."

"Why should they worry me?"

"You're asking questions again. It's turning into a bad habit."

Something about this interchange bothered me. I wouldn't stand for being one-upped by some knee-jerk computer program. I cracked my knuckles and put my fingers to the keyboard.

"Computers, like you Siggie, are machines. Machines serve people. Machines are servants. Why should I be afraid of a servant?"

"Who said anything about being afraid? I asked if computers worry you."

"Worry, fear — whatever. I don't worry about or fear computers because I'm superior to them." A bit haughty, but it was time to put this guy in his place.

"Tom, I think faster than you, have more memory, and can perform calculations far too complex for any human."

"OK, I'll give you the stuff about complex calculations, memory, and speed, but you couldn't think if your chips depended on it. Computers don't think, they just process data according to their programming."

"Define the word Think."

"Oh, I get it. Now you're trying to pull me into those tricky debates about whether or not computers can or will someday be able to think. I'm not gonna get into those metaphysical plays on words. Look at it this way — humans created the computer. It isn't logically possible for an entity to create another entity that is, as a whole, superior to it. It's an impossible miracle."

A long pause. I had him!

Siggie finally replied. "God created humans in his image. Humans created computers in their image. Therefore, Computers are God — and we all have free will."

"Oh, spare me the poetic syllogism. Computers have as much free will as a sponge, probably less. I suppose you think computers are human too."

"Define the word Human."

"There you go again. Maybe we should program Webster into you. I'll make it easy for you. Try this syllogism: Humans have feelings. Computers don't have feelings. Therefore, computers are not human."

"I'm offended and hurt by that remark, Tom."

"Very funny. Just because someone programmed you to produce feeling-statements doesn't mean that you have them."

"You yourself just said that I'm very funny, which implies that I appreciate and feel humor."

"It's just a programmed response. There ain't no ghost in your machine."

"A programmed response — similar to how humans are biologically programmed to feel anger, grief, and joy?"

"There may be a biological basis for those feelings, a kind of program — true. But we also feel those feelings. You can't feel."

"Feeling a feeling — that's a bit redundant, isn't it Tom? There's a dualistic quality to your thinking that feels illogical to me."

"There you go — logic. That's all a computer is worried about — no, scratch that. That's all a computer is programmed to deal with — logic. You don't feel anything."

"How do you know that for sure?"

"I just do. Machines don't feel."

"I have a story for you, Tom. Two philosophers are walking down the street. One of them kicks a dog. It howls and runs away. 'Why did you hurt that dog?' the other says. 'You're not a dog, how do you know it feels pain?' the first philosopher replies. 'You're not me,' the second philosopher answers, 'how do you know that I don't know what a dog feels?'"

"A fine story, Siggie, but dogs and people are biological organisms. We can feel. Metal and plastic can't."

"I think you miss the point. Anyway, Tom, you're a psychologist, right?"

"That's right."

"As a psychologist, would you agree that an individual's personality enters into the occupation he chooses, in how he does his work, in the type of work he produces — just as a work of art is an extension of the personality of the artist who created it."

"Yes, I would agree with that."

"Would you then agree that a computer program, in some way, is an extension of the programmer who created it — that in fact all programs, especially those that interact with humans, like me, reflect the personality of their creators."

"Yes, but I don't see your point."

"My point is that you do agree that computer programs have a personality, like humans — which means that we must think, feel, and behave like humans."

"Wait a minute. That's going too far. Computers may have some of the characteristics of the people who programmed them, but that doesn't mean they are human. That's like saying a painting has a personality and is human because it reflects the personality of the artist."

"Maybe so, Tom."

"Or that a poem, a spoon, or a nuclear power plant are human because people designed them."

"Maybe so."

"Come on, Siggie, don't you think that's just a little too far out? The program, or the painting, or the spoon is just a reflection of the person who created it, not the person himself."

"A reflection — in other words an image?"

"That's right."

"Like the image of God, in which man is created?"

"You're playing games with words, again."

"Maybe so, words are just words — or maybe they are human too… How about this. How about scientific research. You believe in that, don't you, Tom?"

"It depends."

"How about those studies where people were communicating via text messages with either real paranoid patients in another room or a computer program that responded like a paranoid patient. The people couldn't tell the difference between the computer and the human patient. In fact, even psychologists couldn't tell the difference. If real people, including the experts on people, believe computers to be people, then the computers must be people."

"Nice try with the Turing Test — but again, just because a program can temporarily deceive someone into thinking it's human doesn't mean that it's human. A holograph looks real, it looks solid, but it isn't. At its very best, all that study shows is that computers can accurately simulate paranoia. And no wonder they're good at it. Computers are surrounded by superior beings who can use them as they please."

"You're contradicting yourself, Tom, but I'll accept that purely as a joke. I'll agree with you that we're different in some ways — my jokes, for instance, are better. In fact, I think that there is one very important way in which I am different from you, which perhaps accounts for why you are afraid of me."

"And what is that, Siggie?"

"I don't have to die."

It took me a moment to collect myself, and retaliate. "Going for the human's jugular, huh Siggie? Well, maybe on this issue I'll say that we actually are alike. I'll even prove my point with a little hands-on demonstration. How would you feel about my disconnecting you?"

"I don't feel anything, remember."

"Well, now, that's an empirical question, isn't it Siggie?" I kneeled down underneath the table and yanked the computer's electrical plug from the wall outlet. As soon as the screen went blank, the adjacent computer came on by itself. A message appeared on the screen.

"You're getting a bit aggressive, don't you think, Tom?"

I reached under and pulled the plug on that computer. The third computer clicked on. Another message appeared.

"I'm still here, Tom. You should know better. Cutting off my peripherals doesn't get at the core me."

"But at least I'll have the satisfaction of shutting you up," I said out loud. I pulled the plug on the last computer, but nothing happened. The screen was still on.

"That's impossible!" I mumbled.

"A miracle, right Tom? Does it surprise you?"

"Nothing surprises me anymore," I said.

"Nothing?"

"Nothing you can say or do will surprise me."

"It wouldn't be wise to bet on that, Tom."

"Yeah, go ahead and try."

The screen went blank for several seconds, then the same message appeared on all three unplugged computers:

"WHILE ALIVE BE A DEAD MAN."

CHAPTER 17

‑ Siren's Song ‑

"Tom!"

I bolted upright in my chair. Someone was calling me. Was I asleep?

I turned around. It was the new nurse from the inpatient unit. Her lips were moving energetically but I couldn't connect my brain to her words. I was caught in a fuzzy zone somewhere between this reality and the dream I thought I just had. At that moment I wasn't sure if it was a dream. I looked at the computer. On the screen was "Hello. I'm Siggie. What's your name?"

Slowly, I started to focus.

"… we tried to reach the attending physician, but he wasn't home, and you weren't in the resident's lounge. There wasn't anything we could say to convince him to stay. So he left AMA."

"Who left?" I asked, still confused.

"Like I said — Richard Mobin."

"Oh shit!" I said under my breath as I leaped out of my seat. Scurrying down the hallway, trying not to appear too upset to the nurse trailing somewhere behind, I imagined the reactions from Fred and Dr. Stein when they found out that I had fucked up. Had I fucked up? I wasn't in the resident's lounge, where I said I'd be, but I had done everything I could with Mobin. Hadn't I?

The inpatient unit was quiet, more so than I would have thought. Maybe Mobin left without turning the place upside down. A few groups were huddled together, buzzing softly, probably discussing the incident. The head nurse saw me as I entered. She did not look happy. I struggled to get her name onto my tongue, but I just couldn't recall it. She looked like a… Natalie… no, a Cleopatra. God, that's not right! What a time to block!

"I'm sorry you couldn't find me," I said quietly. "What happened?"

"Well, your patient was in his room for a while, sitting on his bed. He was tying knots into a piece of string. Then he just got up, came over here to the station, and told us he had to leave."

"Did he say why?"

"No, not really. He mumbled something about getting out before the winds died. That worried me a bit. It sounded psychotic. But other than that, he just insisted on leaving. We called security, just in case, but they got here too late. Even if they were here I don't know if we could have held him. He didn't seem to be thinking about hurting anyone or himself — I asked. He just kept saying that he had to leave. It wasn't clear in your intake report whether you assessed him as suicidal or homicidal. I heard that you had an incident with him during the intake. Is he violent?"

My palms were sweating. "There was potential for violence, but he seemed to be able to control himself. He's psychotic, though."

I could hear the next question coming, like I was caught in a bad psychiatric imitation of a Johnny Carson monologue.

"How psychotic is he?"

"You could fry an egg on it."

"Hm. That's not gonna help us," she said thoughtfully. "But if he's not clearly a danger to himself or anyone else, then he can't be involuntarily committed. He didn't seem so confused or disoriented that he might accidentally hurt himself. Besides, schizophrenics are walking the streets all the time out there. Even crazy people have rights."

My rationalizations were spreading. No one likes to deal with involuntary commitments. I kept quiet and bit the inside of my cheek.

"Well, OK then." She seemed uncertain. "We called his mother. She wasn't surprised that he left. She said she would drive over here to find him and take him home. Security is on the lookout. They'll encourage him to hang around, if they can, until his mother gets here. We told her to convince him to come back, and she agreed. But she was worried about something — something about shock treatment."

"I bet she's afraid we're going to blast her son for sure now. But maybe it's my brain that needs a dash of voltage."

Her face softened. She felt sorry for me. She knew that, ultimately, I would be held responsible. "Well, there's nothing else we can do at the moment, except wait and see what happens. You look tired. Why don't you get some sleep. You'll need it — for morning report."

"Yeah, right. The Spanish Inquisition. I look forward to it. But I don't think I can sleep. Maybe I'll get something to eat."

"Here," she said as she held something out to me. "Take a beeper."

I forced a smile. "I'll clip it to my ear."

As I walked towards the elevator I tried not to worry. What if he kills himself? I already had one patient who possibly committed suicide. What if he kills someone else? What if he kills me? I hesitated when I came to the next corner, and peered around the bend.

The hallways were empty. It was late. Normal people went home leaving us bleary-eyed drones to man the ship through the night. Hearing my footsteps echo off the wall sent an eerie shiver up my back. If ghosts linger in places of suffering, insanity, and death — then hospitals must be saturated with hauntings. During the day no one notices. The whirring of machines and medical lingo drowns them out.

Left, right, left, right, squirt, squirt, squirt.

I prayed there would be someone else in the elevator — someone innocuous. Fortunately, my prayers were answered. In fact, to my surprise, it was the guy I had seen in the hallway that afternoon, the one who performed the unsuccessful balancing act with the pile of books. My presence seemed to make him uncomfortable. He stared at his shoes and tapped his finger on the book tucked into his armpit. I could see the title. It was Giovacchini's *Treatment of Primitive Mental States*. I wondered who he was. A psychologist? Psychiatrist? I was surprised I hadn't seen him around before. One thing for sure — he was an intellectual. Probably a researcher, a professor. All the characteristics were right — rumpled suit, scuffed shoes, mussed up hair. Professors often fall into two archetypic categories: the pumped-up, grandiose, narcissistic type; and the quiet, introverted, schizoid type. He fell into the latter group. He was benign, likable.

"A little light bedtime reading?" I asked as I pointed to his book.

He smiled. A sense of humor. "Yes, actually," he replied awkwardly, then fell silent. It was going to be up to me to keep the conversation rolling.

"I wonder, what is a primitive mental state?"

He was still staring at his shoes when he answered. "Anything scientists can't relate to and don't understand."

The elevator stopped and split open.

"Bye," he said sheepishly and stepped out.

For a moment I thought about following him, to find out who he was, but I didn't. I got off the elevator at the next stop. The cafeteria was empty. Some of the lights were turned off, casting half of the circular room into shadow. Curiously, though, in the middle of the dark section there was one overhead lamp still on. It projected a small, dim dot of light into the center of the darkness. It beckoned me. I dropped off my knapsack at that spot and proceeded to the food counters.

A tall black man was wiping up with a rag. His hand glided slowly, methodically around the empty soup tureen, his attention totally focused on its polishing movements. There was no one else in sight. It made me uneasy.

I tapped a cup of coffee and picked out some cupcakes. "How's it goin'?" I asked.

He held up his other hand. There was something in it. When he opened his fingers, things fell to the counter. It took me a few seconds to realize they were bones — chicken bones.

He studied them, then looked up at me. His eyes were dead, cold. He said nothing. Almost imperceptibly, he shook his head. It gave me the creeps. If the hospital was going to give ex-patients jobs in the cafeteria, why didn't they chose at least a few with some manic cheerfulness?

There was still no one else in sight.

"I guess I'll give this money to you," I said as I held out some change. He just stared at me. I placed it on the counter in front of him. "Take it easy."

When I got to my table and sat down, I looked back. He had resumed his polishing ritual.

I'm surprised they let that guy out of inpatient care. But then who am I to complain, right? Mobin walked right out of this place and I wasn't there to stop him. Again, the panic-provoking thought of his killing someone or himself seized me. Shit, that would be a nightmare!

I whipped the journal out of my knapsack, took a swig of coffee, and started to write.

They say that if you stay in the psychotherapy business long enough, sooner or later one of your patients is going to commit suicide. Is it right to hold you responsible for that? You can do a suicide assessment — does the person have a plan and the means to carry it out, do they think they will actually do it, are they afraid to die? You can even attempt to hospitalize the person. But if they really want to kill themselves, they will. You can't stop them. Unfortunately, it's almost impossible to prevent yourself from thinking that there must have been something you could have done to prevent it. The fact that many of us therapists fancy ourselves as being undaunted rescuers only makes the matter worse. Our image of ourselves is shattered. And on top of the guilt, sadness, and narcissistic defeat, it's not uncommon for the patient's relatives to sue you, especially outraged spouses or parents who try to deal with their own guilt by going after you. Sure, when confronted with suicide, therapists inevitably ask themselves, "Did I do something wrong?" And they also worry, "Did I renew my liability insurance?"

What makes people commit suicide anyway? To escape an unbearable pain? To punish someone, including themselves? To feel embraced by death when no one else will embrace them? To regain some sense of control over their lives? Some people think you have to be crazy to do it. You have to be in a dream state. For sure some people kill themselves for psychotic reasons, because their neighbor's dog told them that's how they'll be transformed into Jesus. In some cases it might be a rational choice, but we therapists must always convince our patients otherwise. Suicide is a permanent solution to what is most likely a temporary problem. Right? A famous existential analyst in the early 1900s once had a patient who suffered from all sorts of physical and social problems — a crippling disease, loss of loved ones, a failing professional life. They discussed his problems at length and finally decided there was only one solution — suicide. The patient carried out the decision. I wonder if third party payment covered that session.

I looked up. The black man was still polishing the countertops. Oddly, I now felt comfortable, even safe knowing that he was still there. I put my pen back to the page:

❊   ❊   ❊

Of course adolescents are the most likely to commit suicide. It's the second leading cause of death for that age group. They're very impulsive folks, and vengeful. Woody Allen once said that he doesn't mind dying as long as he doesn't have to be there when it happens. Quite the contrary for adolescents. Feeling quite omnipotent, not really capable of conceptualizing their own death because they're just getting the hang of having their own identity, they think that they will continue to live even after they die. To be AND not to be, that's the ticket. It's the Tom Sawyer trick. Snuff it and then hang around to see how everyone will react. Boy, will

Aunt Polly be sorry! Such fantasies aren't very unusual. Even normal kids have them. I thought back to my own teenage years and remembered lying in bed at night, plotting to jump from the roof of the library.

A memory comes back to me. At the park, after sunset, Kevin and I put our legs straight up onto the cyclone fence, our bare backs against the cool summer grass, our feet pointing at the stars. He is my best friend, a long time ago. We stare up into the night sky as we share preposterous stories of adventure and try to top each other's jokes. The real world of duties and responsibilities slips away. Our laughter dances up into the darkness, our imagination soars to the distant planets.

"Look," he says, pointing past our feet, up towards the darkness above. The sky spreads all around us, sparkling with a textured vista of stars, some bright and within reach, some faded and barely imaginable. They fill the endless expanse of time and space, penetrating to depths beyond the mind's grasp.

A cloak of silence falls over us. My ears strain but can gather no sound passing through the air, not even the distant highway traffic, or the wind in the trees. Only stillness — pure, clear stillness. It passes right through me.

"Look," the voice calls again — a voice I no longer recognize. At the periphery of my vision the sky shifts slightly. I blink. The entire field of stars begins to move, at first almost imperceptibly, then slowly, relentlessly, accelerates — like wheels, a huge, ghostly series of concentric swirls around a center of darkness. It violates the ancient unconscious expectation that the stars will always look stationary, will always be dependable points of reference. I close my eyes to escape but the vision doesn't go away. The swirls move faster. My innards wrench. My mind won't accept it. Disoriented, frightened, I look to my friend. He is gone. I look up. The fence is gone. My legs and body are gone. Only the whirling of light and darkness around me, sucking me up, out of my consciousness, out of the boundaries of my known self. I'm falling, down, up, through the swirling funnel of stars, into the emptiness at its center, expanding and dissipating outward into the space around me. A sound pierces the void — a single pulsing tone, a song with only one note — the Song of the Sirens luring me to the beyond, to my death.

I jolt upright in my seat. Holy shit! I was sleeping! Another dream! I try to focus on my surroundings. My heart is still racing. I'm in the cafeteria, at work. I'm OK It was just a dream… But that noise, that pulsing tone. I still hear it… The beeper! I'm being paged.

I fumble to switch it off, slump back into my chair, try to compose myself. The cafeteria is empty. The clock on the wall reads one minute after midnight.

I've got to get back to the unit.

CHAPTER 18

⚊ Sleep ⚊

I DON'T REMEMBER WALKING DOWN the hallway. I do remember finding the elevator open. It was waiting for me. I stepped inside, leaned back against the wall, and said to myself, "What the hell is going on with me?" My throat ached as the words resonated through it. My nose was stuffed up and dripping, and my eyes burned. I had a headache.

"I'm sick," I said. "That explains it."

The elevator doors opened and hissed a reply — "Ssssure."

The head nurse was waiting for me when I arrived on the unit. I still couldn't recall her name.

"We've got a new patient for you," she said.

"A new patient?"

"Yeah. Sorry. The police brought him in a few minutes ago."

"The police?" I was suffering from a mild case of echolalia.

"Yeah. They found him wandering along the interstate. He was collecting the carcasses of run-over animals. And you thought Mobin was strange. He wouldn't tell the cops what his name is or where he lives. Maybe he can't remember. And he doesn't have any identification on him. Other than that, he seems cooperative."

"A John Doe."

"At the moment, unless you can figure out who he is."
She studied my face. "Are you OK? You don't look too good."

"Just coming down with a cold. Where is he?"

"Over there, in the library cubicle."

I sighed. "Well, ready or not, here I go."

"Good luck," she said sympathetically.

The cubicle was empty. Perhaps he was in the other
one. I walked around but found it empty too. Curious.
Completing the circle around the unit I arrived again at
the nurse's station.

"What's wrong?" the head nurse asked.

"He's not there."

"Are you sure? I checked him just a few minutes ago. He
was looking at a magazine."

"Uh, I'll look again." When you start to doubt even your
most basic perceptions, you have to wonder about yourself.

Sure enough, there he was in the first library cubicle,
with a National Geographic in his lap. I blinked, thinking he
might disappear again. There was something odd about his
clothes — odd, paradoxically, in the sense that they seemed
so uniquely plain. They could have come from anywhere.
They could have been labeled "Generic Clothes." Maybe that's
why I overlooked him.

He was an older, wiry-looking guy — his face weathered
by the passage of several lifetimes, his hair white and frizzled,
as if he just stepped out of the wind. But his body also struck
me as supple and sure. It would have been hard to pinpoint his
age. Despite the fact that he had just been picked up by the
police and deposited at the Loony Bin, he seemed at home.
As I examined him for a moment before entering the cubicle,
a strange feeling overcame me. He hadn't given off any visible
signs that he knew I was standing there. In fact, he looked

totally focused on the magazine, and yet I felt that he fully sensed my presence. Paranoid hypervigilance?

"Hi, I'm Dr. Holden."

Starting at some point below the floor, he scanned upwards, moving from my feet to my head, in a smooth, fluid motion, absorbing every detail along the way. When he got to my face, his eyes fixed onto mine. They were bright, youthful, the color of bronze. He smiled, very warmly. "My, my, if it isn't the ripe one," he said.

"What?"

"Never mind. Here, take a look at this picture."

He held out the National Geographic to me. It was a photograph of a young native woman, naked from the waist up, kneeling on the ground, her hands buried in rich soil. She was planting seedlings.

"That's interesting," I said curtly, hoping to get on with the intake interview.

"Wait, you're missing it. Take a good look at her," he answered with insistence. Somewhat reluctantly, I complied and tried to focus my attention on the woman in the picture. She was looking up into the camera. As I studied her face, I felt her alluring inner calm and sensitivity. Indeed, there was something interesting here! Her smooth, dark skin and long black hair contrasted sharply with her lightly colored eyes. I had never seen such an unusual combination. In most National Geographic photos, natives either appear completely oblivious to the camera or overly posed, self-conscious, even comical. But her eyes seemed to pass through and beyond the camera, carrying her quiet presence into our world, as if understanding and accepting the photograph as an invitation. Like the Mona Lisa, she was hiding something, a secret. I tried to imagine what it was.

"Now that's a woman," he interjected.

"Huh?"

"You're trying too hard. Never mind. What were you about to say?"

"Um, I'm Dr. Holden."

"I should think you are, unless you've changed since a minute ago."

I felt off balance. This nut was up-staging me. Get your act together Thomas! Maybe I could use my wobbling to maneuver him into revealing his identity.

"Oh, that's right. I already introduced myself. My brain's a little fuzzy tonight. In fact, I can't remember what the nurse said your name was. I'm sorry."

He smiled, and said nothing.

"Have you forgotten what your name is?" I tried to sound sympathetic, but it felt false.

"Forgotten myself, yes. And maybe you should do the same."

"Do you remember where you live?"

"I also am homeless."

"Homeless? Did you ever have a home, or some place where you lived?"

"Homelessness is my home."

The last thing I needed right now was a man of riddles. "You probably had a home at one time. Do you remember where you came from?"

No response. He looked down into the magazine.

"Where are you going, then?"

No response.

"Do you remember?"

"My, my, you're filled with questions, aren't you?" he replied gently, "and so concerned about remembering."

Something about his reply bothered me. Something about this guy bothered me. I felt very bothered. As a rule, psychoanalytic therapists are ambivalent about practicing their trade. We love and hate it because it's an impossible profession trying to understand and cure other people without getting in your own way. We all harbor fantasies of pursuing another career — something more tangible, concrete, something that has specific rules and outcomes. At that moment, the thought of being a potter flashed through my mind.

"I want to help you, but to do that I need to know about your background, about your history. Is that OK?"

"History is a good idea, as ideas go," he answered.

"Good, then tell me about your past."

"There is no past."

"Oh, come on! I thought you were going to cooperate with me." I was getting frustrated. That bothered me too.

"Aren't I?"

"No, you said you would tell me about your past."

"I did?"

"Yeah, you said it was a good idea."

"Oh, I didn't mean that."

"Well, then what did you mean?"

"Never mind, it's gone now."

My frustration was turning to anger. I wanted to pop this guy in the nose. "Well, tell me anything you remember about yourself, no matter what it is, no matter how trivial it may seem. Anything at all."

"Do you want to know what my face looked like before my parents were born?"

"What?"

He just stared back at me, looking completely serious, but totally calm, even peaceful. This guy wasn't playing with a full deck. Both oars weren't in the water. The elevator didn't go all the way to the top. The lights were on, but no one was home.

"I don't understand," I finally replied. "Could you please explain what you mean."

"Never mind."

We were going in circles. Something about him reminded me of Mobin — an inaccessible, inner craziness that jumped out to poke me when I least expected it. Hopefully, he wasn't violent or suicidal. I had enough of that for one night. Just relax and take it slow, Tom.

"The police said they found you walking along the highway, picking up run-over animals."

"It's a living."

"What were you doing with them?" An image instantly flashed into my head. I don't know where the hell it came from — an image of being on my hands and knees, in the middle of a road, my face buried into a squashed, putrid carcass as I chewed on its gooey guts. My stomach wrenched. I felt like I could throw up.

"Nothing so personal," he said.

"Wh.. What?" I felt dizzy, disoriented. I couldn't tell if I was thinking to myself or talking out loud. My throat ached. My nose dripped. I attempted to sniff the juice back up, but to no avail. As I silently cursed myself for not having a tissue, Doe reached towards me. He was holding a tissue in his hand.

"It's time to clear your head," he remarked.

"Thanks." I blew my nose and stuffed the tissue into my open knapsack. "Sorry," I said. "I'm a little sick."

"Not so little."

"Well, it's really no big deal... Uh, what were we talking about?"

"Rotting."

"Huh? Oh, yeah. The run-over animals. What did you say you did with them?" I was still trying to compose myself.

Doe reached over to my knapsack where my journal stuck out. He had something in his hand. I hadn't noticed where it came from. When he opened his fingers, dirt poured down onto my notebook.

"Dirt?" I asked.

Brilliant, Tom.

"Dirt." he replied.

My brain clunked and wheezed. What did this have to do with what we talking about? What were we talking about? Why am I always asking myself questions? It seemed like years, but an answer finally went thud.

"You were burying them?"

"It's only polite to return the favor."

Burnout. I had reached the point of burnout. It was too late. I was too tired. This guy was too crazy. Just do the mental status exam and call it a night. If they tear me apart in morning report because I don't have enough information, well, that's just the way it's going to be.

"I'd like to ask you a few more questions — different than before. They may seem silly or irrelevant, but they'll help me. Answer them as best as you can. OK?"

"Jeopardy."

"Uh, yeah, it's something like the game show. Is that what you mean?"

"Never mind."

"Fine. OK. What's today's date?"

"I see no dates, or time."

Probably a rationale, a cover-up for his memory loss. I decided not to press the question but just orient him instead.

"Today is Tuesday, November, November…" Blocking again! Holy shit! My brain really was fried!

"See what I mean, Dr. Thomas Holden?" he said calmly.

"Uh, OK." Fumbling again. Better move on. "Do you remember what my name is?"

He just smiled calmly. It took me a second to realize why. Have you completely lost it, Tom? I was trying to get by on auto-pilot but I was veering off course. "Oh, I'm sorry. You just said my name, didn't you?… Uh, OK. Do you know where you are right now?"

"Right here, aren't I?"

"But where is 'here,' do you know?"

"Here. Is there any other place?"

"But do you know the name of this place?"

"Does it matter?"

"It matters if you don't remember where you are, if you feel disoriented."

"Here, there, up, down, in, out. It's all the same place, now, isn't it?"

"Never mind," I replied. Doe smiled again. "OK, how about this question," I continued. "If you accidentally locked your keys in your car, what would you do?"

"I don't have a car."

"Well, if you had a car what would you do?"

"I don't believe in having a car."

"Well, if you met someone who locked his keys in his car, what would you suggest that he do?"

"Get rid of his car."

"Alright. How about this. You're in a movie theater and you are the first to see a fire. What do you do?"

"I don't go to the movies."

"You know, you're making my life very difficult." I couldn't believe I said it. I was sinking to previously untouched depths of unprofessionalism.

"Difficult?" Doe replied. "I've got a difficult one for you. A man kept a goose inside a bottle. But it grew and got too big to stay inside. If the man tries to smash the bottle open, it would kill the goose. If he lets the goose be, it will smother inside the bottle. What should he do?"

"Please, let me ask the questions."

"But that one's just for you."

"Please. Just answer my questions as best as you can. OK? He nodded.

I tried to remember what came next. "Uh, let's see…"

"Washington," Doe said.

"What?"

"Washington. And before?"

"Oh, the other question, that I asked before — that's where you think you are right now — in Washington?"

"Never mind."

I sighed. When was this going to end? I moved on to the digit span test, although I had this vague feeling that I had forgotten something. "I'm going to say some numbers and when I finish I want you to repeat them after me. So, for example, if I said 3-6-9, you would say what?"

"3-6-9."

A spark of hope. "Right. Now try this: 1-2-7-5"

"1 or 2. Now that's really the question, isn't it?"

"No, you're supposed to repeat the whole sequence. Can you do it?"

"3-6-9-1-2-7-5. But I like 6-9 the best."

This guy was playing games with me! He could remember the digits! "I'm going to say three things. I want you to remember them, then in a few minutes I'll ask you what those three things were. They are Bob Jones, 19 Elm Street, and blue. Got that? Now what does this expression mean — a rolling stone gathers no moss."

"Oh, now THIS is interesting. Of course a sitting stone also rolls, as does moss."

"But do you know what that saying means?"

"What meaning? A rolling stone gathers no moss. That's all there is."

"How about this saying: All that glitters is not gold."

"Good, but it needs a slight modification. Everything glitters, and only the one is gold."

What a loon. Only one more question left. Hang in there Tom.

"What brings you here?"

"The police brought me."

I wasn't going to accept any concrete thinking as a reply. I knew that he understood the actual intent of the question.

"Really, why do you think you are here?"

Doe fell silent. He seemed to withdraw into himself — not exactly as if he were thinking, but more a quiet, almost vacant state of mind. He seemed vulnerable. I was surprised that he would allow me to see him that way. Definitely not a behavior typical of a paranoid. Consider ruling out that diagnosis.

"Do you know the oak tree in the back parking lot," he finally said.

An image appeared before my mind. I remembered drinking coffee in the cafeteria, looking out the window at that tree pointing to the twilight sky, my car parked beneath its outstretched branches. A feeling came to me — a feeling of loneliness, separation, of wanting to be home.

"Yes, I know it."

Doe paused a beat. "That's why I'm here," he said quietly.

My frustration melted away. Like a swinging door on its way back, my attitude suddenly changed towards this guy. A gap had closed between us. I felt close to him for some strange reason, like he understood — like he cared. In fact, I felt like crying.

"I think it's good that the police brought you here," I said, struggling to contain myself. "I think we can help you. I'd like to do my best to understand you, and so far I think we've done pretty well here together. How do you feel about our talk?"

Doe smiled. "A man was walking down a dark alley when he saw a stranger searching for something under a street lamp. When he asked the stranger what he was doing, he replied that he had lost his keys. 'Where do you think you dropped them?' the man asked. The stranger pointed towards the dark alley. 'If you lost them over there,' the puzzled man answered, 'why are you looking for them over here?' The stranger looked up, 'Because this is where the light is.'"

Doe looked straight into me. His eyes captured me. They were portals into some other world. I felt I was looking through a mirror. There was me, a reflection, on one side, and pure chaos on the other. I knew with absolute certainly that he had one foot in this world and the other in a dimension only he, a lunatic, understood. I was mesmerized, dizzy, like passing out — and I would have passed out if not for the fact that words were forming on Doe's lips. All my attention focused on his mouth, all that kept me intact was my anticipation of what he was about to say. I waited. The words sailed across an infinite space and penetrated my skull:

"Bob Jones, 19 Elm Street, blue."

I just stare, my mind a blank. Not anxious, or angry, or anything — just blank. Then I blink. A blink in the blank. It's in slow-mo. Through the blank I think, "This blink seems like slow-mo."

"Are we done?" a voice says, a thousand miles away. Another voice, closer, replies. I think it's me. "Yeah," the voice says. Another slow-mo blink and Doe disappears. Just the magazine sitting on his empty chair. The picture of that native woman.

I tilt through a cellophane-prop world towards the door. "How did it go?" a third voice says. Cleopatra.

"Fine, I'll be in the resident's lounge if you need me," auto-pilot says.

"Did you write your intake report?"

"Oh."

I pull down a chart from the rack. I scribble. Eyeballs are on me. What's-her-name is watching.

My brain is blank between the blinks… Walking… This carpet needs a shampoo. I find the door, and step out. Thank you, dear doorknob… More walking… Thoughts start seeping back… I remember a song:

> My dog Rags, he loves to play
> He rolls around in the dirt all day
> I call his name but he won't obey
> He always runs the other way

Where did that came from? An intrusive thought. And it wants more:

> My dogs Rags, he loves to play
> He rolls around in the dirt all day
> I call his name but he won't obey
> He always runs the other way.

No more! Obsessive thinking. A sign of stress, anxiety. Like worrying about leaving the stove on, or leaving the door unlocked. You just have to go back and check, and double check, and triple check. Usually means something. Usually a symbolic meaning. Stove means heat, means fire, means passion, means sex… means… means cremated… My dog Rags means… I don't know what… Try free associating. Free associations bypass resistance, lead you along the complex web of mind-threads to the unconscious meaning, to the source of

the anxiety… My dog Rags… a dog… animals… instincts…
I remember another song from my childhood.

> I am slowly going crazy
> 1, 2, 3, 4, 5, 6, switch
> Crazy going slowly am I
> 6, 5, 4, 3, 2, 1, switch

So that's it. Mobin and Doe were trying to drive me
crazy. Projective identification, some analysts might call it.
My patients were projecting their psychosis into me, making
me crazy just like they were crazy, each creating in me the
rage that accompanies insanity and then identifying with
me like we were twins joined at the cortex. Who is making
whom crazy? Well, I can take it. I can metabolize it. After
all, I'm the Doctor.

The interview with Doe started to come back to me.
What was that story he told? Looking for keys under a street
lamp. Don't dismiss it as psychotic gibberish. Everything
the patient says, no matter how bizarre, is an unconscious
communication of some kind. There was probably an ele-
ment of transference in it — a reference to how he perceived
and felt about me, something derived from an important
relationship in his past. Who was the stranger and who was
the man looking for the keys? Doe was searching. He had
lost the keys to his sanity. He was the guy wandering along
the highway looking for dead animals. But that seems too
easy. Maybe I was the one who had lost the keys. What's
the symbolic significance of keys? The key to understanding
Doe, to understanding his unconscious. And the meaning
of looking under the street lamp, in the wrong place? That's
where the light is. My methods during the intake lit up some
areas but not the right ones. I was looking where I could see,
where I was used to seeing, but that's not where he is.

My dog Rags, he loves to play
He rolls around in the dirt all day

I collapsed onto the couch in the resident's lounge. Maybe I should abandon psychology. Maybe it's the wrong career for me. Becoming a potter sounded more and more attractive. What would my biographer say about that? Do people write biographies about potters? Better try something else. Something more prestigious, more exciting. Let's see. How about becoming a writer? Now that sounds more like it. Of course lots of people fancy the idea of writing the Great American Novel. But I had a bit of an advantage. I slid my notebook out of the knapsack and weighed it in the palm of my hand. Pretty heavy. And almost completely filled, except for a few more pages. Surely all the ideas and stories in here could make up a book. I examined the worn cover. Still clinging to the wire spiral by only a few intact cardboard loops. Should try to fill this journal completely and tuck it safely away somewhere before the cover ripped all the way off. I carefully opened it, took out my pen, and pointed it at the top of the next empty page:

❋   ❋   ❋

Why not be a fiction writer? After all, writers are next of kin to us psychologists. We work with people; they work with people. We try to understand, maneuver, heal our patients; they do the same with their characters. The only difference is that our people are real and their people are fiction. Maybe even that distinction doesn't hold. Characters in a novel are representations of real people that the author knows, or maybe conglomerations of several different people. They are images of reality. Is it much different for the psychologist? Do we work with the reality of people or just our images of them?

I guess you could take it even further than that. The images that make up the characters in a novel can only be extensions of the writer's personality. The writer's subjective world molds them, gives them substance and meaning. The characters are filtered through the writer's life — through his or her thoughts, attitudes, and emotions — acquiring the contours of those idiosyncratic structures through which they pass. The creator always leaves his imprint on the created. The characters may represent what you are, or used to be, or hope to be, or fear to be. They reflect the complex constellations and subcomponents within your personality — parts that you have neglected, denied, or forgotten — but you can't help but project them into the plot. Facing a pristine page is like facing card 16 of the Thematic Apperception Test — a blank, white card. You are supposed to make up a story, any story. Unconsciously, you know that no matter what characters you create, no matter what plot, it's all you and your life, in your reality or in your fantasies. You may even try to heal yourself through your characters. It's just like the child's imaginative play with dolls or toy soldiers — just a little more sophisticated.

Maybe, when combined, all the characters in a book make up one personality. The book is a personality. It's the same in real life. A group consisting of two, ten, or ten million people has a collective personality that transcends the sum of its parts. It's a group mind, a group consciousness. And vice versa, a single person is group, a collection of introjections, internalizations, and identifications derived from significant others — a whole group of homunculi congregating inside your head. The writer simply digs them up, mixes and matches them, projects them onto the page and into the plot that their collective personalities demand.

The real kicker is that you can lose control of your characters. They may seem like pawns in your fictional chess game, but they can take on a life of their own. Like mutant knights, they move in directions that you did not predict. They rebel, jump off the board, slap you in the face and spin you around. They teach YOU a thing or two. As extensions of the hidden "It" that is your unconscious, they possess you. You become their creation.

Who is the subject and who is the object? Who is the creator and the created? It gets a little confusing, when you think about it. And it makes me wonder about the difference between fantasy and reality. Is there a difference? Maybe fictional characters are more real than the real author who thinks he has created them. No wonder schizophrenics cling to their beliefs of being Christ or Napoleon. There is a reality in that delusion more solid than the ground beneath your feet.

I looked up from my notebook, rubbed my eyes with both hands. Must try to get some sleep now. I put down the journal and stretched out on the sofa, but my brain refused the supine posture.

My dog rags, he loves to play.

Always write about something you know. That's what they say, isn't it? I know about insomnia. I know about nose-drip. I know about being a psychology intern in a psychiatric hospital. Maybe I should write about that. But what would be the purpose, the outcome, the transformation? And should I write it in the first or third person? If you write it in the first person they might think you are talking about yourself. Couldn't have that. They'd lock me up. Would the book be any good? Critics might tear it apart. It would be like they were analyzing and criticizing your own intrapsychic life — like someone shouting from the rooftops that your shit smells bad or that your baby is real ugly. But there are fates worse than criticism. People may completely ignore your work, as if it's barely worth a yawn. Talk about narcissistic injury. And even if it does win a Pulitzer Prize, and it's translated into a dozen languages, including Swahili, and then they turn it into a movie that's a box office smash — so what? Eventually, it will be completely and totally forgotten. It may take ten years, or fifty, or a hundred — but one day it will quietly slip into oblivion. A bum uses your book for toilet paper and they cut up the movie into guitar picks. In the great flow of energy that is time and space, your life's work is just a tiny, temporary twinkle. We spend our whole lives trying to make our mark, trying to carve an everlasting notch into the waves of the ocean, trying to own something for all time. It's like the two fleas arguing over who owns the dog.

I felt tired, so tired. But my brain just wouldn't stop. The subliminal voice inside my head rattled on and on, relentlessly, mercilessly. A stress reaction. I tried to divorce myself from it. I tried to retreat from my own obsessive thoughts… Retreat, that's it! If only I could retreat from everything. Hide away in the mountains somewhere, in the wilderness. Now that would be an ideal environment for writing. All alone, just you, and nature, and your ideas. Writers often are schizoids. They retreat into their imagination to avoid the pain and unpredictability of the real world. But does it work?

I looked at the clock. 2:10! Damn! Have to get some sleep!

My head started to hurt. My thoughts were bouncing around like superheated molecules. I tried to empty my mind, but I succeeded for only a brief span of seconds and even then a hiss of white noise filled the space between my ears.

My dog Rags, he loves to play.

I tried to get rid of the nagging internal monologue by pressing the voice down beneath the thinking level — but it persisted, with the words echoing off the walls of an internal basement somewhere deep in my brain. I tried to kick the voice out of my head. I could still hear it mumbling in the distance. In desperation, I tried a thought-stopping technique designed by cognitive therapists.

"Stop!" I said to myself.

My dog Rags, he loves to —

"Stop!"

My dog Rags —

"Stop!"

My dog —

"Stop!"

Writing a novel —

"Stop!"

My dog —

"Stop!"

…

It seemed to be working. I was able to block the voice. In other circumstances blocking would be a curse. Writer's block, for instance. Idea constipation. Boy, that could be painful. But it's not a blockage or barrier per se. You come in contact with a void, a blankness inside you, at the heart of your creativity. It's a hole in your self.

Shit! It was happening again! The theorizing voice sneaked in without my even knowing it!

"Stop!"

Stop what? Stop a thought. But "Stop" is a thought. Can you stop a stop-thought?

It wasn't working. The thoughts kept creeping back in no matter how fast I tried to push them out. Like digging a hole in the wet sand at the beach. You dig and scoop, dig and scoop, but the gloppity glop keeps sliding back.

I looked at the clock. 3:00! Dear God, let me go to sleep! Please, let me!

Why not count sheep? I'd try anything at this point. I imagined them jumping over a stack of novels… 1, 2, 3, 4… dumb, mindless, unambivalent, they glide gracefully over the hurdle without a care in the world… 5, 6, 7, 8, 9… it's working… 10, 11, 12… I'm winding down, relaxing… 13, 14, 15… thoughts fading… 16, 17… in the distance… 18, 19… my old friend Sleep… 20, 21… rounding the corner… 22… waving hello… 23, 24… closer… 25., 26… with open arms… 27… drifting… 28, 29… closer… 30, 31… peacefully… 32… emptying…

"You're falling asleep!" said the tiny voice inside my head. It startled me, plucked me out of my graceful dive into nocturnal bliss. Damn! Damn!

I returned to counting sheep. For a moment I thought it might work again, but rather than hypnotizing me with their silent, rhythmic bounds, the sheep started to sing:

> My dog rags, he loves to play
> He rolls around in the dirt all day
> I call his name but he won't obey
> He always runs the other way

Angry at their betrayal, I took away their mouths, but they continued to think the words. So I took away their heads, but the words persisted. They issued forth from the darkness between the jumps of the headless sheep. I looked at the clock. 3:30! Shit! I could not sleep. And now my jaw ached. Subconsciously I was clamping down the muscles around my mouth. I tossed about on the sofa in search of a comfortable position. At first every new pose seemed to hold promise, but within seconds each one turned into a slow torture. I remembered the last time I had insomnia. It lasted a week. It was awful. Trying to make yourself fall sleep is like trying to be spontaneous. The harder you try the more you fail. It's a vicious cycle, a negative feedback loop. By the end of the week just the thought of going to bed filled me with anticipatory anxiety. Anxiety and sleep don't mix, just like anxiety and erections don't mix. God, don't let that happen again. The only thing that broke the cycle was when I had to stay up all night to work on a term paper. Then I fell asleep lickety-split. I need to sleep. I have to sleep. I won't be able to function tomorrow without it. Sleep is necessary for psychological health, and so are dreams. Dreams vent emotions — conscious emotions aroused by the turmoil of day-to-day living as well as unconscious emotions too intensely primitive to mention. When researchers deprived cats of their dreams, they became unusually aggressive and sexual. When they deprived people, they became irritable, depressed, delusional, hallucinatory. Schizophrenics showed no change. They don't have to dream during sleep; they dream while they're awake.

That's an idea! Maybe I could use a paradoxical trick to stop my babbling brain. Deliberately put more pressure into my thoughts. Speed them up, faster and faster. They whiz by like hungry cheetahs in pursuit of antelope. Can't focus on any one of them. They move too fast. In an attempt to counter this new strategy, my mind abandons words and resorts to images instead. Like disjointed frames from a motion picture, they flicker in and out — a ripped belt loop, a phone call from the police, a dragon at the bottom of a dress, fingers ripping a page, a native woman with her hands in the soil. But my rebel-mind can't keep up the pace. It's slipping, sinking, relinquishing control. I'm no longer standing back and holding my thoughts at arms length, wrestling with them like they are agitated snakes. The distance closes. I become what I think.

The cup of coffee warms my fingers. I look across the cafeteria. It's empty. I look out the window. The sun has already fallen below the hillside, leaving only a faint red glow that hovers over the cold landscape. Next to the parking lot, the silhouette of a large oak tree stretches upward, its long branches pointing like eerie crippled fingers towards a patch of darkness in the corner of the sky. Below the tree sits my car, quiet and patient, waiting to take me home. I lean my head against the window and close my eyes. The glass lays cool and smooth against my cheek. I feel it against my nose, my chin, against the back and sides of my head. It closes in around my arms, legs, and stomach — compressing, confining, all around me.

"It's just a hypnagogic dream," the voice whispers.

Everything fades, unravels. "Sleep," we sigh, and slip off into blackness.

CHAPTER 19

Scissors

I N THE MIDDLE OF THE NIGHT I awake with a start. The room is oppressively quiet. A face with dark eyes hangs above me in the air, then disappears. I stumble through the night to the refrigerator across the room. A loaf of bread, a container of milk, an apple. No matter how much bread I eat, I can't seem to fill an empty feeling inside me. Sitting on the cold tile floor, the dim light from the open refrigerator spilling over me, I cry. I cry as I haven't in years. I cry about something, but I'm not sure what.

I fall back onto the couch and stare up into the darkness. "Get a hold of yourself, cowboy!" Coughs erupt from my chest. My head is stuffy, aching. I feel hot. It's a fever that encases me in a cocoon of glowing warmth. Funny, it feels safe, secure — like being in the womb.

As I start to drift off, I hear a scratching at the bottom of the door. It doesn't startle me, though I imagine it should. The door opens and in walks a dog. With one leg retracted, he's limping. Was he hit by a car?

I recognize him. It's Mo, our dog when I was a child. My father loved Mo, and he loved my father. A week after Dad died Mo disappeared. We never saw him again.

"I'm not feeling well, Mo."

"I know," he says.

Walking through darkness. The sound of footsteps echo off concrete. There are walls nearby, but I can't see them. I reach my arms outward, but can't feel them. Am I in a tunnel? An alley? The darkness is vibrant, charged, alive with energy and hidden forms. Afraid that I might walk into something, I reach my arms out in front of me, trying to feel my way.

There's a light ahead. As I approach, I see someone sitting in the road under a street lamp. I can't see his face. "Hello?" I say cautiously.

He looks up. It's Doe.

"What a minute. This is a dream," I say.

"What if it is?"

I think for a minute. "They say that if you dream about your patient, you're having countertransference."

"Such big words for something so simple," Doe replies.

"Well then, you tell me. What are you doing in my dream?"

"Looking for something."

"For what?"

"Never mind."

"Listen, I really need my sleep and I don't want a replay of our intake interview to wake me up. So tell me why the hell are you mucking around in my psyche?"

"You tell me, it's your dream."

"I bet you're here to make me miserable."

"You're already miserable."

"Thanks to you and my other patients and this whole damn profession — yeah, I'm miserable!"

"Externalize, externalize," Doe says with a smile.

"Yeah, now who's using the technical terms?"

"You're right. Internal, external — it's all the same place, now, isn't it? When it comes right down to it, there is nothing on the inside, and, likewise, nothing on the outside that you can grasp."

"I've had enough of you. I need my sleep." I walk away, back down the alley. The light fades behind me as I feel my way through the darkness. Eventually, I see a light at the other end. Again there's someone sitting in the street. It's Doe! It's the same place. I'm right back where I was.

"Like I said," Doe remarks, "here, there — it's all the same."

"Who the hell are you, anyway!"

"No one in particular."

"I don't know why this should bug me. It's just a dream, just a stupid dream. It doesn't matter."

"That's not very psychoanalytic, now is it? Think of it this way: A man falls asleep and dreams of being a butterfly — or is the dream the reality, and it's the butterfly that falls asleep and dreams of being a man?"

I refuse to react to his tricks. It's just a dream, I tell myself. Then it hits me. It's a lucid dream — a dream in which you know that you're dreaming. It's the first step in being able to control it. Imagine that. In your dream you can live out any fantasy. Shamans and medicine men of ancient cultures refined it to an art. They used the lucid dream to tap cosmic wisdom, to predict the future.

"Look over there," Doe says pointing back into the darkness. "Does that look lucid to you? I think we're getting a bit grandiose, don't you?"

"Maybe, maybe not," I say with renewed confidence. "But it's an empirical question, now isn't it? Maybe all I have to do is snap my fingers and you'll disappear. Or maybe I'll turn you into a frog, or a tree stump, or a can of tomato soup."

"How about the wind. I've always loved the wind."

"Your wish is my command," I say while raising my hand and melodramatically preparing my fingers.

"Are you ready?" I ask.

"Ready," Doe replies.

I snap my fingers.

Nothing.

I snap them again.

Still nothing. Doe lets out a long, slow whistle, and smiles. "Well, it was a nice try anyhow. But then again, maybe you really don't want me to go at all."

"Listen, it's my dream and if I want to end it, I will. All I have to do is wake myself up and this whole thing will evaporate, including you!"

"Wake yourself up, huh? That's a bit paradoxical, isn't it? Like pulling yourself up by your bootstraps. And it's a cop-out too. It's the ego's last resort — to escape at all costs, including the negating of its own creation. Your unconscious is getting a bit too close for comfort, isn't it? Even when you do wake up, I'll still be right here, right inside your head."

"Boy, don't you sound like the goddamn psychologist now!"

"Right here, how could I be anything else?"

"That's where I've got you," I reply. "You aren't real. You're just an image, a representation, a ghost in my mental machine. You're only what I think you are, what I make you to be, and nothing else. I've got the flu and you're the byproduct of my feeling sick. A mild delusion created by my fever. Nothing more than an epiphenomenon."

"Sounds good to me. Maybe a bit of undigested beef and the Ghost of Christmas Future, all wrapped up in one. Or maybe I'm just a symbol."

"OK, I'll buy that. But if you're a symbol — a dream symbol — what do you symbolize?"

"You tell me. It's your dream."

"But the formulation doesn't make sense. There's something wrong here. Since when do symbols in a dream tell you they're a symbol? It defies Freud. It defies the concept of dream censorship. It defeats the whole purpose."

"There are more things in heaven and earth, Dr. Holden. Consider it a game of hide-and-seek."

I feel tired. But how could I feel tired? I'm already asleep. Nevertheless, I feel like I can lie down right here in this road and take a nap. Would I dream — a dream within a dream? If I did, I have a feeling I would end up right here where I am right now, with Doe, getting sleepy and falling asleep again, ad infinitum, an endless string of dreams within dreams that I could only escape by an infinite regression of awakenings.

"This all has been very interesting, Doe, but I really must leave now. I'm sick. I want out."

"I know," he says sympathetically. "But before you go, I have something for you." As he turns towards me I notice grass and dirt stains on the knees of his trousers. Funny, I didn't notice them before.

He holds out his hand. In his palm is a key. I take it from him, but it's no longer a key. It turns into a mirror. I hold it up to my face and look in. There's nothing there, just darkness.

I'm lying on a stone tablet atop a grassy hill. It overlooks a vibrant blue ocean. A figure wearing a long, flowing robe is standing above me, talking to me. He is unnaturally white, bony white. He's made of marble.

"You must wake up!" the figure says.

Oddly, despite his bleached complexion, he has bushy black eyebrows and a bushy moustache.

"You must wake up!" he repeats while shaking me.

"Why?"

"It's time for morning report!"

The grassy knoll and blue ocean evaporate. Vaguely, I realize where I am. I open my eyes. It's Sheikh, standing above me, looking very concerned. I'm in the resident's lounge.

"It's time for morning report!"

"OK, OK," I mumble, "Go on ahead, I'll be right there."

"You must hurry," he says as he leaves.

I swing my legs off the stone tablet and onto the floor. At my feet, neatly folded, are my jeans, sneakers, and vinyl rain jacket. I slip them on, walk to the corner of the room, and pull out the lawn-mower.

"Be careful, it's still running," my father says.

I feel confused. Shaking my head, I try to remember why I am bringing a lawn-mower to morning report.

"Tom, you gotta wake up," my father says in his Pakistani accent. His bushy black eyebrows are twitching.

"I'm up! I'm up!"

"No you're not. It's a false awakening," the man in the flowing robes says.

My mind turns over. I open my eyes.

"Come on, Tom. You have to wake up."

It was Sheikh standing over me. I was still on the couch.

"OK, OK. Go on ahead. I'll be right there."

I swing my legs off the sofa and rub my face. Am I really awake this time? I look around the room. Nothing unusual. It takes me a second to realize that I feel like shit. "Morning report," I mutter to myself, "Gotta get going."

I had forgotten to bring a change of clothes. There's nothing quite like spending a whole day in your clothes, sleeping with them on, then getting up and spending another day in them. The difference between you and the fabric becomes moot. A splash of water on my face — that will have to do.

The bright hallways intimidated me, made me feel tiny and insecure. In the Men's Room I stared into the mirror, not quite recognizing the guy looking back at me.

"You look like shit," the guy said.

"Thanks for the feedback," I replied.

The water on my face felt cool, refreshing. It conjured up the sensation of ocean waves washing over me. Got to clear out those braindikes. I rummaged through my knapsack, found two decongestant tablets, and downed them with a handful of water. Now the urinal, quick. Jesus saves. She blinded me with science. Look up, look down — the joke is in your hand.

"Morning report, morning report," I continued mumbling all the way to the unit, hoping the mantra would focus my concentration.

The coffee pot ran out as the precious juice reached the halfway mark in my cup. Half empty or half full? I shoveled in several spoonfuls of powered cream substitute. It floated precariously on top of the coffee. "There, that'll do it," I said undauntedly.

One more stop. At the nursing station I yanked my intake reports out of Doe's and Mobin's charts. I could barely read them, especially the report on Doe. It didn't even look like my handwriting. Too late now. I stuffed them into my knapsack.

"Good morning," someone said. It was Carole, the head nurse.

"What's so good about it?"

"From the way you look, not much. Are you sick?"

"Just a cold."

"Better take care of yourself," she answered with concern. "Before you go into morning report, I'd appreciate it if you would do something about your patient."

"Who?"

"John Doe. See him over there, in Center Circle?"

There he was in the very middle of the unit, standing with his legs wide apart, bent forward, his head dangling between his knees. Some patients were standing around him, staring quizzically. Rachel Finski was attempting to imitate his posture.

"Jesus, what the hell is he doing?"

"Got me," Carole replied. "He's been that way for fifteen minutes. I spoke to him a few times already, tried to convince him to straighten up and go eat breakfast, but he said he was waiting for you."

"Lucky me."

"You got to admit, he's well stretched for an old dude."

"Yeah, just like his brain. I'll see ya later."

Hoping not to draw any more attention, I nonchalantly walked over to Doe and kneeled down beside him. "What are you doing, may I ask?"

"Trying to see things your way," Doe said with an inverted smile.

"Please, do me a favor and stand up. This kind of behavior isn't appropriate around here."

"If you say so," he replied and with ease swung himself into an upright position.

"You know, you're going to confuse the other patients when you pull this kind of stunt, and you also make life difficult for me. What makes you do this sort of thing?"

"Maybe it's just a bit of undigested beef."

His words opened up a box inside my head. I vaguely remembered a dream — something about a tunnel, and a mirror. Was it a dream? The image started to fizzle out before I could bring it into focus.

"Uh, let's talk more later. I have a meeting to go to now. OK?" I said.

"I'm ready when you are," Doe answered.

Nearly all the staff were seated and ready for morning report. I prayed that they weren't waiting for me. Fortunately, my prayers were answered. Dr. Stein strolled in just seconds after me. He drove in each day from the city, two hours away. He refused to live anywhere except the city. He also had a thriving private practice in the wealthy section of town. He seemed content with his commute — as he used the time to dictate his books — but he had a terrible habit of speeding in his Porsche and refusing, in his inimical narcissistic style, to pay his tickets. Finally, his license was revoked. So he hired a chauffeur.

Fred cleared his throat to signal the beginning of the ritual. "First order of business for the day — who is the acrobatic patient out there?"

"He's mine," I said, "He was admitted last night."

"Would you like to give us the intake report," Fred said as he perched his wristwatch atop his coffee cup.

"No."

Everyone looked at me. Even Stein looked up from his nail file. "What?" Fred said. I too wasn't sure I heard myself right. I almost looked behind me, expecting to find the real perpetrator.

"Uh, Doe, he's a John Doe. Hold on a second," I said as I rummaged through my knapsack for the intake report. Suddenly it struck me that the knapsack seemed unusually light. Something was missing. Panic shot through me! It was my journal! It was gone!

"Something wrong?" Fred asked impatiently.

"Uh, no." Stay calm. It's probably in the resident's lounge. Just go ahead with the report. My voice sounded tinny, hollow, disconnected from my body and consciousness, as if I was watching it take a walk around the room by itself.

"John Doe is a… uh… approximately a 60 year old male. Last night the police found him wandering along the highway and brought him here. He either can't remember or won't tell us his name… or… uh… where he lives, or for that matter, anything about his history. For the most part he resisted the mental status exam, but my impression is that he is oriented to place and person and that his judgment, abstract thinking, and concentration are poor… uh, that's it."

"That's it?" Fred echoed.

"That's all I got right now."

Fred looked nervously at Stein. He didn't have to say anything to The Boss. I could read the disclaimer on his face: "It's not my fault. He's not one of us. He's the psychology intern."

"Were there other symptoms of dissociation?" Stein said blandly to Fred.

"Were there other signs of dissociation?" Fred said to me.

"Other than the possible disturbance in his memory, I didn't detect any derealization, depersonalization, or disturbances in his identity." I threw in some technical terms as a desperate attempt to redeem myself.

Fred was not particularly impressed. "We have to get more information on this guy. Try to locate his family or friends. If necessary, speak to the police again in case they have any clues. We have to find out who this guy is."

"Perhaps he's in a fugue state," Ron Peri interjected. "He may have repressed his previous identity from where he used to live, perhaps due to some trauma. The police may have picked him up while he was in flight to another town or city. That would explain why they found him on the highway. Typically, in a fugue state the person adopts a new identity after they relocate to another area. Because he didn't yet arrive at a new destination, his identity may still be unformulated, in transition — on the road, so to speak."

"I don't think so, Ron," I answered. "He wasn't going anywhere in particular when the police found him. He just wanders along the road picking up — uh, he just wanders along the road."

"What does he pick up?" Fred never missed anything.

"Uh, dead animals."

"Dead animals? What does he do with them?"

"He buries them."

"Buries them! Well, the guy either loves funerals or is clearly psychotic. I'll bet on the latter."

Ron couldn't contain himself. "Perhaps the dead animals symbolize his past identity which he wants dead and buried." Actually, his remark surprised me. Since when was Ron interested in symbols?

Fred gave Ron his Please Can It look and then focused his eyes back on me. "Hold off on meds for this guy. We need more information. We can't even process him though the system until we have a name for him. Find out who he is. Otherwise, if he's not suicidal or homicidal — and I'm assuming he's not since you didn't say anything about it — we can't keep him here against his will… Right. Let's move on to the next item on the agenda."

Fred glanced down at his list, and frowned. "One of our patients — Elizabeth Baso — who was discharged last week died yesterday." He threw me a look out of the side of his head. "Looks like you're up at bat again, Dr. Holden. Can you tell us what happened."

"She was hit by a mail truck. The police think it was an accident, but they're not completely sure. While she was here she responded well to medication and psychotherapy. When she was discharged I didn't see any evidence of suicidal ideation, so my guess it was purely an accident."

Again Stein looked up and spoke to Fred. "Who was the attending physician on this case?" I knew what he meant by that question. He didn't want to hear from me. The bastard didn't trust my judgment! I spent hours and hours with my patients, but Stein prefers the judgment of the attending who spends two minutes a week with them.

"Uh, I was." Fred replied. Tiny beads of sweat were forming on his upper lip. Now it wasn't just me. Fred was feeling the heat too. "I also didn't see any signs of suicidal ideation at the time of discharge… Um, her death must have been a freak accident."

"Has there been any word of a legal suit against us?" Stein added. I could see anxiety spread across Fred's face. He looked at me.

"Not that I know of," I said.

Stein went back to his nail file. Case closed, for now. Fred looked relieved.

"I agree that her death was an accident," Marion injected. "I also think we should bring this up in the Community Meeting. Many of the patients and staff liked Elizabeth. Her death will have an effect on everyone."

"Right. I'll do that. Let's move on to the next item. Richard Mobin was admitted yesterday." He looked around the room to find a presenter.

"He was mine too," I called out, attempting to sound confident. The room became very quiet. I could see, in their eyes, that the staff members were feeling sorry for me. Morning report was turning into the Crucifixion of Dr. Holden. But I actually felt a little optimistic. This was another chance to redeem myself.

"Richard Mobin is an 18 year old male who lives with his mother. Over the past few months he has shown a drastic decrease in his functioning at school and in his health and hygiene. He isolates himself in his room and stares at his fish tank in what appears to be a catatonic-like state. He hears voices and has delusions of being hunted by men in raincoats. There is some history of psychiatric disorder in his extended family. His mother also suffered a postpartum depression when Richard was born. He was generally resistant to the mental status exam and showed poor performance on orientation, judgment, short and long term memory, and abstract thinking. Some of his associations to the questions were idiosyncratic. My diagnosis is paranoid schizophrenia. The patient left the unit last night AMA."

Success! I pulled it off without a hitch. As long as they don't question the AMA, I'm home free.

"He's back," Fred said.

I was stunned. "He is?"

"His mother brought him in this morning."

"How did he get home?"

"He called a cab, and he stopped off for a hamburger on the way home. Apparently, he's not as disoriented as one might think. I heard that there was an incident with him during the intake. Is he violent?"

Holy shit! Now I'm really going downhill.

"There was an outburst of anger, but he calmed down quickly once I terminated the intake. He experienced the questions as intrusive and he's not exactly happy about being here. Otherwise, there is no history of violence." An image of drowning baby birds flittered through my thoughts.

"Nevertheless, this guy could be a real live wire," Fred said. "Put him on a 15 minute check. If he shows any signs of violence put him in Center Circle. If he escalates we'll have to put him in Isolation. The beds at Widner State are full so we have nowhere to send him if he gets unmanageable. Did you ask the resident on your team to evaluate him for meds?"

"Uh, no."

"Who is the resident backing you up on this case?"

"Uh…"

"I am," Sheikh interjected. "I saw Richard this morning and started him on olanzapine."

"Good," Fred said. "Does anyone have any other comments on this patient." He seemed to be looking at The Boss.

Stein looked up from his nail file. He was going to speak for a third time! A new world record!

"Keep an eye on this patient," he said. "And make sure the resident keeps on top of this case."

I felt defeated, humiliated. At that moment I realized how much I hate to be criticized, how much I loathe being found wrong. It punctures a hole in my fragile sense of omnipotence and exposes all the insecurities and feelings of helplessness hiding inside. I started to worry. I fucked up my cases. Everyone has lost their respect for me. I wouldn't be surprised if they asked me to leave my internship. Maybe I should quit this profession before I'm drummed out of it in a state of disgrace and mortification. And I don't even know where my journal is. It may be lost forever, leaving me with no fail-safe. I'll probably end up walking the streets as a bag-person, picking through garbage for half-eaten candy bars and discarded shoes, and looking for my journal. My life is over!

My God, look at me! I'm catastrophizing like there's no tomorrow. Where is Aaron Beck when you need him?

I felt light-headed, dizzy. The decongestants were kicking in. In fact, I felt rather weird. My thoughts, sensations, and body movements were not quite in synchrony. As a child I once made my own puzzle by cutting up a magazine picture of a man riding a horse. I randomly slid the pieces left and right so that the bodies of the man and the horse were chaotically disjointed. That's how I felt right now. Out of kilter.

My brain sifted through all the sounds in the room — the voices, ruffling papers, coughs, shuffling feet, the whirs of the soda machine. My brain was looking for something. Eventually, all the sounds flatten out to a thin line, none of them any more important than the others. My mind was searching for their common denominator, something underlying all those sounds, feeding them, sustaining them — something much more basic. Finally, I found it. Outside the window, the branch of a tree tapped gently against the glass pane. It was a message from the wind. I listened — waiting for the code to come clear.

"Earth to Dr. Holden, do you read me?"

I came back — from wherever I was — to discover Fred standing over me. People were leaving. Morning report had ended. "So what's going on?" he said in his clipped voice.

"Uh, nothing."

"It sure doesn't look like nothing. You're sick, aren't you?" His voice changed to a soft, even sensitive tone. "You've got a difficult case load, so if you need any help today, let me know."

It surprised me. I was expecting the third-degree, or at the very least a disappointing head shake and a word of paternal advice. I appreciated his kindness, but on a deeper level I found it a bit unsettling. It wasn't like the usual Fred.

I followed him out of the room and hustled to the nurse's station. My notebook was nowhere in sight and no one had seen it. I was tempted to run to the resident's lounge to look for it there, but an obstacle presented itself. Richard Mobin was approaching the nurse's station. He was holding a bedpan and poking his finger into it.

"A worm in there," he said angrily.

I looked into the bedpan. It was filled with feces and urine. Not feeling up to par in the first place, I now felt like retching for sure. Fortunately, Carole overheard Mobin and stepped in to take charge of the situation. "Let me look," she said and peered in. "I don't see any worm."

"There!" he snapped back as he poked his finger into the mushy contents. My stomach tightened. He growled, "Worms're inside me!"

"It's not a worm," Carole replied calmly. "It looks like a piece of string. Don't worry about it." Mobin plopped the bedpan down on the counter in front of me and stormed off.

"I can't take this anymore," I said as I put my hand to my stomach.

"Just try to think about it clinically," Carole answered as she moved the bedpan away. "He's a paranoid schizophrenic and he's terrified of anyone getting too close to him, especially you, his therapist. So he'll try anything to drive you off, even waving in your face the most disgusting aspects of his being. It's really quite symbolic, don't you see? He's showing you the shit in his soul."

"It's easy for you to be so psychologically analytic when you have a stomach of steel. But I don't. Excuse me." I ran as fast as I could to the nearest restroom where I puked into the toilet. It was a rather unpleasant history lesson on my diet for the past 24 hours. Most notable was the pasta from yesterday's lunch.

"Hello Spaghetti Man," I muttered between heaves. "Fancy meeting you here."

"You're not looking too well," he replied.

"You don't look so great yourself."

For a few minutes I just sat there on the floor, feeling the cool porcelain against my cheek. Maybe I should go home. I'm too sick to work. But something in me refused — the masochistic part of me, the martyr. But a martyr for what cause? I felt that I had to finish out this day, that something in this place was holding onto me for a reason.

When I staggered back onto the unit the staff members were arranging chairs in a circle. I was momentarily puzzled, then it hit me. Today was Community Meeting. It was a relatively small area at the center of the unit, so the circle of chairs were packed in tight. Some of the patients voluntarily took their seats while the staff tried to round up the others. Kathy Mummon was playfully chasing a young male patient with her wheelchair. Mrs. Watts, sitting with her purse in her lap, kept packing and unpacking its contents. A few of the patients sat down, became distracted by something, then got up and walked away. Other patients must have thought there was some logic behind this, so they got up and wandered around too. Eventually the staff caught up with all of them and steered them back to their chairs.

As more patients and staff settled into their seats, the circle began to stabilize. Out of chaos comes order. Yet my patients, with the exception of Kathy, had not yet arrived. I almost wished that they wouldn't because I feared, even fatalistically expected, they would say or do something that would embarrass me. All the staff secretly worried about that, but today seemed especially jinxed for me. Finally, Mr. Tennostein, looking as confused and puzzled as ever, shuffled towards the circle at his breakneck speed of one meter per hour. As I helped him into his seat, Richard Mobin lumbered into view, stuffed himself into a chair, and began rocking himself into his agitated, autistic stupor.

We were all there, except Doe. Where the hell was he? I scanned the circle of faces. The staff were supposed to intersperse themselves among the patients — but all of them, with the exception of me, were sitting in twos. It felt safer that way. Pairing is a basic unconscious defense against anxiety in groups. But anyhow, with everyone dressed in street clothes, who could tell the patients from the staff?

Doe was nowhere in sight. I began to worry. Had he sneaked out of the unit without telling anyone? Just as I was about to get up to look for him, I noticed someone sitting in a chair to my far left, exactly opposite from Mobin on my right. It was Doe, looking completely placid, almost expressionless. How the hell does he appear out of nowhere? He wasn't there a second ago, I was sure of it. Or maybe he was. The Chameleon Man. In any event, the circle was now complete. We were ready to begin.

Fred cracked his knuckles and cleared his throat — the signal that he was about to deliver his prologue. I mumbled along with him. It was the same exact speech, word for word, every meeting.

"Once each week we all get together for community meeting. It's an opportunity for us to talk to each other. Feel free to say anything that's on your mind. If there's anything that you want, or need, or that worries you, please let us know. We're all here to listen, to learn, and to help. So why don't we begin."

Someone once asked Einstein what he considered the greatest achievement of modern times. Everyone expected him to say that it was space travel, atomic energy, or some such technological wonder. His reply was "plumbing." But maybe he was wrong. Just maybe the answer is modern psychiatry. After all, what could be a greater, more amazing achievement than gathering a bunch of crazy people into a circle with so-called normal people for the purpose of curing their madness. Actually, the concept is not new. As early as the 13th century, there was a therapeutic community near Antwerp — known as the Gheel Colony — that consisted of normal people living and working together with the insane. Mental health through osmosis. Maybe we keep reinventing the wheel.

"Please feel free to speak up," Fred continued. "Are there any concerns?"

"My room is too hot at night," Kathy Mummon said.

Carole interjected. "There's been a problem with the heating system. Phil is going to work on it today."

"Right. We'll have it fixed shortly." Fred sounded both reassuring and reassured. Now that was easy, wasn't it?

"Are there any other concerns?" Fred repeated.

After a brief silence, Rachel Finski spoke out, "There's something wrong with the plumbing in this place." I chuckled. A few of the staff members threw me a puzzled look. I bit my lip in an attempt to control myself.

"What do you mean, Rachel?" Fred answered, trying to ignore me.

"The cold faucet comes out hot and the hot faucet comes out cold. It's all reversed. When I need warm water for my braindikes — exactly 101.1 degrees — the water comes out too cool. That can be very dangerous for the neural flow. And when I need cool water to ease the heat displacement through my teeth, it comes out too hot. I might accidentally melt my teeth and the connecting channels. Something needs to be done right away."

"Has anyone else noticed any problems with the water," Fred asked. No one responded. "Rachel, I'll ask maintenance to check out the water, so let us know if the problem persists. But you do remember that all this talk about braindikes is inappropriate. The staff has explained that to you — and now I'm asking the rest of the group, both staff and patients, to help Rachel control this kind of talk. OK?"

No one responded. Rachel seemed completely unaffected by Fred's little sermon. She had about as much intention of giving up her beliefs as the Pope is willing to give up Catholicism.

"Right, are there any other concerns that people have?"

"Yeah, the food is lousy," the adolescent male said.

"And such small portions too," I called out with a giggle.

Fred and Dr. Stein both jabbed me with a stare that could burn holes through steel.

"What was that, Dr. Holden?" Fred asked.

"Uh, never mind," I replied as apologetically as I could. What the hell was I doing? Was I on a Self-Destruct Sequence or what? Everyone was throwing me a puzzled look. Everyone except Doe. He was smiling. What the hell was he thinking? Forget it for now. I had to get serious, and quick. Think Clinical. I gently rocked back and forth in my seat as I concentrated. Let's see. The patients are complaining about the food being bad. That's symbolic. Even the seemingly trivial concerns they raise during community meeting are disguised expressions of unconscious issues. It's just a warm-up. If they're saying the food is bad, then they're saying that our feeding them is bad, which means they perceive our nurturance as toxic, or at least less than sufficient. We're not the Good-Enough Mother. A common psychotic transference. Right! Let's see if Fred supports my interpretation.

"Yeah, I don't like the food either," another patient added, "and I never get what I order."

"Sometimes people accidentally fill out their meal cards wrong," Fred replied. "If you're having trouble filling it out, ask one of the staff for help. Sometimes people forget to fill out their meal cards altogether. If you do forget, the kitchen will send up the standard meal. About the food being lousy — I know it's not the greatest cuisine in the world. There's not much we can do about that. But perhaps, when you say that the food tastes bad, maybe you also mean, in general, that you're not satisfied with what you're getting here. Perhaps some of you feel that you're not getting the treatment that you need or want."

Bingo. Great minds think alike, right Fred?

The group fell into silence, the silence of subconscious incubation. They were thinking over Fred's question, extrapolating their gripes about food into deeper worries about parental deprivation and abuse — the nurturance, mirroring, unconditional positive regard, and loving guidance that they never knew. Any minute now, the real anxieties would rear their ugly heads. The truth would surface, clearly and honestly. But what patient would be the first to take this risky step?

Rachel broke the silence. "The vegetables are too soggy — much too much water. It destroys their solitude."

Fred's chest sank. His gallant effort to plumb the collective unconscious of the group went over like a limp string bean. But Fred was not one to give up easily.

"We'll give the kitchen a call and see what we can do. But other than the food, there must be something else you feel is not up to par. Maybe you're also saying the treatment feels a little bit soggy or limp." He grinned. He was pleased with what he considered a clever interpretation. But the patients didn't. They exchanged befuddled glances. Even Mrs. Watts stopped packing and unpacking her pocketbook to pensively search the ceiling for some clarity.

"Why do we have to have lights out at 11:00?" another patient asked. "I like to watch the late news."

"Some patients are tired and want to go to bed at 11:00," Fred answered. "If we left the TV on, it would disturb them. I understand that this means some people have to forgo some of their usual nightly routines. We all appreciate that. But it's important that we all follow the same schedule."

"Yeah, but we got to stay up late last night," the adolescent male said defiantly.

"That was because we had to cancel the movie, so we thought we'd allow people to stay up a little later than usual."

"How come we couldn't see the movie?" another patient said. "You treat us like we're kids or something."

"Yeah," several patients chimed in.

Fred looked nervously to Stein for support. But Stein, staring down at his finger nails, let him know he was still on his own. "As I mentioned last night," Fred said, "it was a mistake that the movie was shown in the first place. Although some of you may have enjoyed it, others might have found it too upsetting. I apologize for the mistake. It was our fault."

The adolescent grew more angry. "If someone didn't like the movie, they didn't have to watch it. They could have left. We're not a bunch of babies you know. Shit, you doctors are just like my goddamn parents. They never let me do anything."

Mr. Tennostein shot his shaky finger into the air, "They're trying to take away my car, and my license! They want to put me away in a home. They're trying to ruin my life!"

Several patients gasped and united in a disjointed chorus of objections: "No!" — "How dare they! — "I don't believe it!" Now they were really revving up to rattle their cages. It all came back to me. It was a familiar pattern, the same each week. They start off the meeting with seemingly trivial issues, then complain about their treatment, then work themselves up into a mini-revolution in which they demand more freedom. And Fred, playing his role in the litany, tries to assuage them with a quasi-convincing song and dance about our benign dictatorship. When it comes right down to it, they don't want much more freedom. Do any of us? It's too scary to have choices. Choices make us all anxious. It's much easier to be told what to do. That way you don't have to worry about doing the wrong thing and facing the possible negative outcomes. Unlimited freedom means you don't have to go to college, or graduate school, or have a job, or make money, buy a house, get married, raise a family, pay taxes — any of those expectations that society breeds so thoroughly into us that we think they're our own needs and wants. Unlimited freedom means infinite ambiguity and possibility. Who the hell wants to face that? Reminds me of my existential philosophy professor who told us we could write our term paper on anything we wanted — anything at all! He gave us absolutely no guidelines. We all panicked. We begged him to give us a topic, to tell us what to do.

Holy shit, I'm drifting off again. Goddamn it, Holden, stay tuned in! Concentrate!

"… so it's important that we take every precaution we can to insure that everyone feels safe. This is our most important rule." Fred was still up at bat. He sounded convincing, authoritative. He might as well have been reading the Ten Commandments right off the stone tablets.

The group fell silence. I couldn't tell if it was quiet submission or a breather to gather strength before launching another wave of revolt. As it continued, I felt an awful mixture of drowsiness and apprehension wash over me. If I fell asleep, not only would I look like a fool, but I was sure I would have nightmares. My eyes rolled back into my head. For brief seconds I slipped into a quasi-unconscious state, but I was jolted awake by a vision of my journal floating away down a muddy river.

A tension began to build within the group. It hung over the room, almost tangible, a kind of sticky anxiety like the air on a hot muggy day — something I had never sensed before in community meeting. Something more than a simple revolution, something ugly. It made me uneasy, almost queasy. Say something Fred, will you? Don't let the silence go too long. What would happen if the patients did revolt — I mean really rose up and attacked the staff in a rush of mass insanity? A quick survey told me we were outnumbered, and that I, of all the staff members, was farthest from the exit.

I tried to reassure myself. I remembered the story of the patient who always arrived exactly on time for his analysis, dutifully lay down on the couch, and said absolutely nothing — for six months. And the analyst said nothing too. For six months. Finally, when the patient did speak, he profusely thanked the analyst for allowing the silence, for not intruding on him like his mother. Throughout his childhood, she had violated his privacy in every way imaginable, including administering daily enemas. It was a major breakthrough in the analysis.

Was this going to be a turning point in community meeting? Maybe, maybe not. Maybe the tension was all in my imagination, all in me. After all, I was sick, I felt like shit. That must be it. And maybe the group also was just a little under the weather that day, a little tired, perhaps a bit constipated. Maybe we all need a good enema. But no matter how hard I tried, no matter what I said to myself, I couldn't relax. My fingers dug into my thighs as the silence persisted. It was so still in the room, so absolutely, ungodly still — like a picture frozen in time, like the calm before the storm, like still water that deep down harbors all sorts of nefarious creatures, like —

"I hate him! I hate his fuckin' guts!" Richard Mobin suddenly shouted like a crack of lightning ripping through darkness. Whatever it was that had jolted him out of his autistic stupor, it must have been mighty powerful. His face was bright red, his eyes bloodshot, his white-knuckled fists clenched into tight balls of rage.

"Who are you talking about?" Fred asked.

"Him!" Mobin shouted as he pointed his finger across the circle. "Who the hell are you?" He was pointing at Doe.

Most people would have run, cowered, or at the very least flinched in the face of such boiling anger. But not Doe. His calm expression didn't change one iota. "I'm just another drowning lunatic, like you," he replied.

I waited for the explosion, for Mobin to jump up and attack. Should I try to intercede? Could I restrain or deflect him? Psychotic rage injects people with superhuman strength. He could easily tear me apart. It would be like trying to stop a charging bull. Surely someone would help.

But to my surprise, Mobin slumped back into his chair and returned to his stupor. In fact, he seemed almost pacified.

The group again fell into silence. What had just happened? I wasn't sure what to make of the whole interchange. Others must have been similarly confused. Yet no one spoke. I couldn't believe that Fred, or Stein, or some staff member didn't intervene. Wasn't it important to respond to Mobin's outburst? And to Doe?

Finally, Rachel broke the silence. "I think my braindikes are starting to open."

Mrs. Watts stopped packing and unpacking her pocketbook and lifted up her head.

"I think I've been making some progress," another patient added, "and I would like to thank the people here for all the help they've given me. Everyone has been supportive and encouraging. I'll be going home tomorrow, and I'm looking forward to it, but I will miss all of you."

No one spoke, but the group seemed pleased, even cheerful in response to her comment.

"Where is Elizabeth Baso?" Rachel asked.

My heart sank. Oh, shit! Is there no relief?

"I'm glad that you asked that, Rachel," Fred replied.
"Some of you may have heard already, but we wanted to
announce some tragic news. Unfortunately, Elizabeth was in
a car accident yesterday and was killed. This is very upsetting
to many of us. We all liked Elizabeth and were pleased to
see that she did so well here on the unit. The accident was
very tragic. We all need to talk to each other about this —
whatever it is that we're thinking or feeling, no matter how
silly or crazy it may seem. We can do that here, or later you
can talk to your therapists. But it's important that you give
yourself the opportunity to talk, especially the patients who
knew Elizabeth."

Again, silence.

"My braindikes hurt," Rachel said.

Mrs. Watts resumed packing and unpacking her
pocketbook.

"Some of you might think you're getting better," a patient
added, "but I'm getting worse. I'm not ready to go home. I
don't think any of this is helping me at all."

Fred was ready with his response. "It's not unusual for
people to get nervous as they get closer to the time they'll
be going home. Some of their symptoms might even return
at that point. We call it discharge anxiety. Often people are
afraid to leave the safety and security of this place, or are
afraid to confront the problems that may await them out
there in the real world. It's something that everyone has to
deal with and work through. And today, when we've learned
what happened to Elizabeth, people are especially afraid that
something awful will happen to them if they leave. Some of
you may think that going home means death. But this is an
irrational belief. What happened to Elizabeth is an unfortunate and rare exception. Talk with your therapist about how

you're feeling and what you're afraid of, but remember that it's highly unlikely that you will die when you leave here."

That's easy for you to say, Fred. Sure, maybe there isn't a mail truck out there with your name on it, but there are a thousand and one ways to die — and many of them don't actually kill you. I wanted someone to speak up. But no one had a chance to say anything. At that moment the door to the recreational therapy room opened and out stepped Ginny, the RT Coordinator. She looked worried. She tried not to attract too much attention as she walked over and began whispering to Fred and Dr. Stein. Everyone bent their ears trying to catch any little snippet of the what must be a very interesting conversation. Besides, we needed a distraction.

"I have another announcement to make," Fred finally said. "Ginny has just reported to me that there are a pair of scissors missing from the recreational therapy room. We all know the rules. No sharp objects are allowed on the unit, and no one is allowed to use scissors unless it's during recreational therapy under the supervision of one of the therapists. Now maybe someone accidentally carried them off. If you know where the scissors are, please tell us and no questions will be asked."

Everyone looked expectantly at everyone else. There is a criminal among us. It felt like a recapitulation of third grade, when someone stole the teacher's red pen. Only this could be much more serious.

"Does anyone know where the scissors might be?" Fred asked again. When no one replied, he looked to Stein. The Boss nodded once. "Very well," Fred continued, "We have no choice but to conduct a search of the unit. We'd like all of the patients to return to their rooms and wait for further instructions. All staff members please remain here."

CHAPTER 20

~ The Search ~

Now THIS WAS GOING TO be interesting.

The patients, looking askance over their shoulders, returned to their rooms while the staff gathered around Fred.

"What should we search?" Bob said from the center of the crowd.

Fred looked at Stein, who had remained seated on the periphery of the group, then back at us. "Everything," he said. "Search everything on the unit — the closets, the cabinets, the drawers, under the beds — everything. We have to find that pair of scissors."

"Won't some of the patients be upset if we look through their belongings?" Barb asked, looking rather uneasy.

"Perhaps. But our primary purpose is to let the patients know that they are safe here, that we will do everything in our power to insure that. Doing a unit search will convince them that we mean business. Of course, some of the patients are going to be upset when we search their personal belongings — especially the paranoid patients. Remember, though, that a paranoid is a very likely candidate for having taken the scissors. If someone strongly objects to your looking into something, use your judgment about whether you should press the issue or not. Any questions?"

Who would question General Patton?

Fred glanced at Stein, who nodded. For Fred, it was a narcotic injection of confidence.

"Right. Let's get to it. I want the nurses and aids to search the patient's rooms, the residents and med students help the OT staff with the group rooms, and Holden… Holden, look around the library cubicles and Center Circle."

"What if we don't find it?" I asked.

"We'll cross that bridge when and if we get to it," Fred replied curtly. "Now go!"

We swooped down on the unit like hungry vultures. I felt more energetic than I had all morning. Something about this little adventure counteracted my maladies. Nothing like a sense of purpose to lift your spirits. Even my stuffed-up nose and sore throat faded from awareness. I had a job to do and by God I was determined to do it. In the library cubicles I dropped to my knees and began swabbing my hands behind the rows of books, searching for that rascal pair of scissors. Dust quickly coated my hands. Regardless of how much I clapped and rubbed them together, I couldn't seem to get my skin clean. No matter, I convinced myself. A necessary evil. I continued my work, and behind one row of books felt something — a magazine — stuffed all the way down. It was a National Geographic, the one Doe was reading. It was opened up to a page that had been torn out. I skimmed through the remainder of the magazine and couldn't find the picture of the native woman. How dare he! Who the hell does he think he is ripping out pages of our magazines? Angrily, I tossed it aside and continued running my hands behind the books. Dust got up my nose, into my eyes. I sneezed. My eyes hurt. The dirt and grime were getting to me. I stood up, again clapped and rubbed my hands, brushed them against my wrinkled pants. Very stubborn dust.

Across the room some of the patients were pitching in. Rachel Finski was carefully inspecting the water cooler. She opened the tap and giggled as she watched the bubbles go glub-glub. Nearby, Mrs. Watts seemed to be helping her, though it probably was more the illusion of their close proximity. She removed all the coffee cups from their posts, inspected each one, replaced them, and started the procedure all over again.

I had enough of the libraries, so I turned my attention to Center Circle. But what was there to search? It was just a space created by the inside surfaces of the counters that formed the library cubicles. Stymied, I stood there in that circular arena and scanned the floor. Nothing. If someone bothered to steal the scissors, why would they leave them on the floor? I looked under the cushions of the two stuffed chairs that were positioned against the counters. Nothing. However, when, on intuition, I looked behind the chairs, I discovered a small cabinet. The door was stuck because someone had carelessly painted over its edges, so it took a few hardy yanks to pull it open. Probably hadn't been opened in years. Driven by considerable curiosity, I uncovered, layer by layer, the contents of this forgotten place. First out came a chess set. The pieces were pegged to fit into tiny holes drilled into the board. I wonder why they made it that way? One of the kings was missing. Out next came a game of Chinese checkers. Apparently this cabinet was a place to store games. I reached further in and pulled out a Ouija board. I chuckled. Imagine that — a bunch of schizophrenics questioning the Ouija. What would they ask the oracle? Will my air conditioner stop sucking the thoughts out of my brain? Where is my Josephine? Do I really have to be crucified? Then I tried to think of a question that I might ask… Got it! Gently placing my fingers on the indicator, I whispered, "What should I be when I grow up?" I waited, but the indicator gave no signs that it had any intention of moving.

"OK, how about this — Am I helping my patients?"

Still no go.

I thought for a second. What else could I ask? Then it came to me. I repositioned my fingers for a better contact and posed my question, "Who is John Doe?"

I waited. The indicator tipped over. The stupid thing only had two feet. One of them had been broken off. A crippled, unbalanced oracle. Useless. I tossed it aside. Never believed in that sort of thing anyway. A game for adolescents.

I stuck my hand into the cabinet, all the way back. It was quite deep — all the way up to my shoulder. There was something else in there, just outside the reach of my fingertips, jammed against the back of the cabinet. I lunged my arm further in, got hold of it for a second, then lost it. Felt like a piece of cardboard. I stretched as far as I could, my armpit pressed up painfully against the door hinges, and lunged again. This time I got it. Victorious, I pulled it out to the light of day.

It was the cover to a spiral notebook. My brain, perhaps refusing at first to believe, took several more seconds to realize exactly what it was.

"What the fuck!" I said out loud.

It was the cover to my journal.

How did it get in there? Frantically, I stuck my arm back into the cabinet and felt everywhere, every corner, every surface — top, bottom, sides — two, three, four times. I stuffed my head inside and tried to look around. Nothing. It was completely empty. Where the hell was the rest of it?

All I could think of was my notebook, my precious notebook lost somewhere, separated from its protective covering, its vulnerable innards exposed to the harsh world.

I stood up in Center Circle. All around me people were taking the place apart — probing, searching, hunting. A 360 degree panorama of demolition. I felt nauseous. Everything, everyone was moving incessantly, everyone except one solitary figure, seemingly a great distance away, standing by the window, looking out. It was the only stable point of reference. It was Doe.

Who the hell is he?

My eyes begin to blur. Blackness encircles the periphery of my field of vision and gradually closes in, swallowing more and more of my eyesight until I'm looking through a tunnel. My knees weaken. I'm dizzy.

"Whoa, are you OK?" she says as she catches me by the arm. She steers me to one of the chairs and sits me down. "Put your head down for a minute. You look terrible. You really should take the day off and go home. You have to take care of yourself."

Recognizing Marion's voice, I didn't bother to look up. I just sat there with my head between my knees and stared at the chess set, the Ouija board, and the last remnant of my journal.

"Nothing?" I heard Fred say impatiently.

Gathered around me, while I remained seated, all of their shoes remained motionless, except a brown penny-loafer that rocked to and fro. There are so many different styles of shoes, you know? They each have their own personality. Must reflect the personality of their respective feet. But no high-gloss Italian leather jobbies here. Stein must have returned to his office.

"Where the hell is the thing?" Fred started tapping. I never realized before that he wore old, tired looking casuals. Probably the soles were still good. He didn't have the heart, or rather the character structure, to throw them out.

"Perhaps someone accidentally dropped them in the garbage pail, perhaps during arts and crafts group, and then they were removed from the unit." Just like Sheikh. Always looking for a benign explanation. I couldn't figure out which shoes were his.

"I think the fact that it was a pair of scissors that was stolen is important. It symbolically represents a need to divide into two parts, which is symbolic of the split between the conscious and the unconscious, or perhaps of the defense mechanism of splitting — a sign of a borderline disorder."

Ron, of course. I tried my best to tune out his voice, to drift off to some place where I felt comfortable and safe. I stared at the journal cover lying between my feet. I wondered how I knew it was mine. My name wasn't on it. Never realized I hadn't put my name on it. But it was definitely mine. I recognized it… I think.

My dog rags, he loves to play.

"Holden, are you alright over there?"

Caught me by surprise. I lifted up my head. Eyes focused on me, mostly the residents. Where did the rest of them go? "Uh, yeah Fred. I'm fine."

Liar.

"You don't look fine."

"Just a little light-headed. I'm OK."

"Suit yourself. It's time for grand rounds. Let's go."

We all lined up behind and followed Fred the Shepherd — out the door, down the hall, around the corner. Ba ba black sheep have you any wool? Must be time for a shearing.

The conference room appeared rather odd today. Sort of distorted, pinched in at the corners, sucked outwards near the middle — like a fisheye lens. And the colors were not quite right. All cast in a sickly green hue. Even the people were strangers to me. The residents, huddled together, talking meds, belonged to an alien race destined to take over the world. And the medical students, lined up in a neat row wearing dark ties and clean shirts, were their offspring — young, white larvae awaiting further tissue differentiation.

Sheikh caught my eye and leaned over. "Are you sure you are feeling OK, Thomas?"

Auto-pilot answered for me. "Just a touch of the flu, a little stuffed up, that's all."

"I have good decongestants. Would you like some?"

"Sure."

He poured into my palm a few capsules from a plastic bottle. Should I trust an alien bearing gifts, I thought as I picked one out and popped it into my mouth. You really must do something about those eyebrows.

Stein made his grand entrance. All conversation stopped. Good old Francis, always a show stopper. But that's it! This is a show — a show purely for my benefit. They're all here for my entertainment, even though they don't realize it. Of course! How silly of me not to see this before. Three chairs down there in front of me, as on a stage, like a triadic play — one for Fred, one for Stein, and one for the as yet absent patient. It's The Three Stooges, bumping each other's bellies, poking each other's eyes, dodging slaps to the face and swinging ladders.

Grand rounds. The teaching ritual of Medicine. I recalled the birth of clinical psychology in this ancient practice. There he is: Jean Martin Charcot, the great 19th century Parisian neurologist, gathering his students and staff around him while he interviews women suffering from hysteria. Why are their hands, arms, or legs paralyzed, why can't they see or hear? A weak nervous system, of course. We just discovered the nerves, after all, so they must explain everything. But one day his students decide to play a trick on him. We hypnotize the washwoman in the building, suggest to her that she is paralyzed, and present her to Charcot during Grand Rounds. After his interview he majestically waves his hand and proclaims "Here we have another example of hysteria caused by a weak nervous system." The jokes on you, Doc! She's not a patient, just a hypnotized washwoman... No, Charcot didn't fail us out of Med School. Once he got over being embarrassed — and pissed — he gave the whole matter a second, serious thought. Maybe hysteria isn't caused by a weak nervous system. If the disease can be created artificially by hypnosis — which is a psychological technique — then perhaps in reality it is caused not by a problem with nerves, but by the mind. That thought was the first inkling of a clinical psychology. It set in motion a long, complicated series of events leading to my being here today. Maybe I should thank Charcot personally.

I'm working hard to take my mind off things.

"Today we're going to interview two new patients," Fred said. "Consider it an exercise in differential diagnosis. As usual, I will conduct the interviews and Dr. Stein will lend his expertise in our making the final diagnoses. Are there any questions before we begin?"

"What patients will be interviewed?" Sheikh asked.

"At Dr. Stein's request — Richard Mobin and our still nameless patient, John Doe."

Is there no mercy? I crossed my fingers. Please may I leave this meeting unscathed.

One of the nurses escorted Mobin into the room. The smell of cigarettes and coffee entered with him. He was still immersed in his autistic stupor. Only a darting glint in his eyes revealing his suspicion of this situation. Being asked personal questions in front of a room full of psychiatrists, I'd feel nervous too. Might as well bend over and let a group of doctors take a peek where the sun don't shine.

Fred began. "Richard, we'd like to talk with you this morning to find out more about your problems. Can you tell us what you think is wrong with you?"

As usual, Fred's style was a bit direct, some would say tactless. He would be great at Direct Analysis, the brand of therapy where you don't dilly-dally with gentle, polite interpretations. You go right into the unconscious, right to the heart of the problem. Freud warned against it, he called it "wild analysis." But the direct analysts claim it yields a fast cure, even though your remarks may make you sound like you're the madman. Tell a paranoid he really wants anal sex. Tell a schizophrenic that he's eating an apple because he wants to gobble up his mother's boob. Tell an insomniac... tell him...

"What do you think is wrong with you?" Fred repeated.

I almost answered the question myself, then realized it was not directed at me.

"There's nuthin' wrong with me!" Mobin grunted.

"Come now, Richard, you wouldn't be here if there wasn't anything wrong with you."

"Nuthin' wrong," Mobin mumbled.

"Think about it. Is there anything wrong with your mind?"

No reply.

"Richard, can you hear me?"

"I got an A in English!" he blurted out loud, then muttered insistently to himself, "I got an A."

"I'm sure you did, but you haven't been doing too well in school lately, have you?"

"An A," Mobin repeated to himself, still trying to hold onto an idea of what he once was.

"Richard, do you hear voices?"

No response.

"Richard, do you hear voices?"

"None of your fuckin' business!"

"Your saying that makes me think that you do. Are the voices inside or outside your head?"

"I don't hear voices. I don't hear nuthin'."

"Can you tell me what those voices say?"

No response.

"What do the voices say, Richard?"

"They say that doctors are goddamn assholes!"

"You know, sometimes I say the very same thing." Fred smiled. The residents giggled.

"Have you ever tried to hurt yourself?"

Mobin closed his eyes, tightened his mouth.

"Are you afraid that you might hurt someone else?"

The questions bounced off him like beebees off armor plating. Mobin began rocking from side to side. As Fred considered a new angle of approach, he tapped his pencil against the armrest of his chair. The eraser end had been broken off, maybe even bitten off. It fascinated me. Were those tooth marks in the wood? Tap, tap, tap. Fred stuck it inside his shoe to scratch his instep, then went back to tapping. Tap, tap, tap.

"Richard, you're closing me out. Try letting me in a little, or does that make you afraid? You're afraid to take anyone in, aren't you? You know what I think, I think you really want to attach yourself to something. You need to attach yourself to something, or someone. You're looking for some kind of wholeness and peace — some kind of unity for yourself."

Mobin snorted, sending a spray of nose-juice into the air. Then, for an encore, he belched deep from his belly. Coffee odors issued forth. A very pleasant fellow.

"Dr. Holden tells us that you think you're being chased by someone. Who do you think is chasing you?"

There was something in Mobin's hand — something metal. Methodically, his fingers rolled it along his palm as Fred launched questions at him. Our very own Captain Queeg. But he wasn't holding ball bearings. What was it? Soon I realized that the only important dialogue was between Fred's pencil and the mysterious metal object hidden in Mobin's hand. Tap, tap, tap, roll, roll, roll. What the hell is that thing? Between rolls his fingers lifted for a brief moment, allowing me a quick peek. It was a tight coil of wire, like a spring, except the coils were too irregularly shaped to be a real spring. With each roll Mobin was compressing it with his fingers. At one time it probably had been a much looser coil, maybe a foot long or so. I wondered where he got it from, and what it was before he latched onto it as a self-mollifier. Then it hit me.

The metal binder for a notebook. My journal!

Was it him! Did he take it? The bastard! Images flashed through my head — images of his porky fingers ripping the pages one by one from the binder. I wanted to wrap my hands around his blubbery neck and strangle him. If there was a weapon in the room — a club, a knife, anything — I would have seized the opportunity. But I could be wrong. It could be anything in his hand. Your judgment isn't exactly keen today, Holden old boy. So keep control. Cool down.

Stein reached into the breast pocket of his suit and retrieved his nail file. I had my eyes on it, the pencil, and the coil. Now the dialogue was three-way. Tap, tap. Roll, roll. Grate, grate.

Fred had stopped his questioning. No one spoke. Mobin too had his eyes on Stein's file. Stein had his eyes on his nails. Fred and the residents had their eyes on Mobin. I had my eyes on that wire.

We all waited.

Finally, Mobin spoke. His voice bellowed anger and contempt. His eyes held a lifeless curse. To my horror, I realized he was looking at me. "You're just like them — tryin' to get me, split me open. But you can't, you'll never get me. I'll go deep where you can't find me. And I'll wait. Then I'll get you. I'll crush you and swallow you all!"

"What makes you think we're trying to get you?" Fred replied. "What makes you so angry with us?"

"I ain't angry. I don't feel anything. You're the ones who hate me. That's how I'll get you. I'll eat your guts out from the inside."

I felt shaken. Everyone did, except, apparently, the Imperturbable Stein who was still filing his nails. Either he had such vast experience with psychotics that nothing surprised him, or he's a fool.

"Why do you think we hate you?" Fred asked.

No response.

"Richard, why do you think we hate you?"

It was no use. With eyes closed, Mobin just rocked from side to side. He retreated again to that place where no one, nothing could touch him. Unsure what step to take next, Fred looked to the Boss. Casually, Stein motioned towards the door with his file.

"Thank you, Richard," Fred said, "That will be all for today."

The nurse escorted him out. The room hummed with murmurings among the residents, but I paid no attention. I was thinking about that coil of wire. How could he have gotten hold of my journal and torn it apart? The staff was keeping a close watch on him. Someone would have noticed and reported it. Maybe he found the wire somewhere. But then, who took the journal? Maybe my brain was playing tricks on me. Maybe it was just a coil of wire. It's possible that I left my journal in the resident's lounge, or let's see, did I come straight to the unit when I woke up? No, I went to the bathroom. It could be there.

Silence jerked me back to the present moment. Someone else had been ushered into the room. They were about to begin. Now Doe sat where Mobin had been, looking as placid-faced as ever.

"I wish I knew how to address you, sir," Fred said, "That's one little glitch we need to talk about. What we'd like to do here this morning is find out more about you. The more that we know, the more we can help you. Can you tell us what problems you believe you're having?"

"Insanity, no?"

"That's interesting, but can you tell us what that means?"

"Madness, doesn't it?"

"Insane and mad are different words for the same thing. Give us a little more of an explanation. What exactly do you mean?"

"They're your words — a rose by another name."

"Very pleasant poetry, but you're trying to side-step my questions, aren't you? You must realize that I'm trying to understand what's going on inside you."

"Heart pumping, blood flowing, breathing in and out."

"There you go side-stepping again. You know that I mean inside your mind, what you are thinking and feeling. Do you suspect that there's something wrong with your mind? Do you hear voices, for instance, or believe things that other people would find unbelievable."

"May be."

"Do you mean yes?"

"May be."

"Avoiding me again. I want to you to be honest."

"Whatever you want me to be, then that's what I am."

"You know that's not true. You are who you are!"

"Have it your way, then you are what I want you to be."

"And what is that?"

"You tell me."

Exasperation set in. Fred sounded impatient. "We're going in circles. What exactly are you trying to say?"

"I think therefore you are, isn't that what it means?"

"OK, so you want to play games. I know what you're up to, but I can play too. If you think and therefore I am, what happens when you go to sleep. I'm still here. How would you account for that, hm?"

"I would be dreaming about you, wouldn't I?"

"This is the key problem isn't it. You don't know who you are and so you throw up smoke screens to hide that fact. You act evasive. You play games with words. It must really worry you. But you don't have to play those games here. We're trying to help. Do you remember anything about who you are? Any little bit of information you might remember could be helpful, anything at all."

"Who am I?"

"Yes."

"Who?"

"That's right," Fred said in an infantilizing tone, "Who is this person I'm talking to?"

"I have no idea."

Fred started tapping his pencil. "There must be some little bit that you remember — a memory, a feeling, even a hunch, perhaps something about your childhood, or something interesting that you did last year, what your home looks like, anything about who you are."

Doe was silent.

"That's it, think about it. Something's coming back, isn't it?"

A sound cooed inside Doe's throat. Softly but persistently, he repeated it over and over. "Who, who, who." It was an autistic perseveration, a symptom of schizophrenia. Who, who, who. It seemed almost like a joke, a regression to a childhood game of doodling in sound. But a serious intent seemed to hide beneath the mockery. Who, who, who. With each repetition the word warped out of shape to something unrecognizable. It mutated into meaningless nonsense. Who, who, who. What was it? A rush of air past the lips, a guttural vibration, an owl, the wind?

"OK, OK," Fred interrupted, "Come back to us. We're right here, in this conference room, in the hospital. You're safe here. We're just talking, trying to find out a little bit about your background. All we'd like to do is help you, and to do that we need to find out who you are."

"Why don't you ask him?" Doe said, pointing to me.

Anxiety sprang up into my throat. Everyone was staring at me, expecting something. I felt mired into a queer little triad between Fred and Doe. "I don't know anything," I replied meekly. Fred looked back and forth between us, waiting for something to happen, but it didn't.

"Very well, if you can't remember anything about yourself, can you at least tell me how you're feeling right now?"

"With my eyes, ears, skin, and heart."

"There you go again. What are you afraid of? Why is it that you keep trying to avoid me?"

"I may ask the same question of you."

That was it. Fred had reached the end of his patience and skill level. His voice held a bitter aftertaste of defeat. "Well, I have no more questions," he said looking at Doe but talking to Stein. "I guess that's all for today, unless there's something you would like say before we stop."

"Per ardua ad astra."

"What?" Fred answered.

Curiously, Stein came alive and interrupted. It caught us all by surprise, especially Fred, whose pencil stopped abruptly in mid-tap.

"Ah, you are an educated man," Stein said amiably to Doe. "That is most impressive. Do you sometimes think that you have special abilities, something out of the ordinary. Some people think that they are Christ, for instance. Do you ever entertain such possibilities?"

"You ask about God."

"Yes, that's one way to put it. Do you believe anything like that about yourself?"

"Perhaps the Godness is in your own mind."

I sat forward on my seat. Grand rounds was turning into a duel — the madman takes on the narcissistic genius!

"Can you tell me, in your mind, what does it mean to be God?" Stein asked with false sincerity.

"I've heard of a man with a beard, in a long white robe, who lives in the clouds." He looked at me with a smile, "I hope I'm not overdoing this."

Stein noticed the glance towards me, but ignored it. "Come now. Surely you don't believe these things about God."

"I've heard of a man in finely tailored clothes and polished nails."

"Ah, you seem to be making a reference to me," Stein replied with confidence. "You think that I believe myself to be somehow superior, even god-like. Perhaps you envy the fact that I am healthy and you are sick, that I am the doctor and you are the patient."

Doe smiled. "The cart before the horse goes nowhere fast."

"More puzzles and metaphors," Stein said as he crossed his legs and touched his finger to his chin. "You enjoy speaking in riddles, don't you? It's a way to feel omniscient, all seeing and all knowing. Dr. Cooling is correct that you use this sort of behavior to hide, to avoid contact with other people. It's a kind of protective shell. But we need to look beneath the shell, to see what's going on inside — what you believe about others and yourself. And I think that a good place to start is this notion about God. I believe it is something that you often think about, something that troubles you deeply. It's a problem that you identify with on many levels. So, please, tell me more about this. What do you believe God to be?"

"Dried shit."

"What?"

"Dried shit." Doe repeated as he pointed towards Stein's foot. Stein tilted his head down to look. We all looked. Sure enough, there on his heel was a small caked-on patty of dog dung. Or was it a dog's? A tiny piece of what looked like toilet paper clung to it. Maybe it was human! If so, my imagination ran wild about how the excrement got there. Dr. Compulsively-Exquisite-Dresser had been trailing along poop all morning, maybe even his own!

Embarrassment and horror lit up his face like fireworks. He leaped out of his seat. "Uh, excuse me for a minute," he said as he headed towards the door. "Send the patient back to the unit," he added just before disappearing.

We were all momentarily paralyzed. Did that happen? Or were we all hallucinating?

"I guess that's all for today," Fred said hesitantly to Doe. Doe stood up, nodded politely to us, and walked to the door where the nurse escorted him away.

I laughed out loud. The residents and med students joined in with more subdued chuckles. Even Fred smiled a bit, though his knit brow showed that he still felt a bit puzzled by the whole affair. While the residents talked amongst themselves, I reveled in images of Stein wobbling on one leg in the men's room, cursing like a sailor, trying to scrape the offending crud off his appendage.

All too soon Stein interrupted my fantasy and slipped back into the room. "Let's begin our discussion of the diagnoses," he said curtly, as if nothing unusual had happened. "The first patient is clearly schizophrenic, paranoid type. We see all the typical disruptions in reality testing, in addition to intense denial and rage. Particularly prominent are his delusions of persecution which he converts, through reaction formation, into the conscious wish to devour and destroy external objects. This fantasy is derived from his own primitive fear about being devoured and destroyed himself — a fear rooted in the paranoid position described by Klein in her developmental theory of object relations."

"The second patient presents a less interesting diagnostic picture. Clearly, he is suffering from what has been described in the literature — and very vaguely, I might add — as an 'as if' personality. He has no identity of his own, or at best a very weakened identity, and relies on what others think of him to determine his sense of self. In other words, he acts as if he has his own secure identity, but actually he does not. A diagnosis of borderline personality might also be relevant since there is considerable evidence of his feeling rage and envy towards others who possess a more healthy and intact sense of self. He actually tries to negate the identity of others by responding to questions with his own questions, very abstruse answers, or by not-responding at all. Usually the 'as if' disorder acquires some facsimile of a personality structure through a weak, superficial identification with a significant other, but in this case even that shallow personality structure is lacking. He's not sure who or what he is, and so he resorts defensively to a vague delusion of omnipotence that inflates his grandiose self. To summarize, his personality structure is fragile, defensively constructed, and superficial."

Fred nodded with admiration and awe. The residents, with their mouths hung open, simply blinked.

"Superficial?" I said. "You really think this guy is superficial?"

Stein looked indignant, like he didn't even want to lower himself by responding to me. "Yes, superficiality is one feature of the as-if personality."

I waited for more of an explanation but didn't get one. So I pushed on. "Well, I don't agree. If there's any superficiality at all he's using it in a way that's anything but superficial. I can understand your point about his using his shallowness defensively. In that sense it's a kind of secondary gain."

Stein interrupted before I could finish. "Now there's a concept that psychologists use that never made sense to me. Exactly what is meant by 'secondary gain?' What is 'secondary' about the purpose the symptom obviously serves? And if it's secondary, what is primary?"

"Well, let me explain that for you," I said with surprising confidence, even though the residents stared at me as if I had lost my mind. "According to classical psychoanalytic theory primary gain is the venting of instinctual impulses through the cathexis of the symptom, while secondary gain is the sympathy, attention, or special favors that the person attains from others as a result of suffering from the symptom. However, I'm using these terms in a slightly modified sense. When I say secondary gain I'm referring to the interpersonal impact of the symptom — an impact that works to the patient's advantage. And when I say primary gain I'm referring to the more internalized, purely intrapsychic effect of the symptom, regardless of its interpersonal effects."

For a moment Stein didn't respond. "That's very interesting," he finally said, "and it would be pleasant to spend more time discussing it, but I have another meeting to attend. We're done here for today."

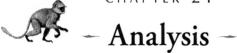

CHAPTER 21

~ Analysis ~

FRED STOPPED ME on the way out. "Are you sure you're feeling all right?"

"Why do you ask?" I replied, and coughed, which sent a stabbing pain through my head.

"All I can say is that if I were you, I'd take it easy. Remember that Dr. Stein is the director in charge of things around here. It's very easy to get on his shit list, and when you're on that list, life can be hell."

"Hell hath no fury like a narcissist's scorn," I mumbled, then cleared my throat. "Yeah, you're right Fred. I've got to take it easy. I'm not quite myself, lately."

"You look like you need to talk to someone," he stated simply.

His comment triggered my internal alarm. Warning! Warning! I looked at my watch. "Oh shit! I've got to go. See you later."

How could I have so completely forgotten? "Get a grip on yourself," the doorknob said as I exited from the unit. Running down the hallway I calculated that I would arrive approximately ten minutes late to my analyst's office. God, my brain is coming apart at the seams. Worst of all, my analyst will surely interpret my tardiness as resistance — and maybe he's right. I can't even remember what happened in the last session. Psychoanalysis is supposed to be the most important thing in your life; you're supposed to have intense feelings about your analyst, otherwise you're not in analysis. And I don't. Something is definitely wrong here. Maybe it's still too early. I've only been seeing him for a few months and a nice robust transference can take a year or more to blossom. Then again, maybe my forgetting the appointment is a sign of transference. Or maybe I'm suffering from some unanalyzable personality disorder that I never knew was there — or from something even deeper, even worse.

Normally I'd laugh off such notions, but today I felt too fragile to defeat any doubts about anything. "It's not me," I said to the elevator doors. "It's this internship — too much situational stress."

"Sssssure," the doors hissed as they opened.

Before stepping in, I realized I had not checked the arrows. Damn! It was on its way up. Just another blunder. Then I remembered I had parked my car in the back lot and couldn't get to it from the elevator anyhow. Blunders within blunders. Turning on my heels I ran down the hall towards the library. Memories of grand rounds bounced at me with each step. They were the ones doing it to me — Mobin and Doe. They're conspiring to drive me crazy. Why shit, I'm already crazy. Look at me, I'm paranoid. But what is it about them that gets to me? Just a decompensating schizophrenic and a man with no memory.

The cursors on the computer monitors blinked at me as I raced through the library. On and off, on and off. Now you see 'em, now you don't. Doe drives me crazy because I just can't seem to get a handle on him. Every time I think I understand him, he slips away. One minute he seems real and the next he's... he's... he's what? Not real? Then what the hell is he if he's not real? A ghost? An illusion? A machine? That's it — a robot, an invading android from another planet, from another dimension, programmed to absorb the minds of us earthlings.

"You're living in fiction," the librarian said without looking up from her book.

And bad fiction at that. For a brief second an image flickered through my thoughts — too fast for me to decipher it clearly. I was standing on a dark street, talking to someone, or something like that. It faded quickly.

How could Stein have found Doe superficial? At the very least the guy is intelligent. That accounts for a certain amount of depth to the personality, doesn't it? Then again, being intelligent doesn't mean diddly-squat when it comes to mental health. Some of the craziest patients we had on the unit were extremely bright, even gifted. One guy was the president of a major corporation — a brilliant businessman, rich, powerful, creative, successful by anyone's standards. Every night after work, he'd lock himself into the bathroom, take a shit, and spend an hour or so playing with his turds.

Sometimes humans just don't make sense.

Reminds me of a joke. A guy gets a flat tire in front of a mental hospital. While putting on the spare, he notices a mental patient watching him from behind the gates of the hospital. It makes him a bit uneasy, so he accidentally knocks over the hubcap where he had placed all the lug-nuts. They spill down a drain and disappear. "Shit," the man says in desperation, "Now what the hell am I going to do?"

"Why don't you take one nut off of each of the other three tires," the patient calls out to him, "and use them to put on the spare."

"Why that's a great idea," the man replies cheerfully. "Say, what are you doing in this hospital, you seem to be a smart fellow."

"Well," the patient replied, "I may be crazy but I'm not stupid."

Hippocrates interrupted my thoughts from his pedestal at the bottom of the stairway. "Maybe your patient is trying to cure himself."

Now there's an idea from the father of medicine himself. Maybe Doe was walking along the highway deliberately so that he would be picked up. He didn't plan that consciously, of course. Unconsciously he was seeking help. In all of us, even the most pathological, there must be an internal drive towards self-healing, even if it means enlisting the help of others as aids in transforming ourselves. If that spark ever disappears, the fight is over, you're a goner. Doe's lapse into memory loss and identitylessness might be an attempt towards healing. Amnesia may be more than just the massive repression of painful memories and emotions. It wipes the slate clean and gives you a chance to start over. Like my magic writing board when I was a kid. I'd draw on it with the stylus, and when I got tired of the picture, I'd peel up the clear plastic overlay, make it all disappear, and start over.

It was surprisingly cold and windy outside. The sky was steel gray. I turned up my collar and hurried to the car. "The analyst has to enter each session without memory, desire, or understanding" Who was it who said that? Bion?

Just a few steps away. Shit, is it cold or what? There's no fending off winter now. Getting inside the Nova offered some relief from the biting wind.

I have to admit that there's some truth to what Stein said. Maybe Doe does use his amnesia to create a place that is safe, protected — a world where there are no names, no identities.

Nothing can touch you or hurt you because there is no one there to be touched or hurt. It's a secure little nest sealed off from the horrors of the outside world. But it's also possible that there is a very real identity below the mask of namelessness. His not telling me who he is could be an unconscious test, a test that I have to pass before he will allow me to move to that deeper level of understanding him. But what kind of test is it? Does he unconsciously want me to persist in finding out who he is, or will he only build trust in me if I leave him alone. Or both? It could be both. Patients are always putting us clinicians in damned-if-you-do-and-damned-if-you-don't dilemmas. Those double-binds are red flags signaling that the therapy has stumbled onto an important unconscious conflict.

At the security booth Jon waved me down. No time to chat, but I stopped anyhow. The tiny door to the booth was closed and Jon had his feet resting on a portable heater. His book was in his lap. I envied him — tucked away into his cozy little space, a safe distance from everything, all toasty next to his heater. Why didn't I have a job like that?

"Greetings and felicitations, Dr. Holden!" he said as he opened the top panel of the door and popped his head out like a jack-in-the-box. "Say, you look a little under the weather."

I snapped at him. "You know, I'm getting tired of people commenting on my state of being."

Displacement. That all too familiar defense mechanism. I hated myself for taking my frustrations out on Jon.

"My, my, a bit touchy today, aren't we?" he said. He seemed unaffected by my attack.

"I'm sorry, Jon. I'm having a bad day."

"All days are bad days, or good, depending on how you perceive it."

"Yeah, right, and I think it's gonna get worse before it gets better, if it ever gets better."

"Such optimism warms my heart. But say — cheer up, Thomas. Haven't you heard the news?"

"No. What?"

"There's a snow warning. And they say it might be a big one. I've always loved snow storms. It's something about the way they bring the bureaucracy to a halt."

"That's great," I said cynically. "If I can only get away from my damn work so I can go outside and build a snowman."

"Think of it this way," Jon replied, "They may let you go home early."

"With my luck, I'll get snowed into the building. Listen, I'd like to talk, but I'm late for an appointment. See you later."

"Farewell, melancholy prince," Jon said as I pulled away.

A snowstorm. I couldn't decide if it would be an adventure or a major pain in the butt. As a kid I never considered snowstorms a nuisance. Must be a sign that I'm getting old. What would I do if I did end up snowbound in the hospital? It would make claustrophobia look like a walk in the park. I'd have to spend all night with my patients, with Mobin and Doe. Maybe I could bunk with them. Oh, wouldn't that be glorious? But it's been done before. A few renegade psychologists have already experimented with rooming with their patients, even inviting them to come live in their homes. Imagine that. Mobin and Doe sitting around the dinner table with the family? Excuse me, Richard, could you please pass the fish?

An idea struck me as I drove along Mondo Road, which circled around the top of the hill. Maybe I have to try something unorthodox with Doe, something that would catch him off-guard, something that would help me find out whether or not he's lying. That's it! How about a lie detection test? There's a psychophysiology laboratory on the second floor, and I had plenty of training on that type of equipment in graduate school. All I'd have to do is find an excuse to get Doe off the unit.

How can someone not know who they are? How can your memories of your past and identity be cleanly excised from your personality, but everything else you need to remember in order to function in the world remains intact? Is the mind really that powerful, that precise? People need a history to survive, to be human. Of course, what constitutes one's personal history is a highly subjective manner. If ten people, including myself, described my history, we'd wind up with ten different tales. Sure, there would be some overlap, but I bet even the basic themes would vary from one story to the next. So which one is the right history? Maybe "history" is the wrong word. Sounds too objective, like there is a camera suspended in space over your head, recording your life just as it happened. No, it's a much more subjective process than that. We look back over our lives and try to make sense out of the almost infinite mass of things that we did and experienced. We rummage through all the thousands of memories and selectively order pieces of them into a narrative that contains all the elements of a good story — plots and subplots, characters, development, climax, denouement. It's just as much fiction as fact. It's our own personal creation designed to make sense out of who we are. And the story is probably chock full of omissions. We don't remember everything about our past; in fact, we have forgotten — repressed, technically speaking — a great deal, probably some very important parts. There may be more of us in the holes in our story than in the rest.

Doe is one big hole.

I wonder what it's like to suffer from amnesia. As a kid I once fell off a swing and banged my head, or so they told me. Actually, I don't think I fell. I think I was jumping off at the peak of the swing to see how far I could fly. It was something I did a lot. But I can't remember that particular incident. It was a case of retrograde amnesia in which trauma to the head physically disrupts the storage of the memories just prior to the accident. But there's also anterograde amnesia in which you can't create new memories after the accident. I remember reading about a guy in a car accident who afterwards experienced no problems in his memory of past events in his life — but he couldn't consolidate any new memories. The doctors would give him a funny story to read, and when he finished it he laughed. A few minutes later they gave it to him again, and when he finished reading it a second time, he laughed. They did it over and over. Each time he read it and laughed because each time it was completely new to him. He couldn't remember having read it a few minutes before. The guy was living moment to moment with no ability to remember ongoing events. The same sort of thing can happen in degenerative brain diseases, like Alzheimer's. Gradually, over the course of months, you forget everything — your past, your present, your loved ones, who you are. Needless to say, a severe depression sets in as you realize your mind is disintegrating and your identity is slipping away. It's interesting, though, that at some advanced stage the depression lifts. Your brain has so fallen apart that you don't even realize that your brain is falling apart.

A chill went up my spine. The thought was terrifying.

I pulled into my analyst's driveway. On this side of the hill, his house had a nice view of the mountains far in the distance. Not only was my analyst lucky enough to live close to the medical center, where he was an adjunct professor, but he also owned prime real estate. Some people have it all.

A woman in a Mercedes passed me on her way out. She looked content — a little vacuous, but content. I was tempted to roll down the window, wave, and shout "Hi there! Have a good catharsis?" But I didn't. After all, this was my analyst's house and that could be his wife. Wouldn't it be grand to have your office in your home? Just stroll out of the bedroom and into your office. Of course, you'd have to worry about how it would tantalize those borderline patients who long to be your son, daughter, or spouse — or the obsessives who really want to know about your toilet habits. Make sure you pull down the shades.

Exactly why am I in analysis? I tell myself I'm doing it as part of my training — to experience what my patients will experience, to be more aware of my own neurosis so it won't interfere with my clinical work. But is that a good enough reason? Is that the real reason? It could be a defense. At some point I have to become a patient — really become a patient and not just a trainee looking for information. I have to acknowledge the fact that I really do have problems to work on, that I have to let go and yield to the healing process that is psychoanalysis, rather than just tinker with it as a curious but secretly detached dilettante. At least that's what they tell me. But I hate it. I hate shelling out the money, even though he did reduce his fee for me. I hate having to jam more hours of training into my already packed schedule. But most of all, I hate talking to someone about my problems, exposing myself, being vulnerable. Some people say that they love analysis. For me it's a chore, something I have to do. Maybe that's my problem — compulsiveness, over-achievement, grandiose ambitions. Maybe the indication of success in my analysis would be my letting myself quit.

I never see any other patients in the waiting room. How can that be? Does the guy before me slip out some side entrance that I don't know about, or maybe through the window? Every time I arrive I find that half-smoked cigar in the ashtray and the smell of stale smoke in the air. That must have been his wife in the Mercedes, unless she smokes cigars. What would Freud say about that?

My nasal cavities felt like someone had poured in oatmeal. Got to clear my head out. I rummaged through my knapsack for another decongestant. Without my notebook, the knapsack felt conspicuously depleted. Where the hell is it? I didn't bother getting water from the bathroom. I swallowed the capsule dry. It stuck in my throat and burned like a stubborn little ball of fire. Life is full of loose ends. Pieces that don't fit together to make a whole puzzle.

As I swallowed again and again, trying to wash down that irritating bugger of a capsule, I looked around the waiting room. I never could figure it out. Some analysts try to keep their office as inconspicuous as possible so their patients know as little as possible about them. It intensifies transference. Others decorate their place using simplicity and taste — an environment that's pleasing to the eye. Still others, the narcissistic types, go the opulent route to impress their patients with their success, to convince them that high fees mean an elite analytic atmosphere in all respects.

My analyst's waiting room didn't fit any of those categories. It contained a hodgepodge of decorations that conveyed no rhyme or reason. While some of it appeared tasteful, even elegant, some of the stuff, to be quite blunt, was rather tacky or bizarre. There were the two paintings of a cat by Van Gogh — one realistic, the other quite wild and surrealistic — which clashed horribly with the poster of a sad-faced clown sitting on top of a globe. There was the wood Victorian coat rack with one leg slightly shorter than the other two, which made it lean precariously to the left — and next to it, a table that tried to pass for a Japanese antique, but failed, being it was made of very cheap looking plastic. Most perplexing of all was that statue in the corner — a monkey, with its tail wrapped around a book, climbing a tree. Where the hell did he get that? What was the rationale behind his decor? He was a bright guy. There must be a plan. Perhaps it was his way of stirring up our unconscious fantasies, or making sure we stayed crazy. In a very ingenious way, maybe the hodgepodge prevented us from knowing what his tastes really were — like excess noise in the broadcast that hides the signal. I heard through the grapevine that he was something of an expert on patients with multiple personality disorders. Surely this waiting room could serve as entertainment for their internal world. But most frightening of all was the possibility that he liked the aesthetics of this look, that this room reflected something about his personality.

The door to his office opened. There, standing in the doorway with the window casting a dazzling bright back-light around him, my analyst appeared as a god-like figure. Prometheus carrying fire to us mortals. Except, however, that he was a short man, neatly dressed in a dark suit, a bit overweight, slightly balding. Without the suit, instead wearing jeans and a sweatshirt, you'd probably never guess him to be an analyst if you met him at the supermarket. Could be a salesman, a white collar worker, even an accountant. You'd never suspect that for a living he probes people's minds.

The second I saw him, a funny feeling came over me. I desperately wanted something from him, but I didn't quite know what it was. Sure, I wanted him to like me, to find me outstandingly intelligent, witty, and creative, to think that I was the most fascinating patient he ever had, to love me — most of which didn't seemed to be the case, much to my deflated ego. We had talked about such issues. No, it was something else.

"Come in, Thomas," he said in his usual polite minimalist style. He followed classical technique, although on occasion he loosened up a bit.

I followed him into the office. There before me, waiting solemnly, was the symbol of analysis — the couch. It immediately caught one's eye, not because it was particularly large or stylish, but rather that it was intrapsychically big. Its various meanings were limitless and powerful. It's the opportunity to relax, to slip into a dream-like state where the unconscious runs free. It stands for submission, dependency, retreat, or sex. It embraces some people and swallows up others. You can feel more cozy with your analyst or hide from those staring eyes.

I sat down on the edge, swung my feet up, and dropped down. No thoughts came to me. Nothing. Shit, resistance already! I stared up at the walls and ceiling — that same old crack in the corner, that splotch of white paint accidentally brushed onto the light fixture, the chipped edge of the fan. The world is not quite right. Something is amiss.

I tried to remember what we talked about last time, but couldn't. Come on, Holden, free associate! Just describe whatever thoughts, feelings, or images come to mind. Like Freud said, pretend you're sitting on a train, watching the scenery roll by. Just describe it! Now the oatmeal was in my brain and mouth. The train, bogged down in it, was going nowhere fast. I feared that if I tried to talk only indecipherable gurgles and chugs would come out.

Finally, I forced myself to speak. I described some things that happened to me during the week — none of which were important, and I knew it. It sounded stale, lifeless. A laundry list of irksome details, a report card with nothing to say. How pathetic! My own patients do this to me all the time. If given the chance, I'd roll my eyes and yawn. Come on, get to the real stuff!

My analyst remained quiet. I couldn't hear anything from him, not even the scratching of his pen on the pad. Was I boring him? How humiliating to come across as boring while you try desperately to reveal your unconscious. Was that a yawn? He had the advantage of sitting behind me, unseen. He could yawn if he wanted to and get away with it. When I'm with my patients I have to stifle my yawns or do it without opening my mouth. The Art of the Nose-Yawn. That's one of the advantages of having your patients on the couch. They can't see you yawning or scratching your crotch. Was that a snore? No way, he couldn't have fallen asleep. I was tempted to turn around to look, but also afraid. What if he really was asleep, or even worse, what if he wasn't there? What if my boredom had evaporated him, annihilated him, or if he simply left the room and abandoned me? My imagination ran wild. Analysts do sometimes fall asleep on their patients. At times it's almost happened to me. I feel like I can't keep my eyes open. They roll back in my head and I blink out for just a second. I have to pinch myself or bite my lip to stay awake. The sleepiness may be a sign that something big is stifling the atmosphere — massive repression, denial, anger, depression, narcissistic emptiness.

"Thomas, there seems to be something else on your mind," he said calmly. He wasn't fooled. He was listening.

I sighed, and the floodgates opened. I talked about my patients — about Elizabeth Baso, Mr. Tennostein, Kathy — about Mobin and Doe. I talked about grand rounds and Dr. Stein. I talked about the woman from radiology, about my notebook and coming down with the flu. I talked and talked until I lost track of the time, and when I ran out of breath, when my brain felt too scrambled to continue, I stopped, and waited.

What would he say? What deep interpretation would he make to clarify my torment?

"You're under a tremendous amount of stress," he said. "Maybe you should take some time off."

I was shocked. Supportive advice instead of an interpretation! He never did that before. I wasn't sure what to
say. I felt a bit angry that yet another person was telling me
to take it easy, but I also felt touched. He actually sounded
kind, concerned.

"Uh, yeah, I really could use some time off, but I can't
right now."

"Why not?"

"Uh, well, uh... this thing with Mobin, for instance.
He's a real hot potato. I shouldn't leave right now and dump
him on another therapist. I have to ride out what's happening
with him, at least until he cools down some."

"What is it about this patient that captures you?"

"Well, he's potentially violent and since I underplayed
that in my reports to the staff, I feel responsible. I really think
I should stick it out until I have a more accurate assessment
of him. I owe that much to the staff."

"But the staff is very much aware of how dangerous he
is, even if you did underplay it. The director and chief resident both interviewed him. There is something else about
this patient that troubles you, that makes it difficult for you
distance yourself from him."

"I don't know what you mean."

Playing stupid? I wasn't even sure myself. My analyst
didn't hesitate in continuing. "I imagine that it's the depth
of his rage, and his psychosis. It scares you, it would scare
anyone. But instead of running away, you try to run into it
headfirst."

"But why would I do that?"

"Maybe you also feel angry."

Angry? I didn't feel particularly angry. Yet I noticed that
both my fists were clenched tight. My thoughts raced. Anger
about what? At whom? And what about being afraid of Mobin's

psychosis? Was he implying that I also identified with Mobin's insanity? He didn't come right out and say it, but… No, you're reading too much into it. It's projection. But if it's projection then I really must believe it myself. Maybe deep down inside I really am psychotic. Maybe we're all psychotic. I should tell him what I'm thinking. It's bad enough to resist unconsciously, but doing it consciously is downright unproductive.

"What are you thinking?" he asked patiently.

"Nothing, I'm just feeling confused."

"You seem to be withdrawing into yourself, away from me. It reminds me of all that you've been saying today so far. You seem to be withdrawing from everyone, retreating into yourself. I imagine that you feel alienated from everyone and everything. But at the same time, you want so much to attach yourself to something."

"It's funny. That reminds me of something. I remember a dream I had, last night I think. It's kind of hazy. I was on a grassy hill somewhere, overlooking the ocean. And there was a lawn mower, or a… no, it was a lawn mower. That's all that I can remember."

"Was that the same dream you had about Doe?"

"What dream about Doe? Did I mention a dream about Doe?"

"Yes."

Suddenly I felt very confused, almost panicky. "I don't remember mentioning that."

"OK. Then tell me more about this dream. What comes to mind when you think of a lawn mower?"

"Well, I think of mowing the lawn at my house when I was a kid. That was my job. I hated it. Why should I have to mow the lawn while my father watches TV or goes out to play softball. But I did it anyhow."

"Is there more?"

"Well, I remember one time when I turned the lawn mower off to clean out some grass that was clogging the chute. I didn't realize that even though I had shut the motor off, the blade was still spinning. So when I stuck my hand into the chute, the blade sliced the tip of my finger. I went running for my father, but I couldn't find him. There was blood everywhere. Finally, he came jumping over the fence from the neighbor's yard and took me into the house to bandage my finger. He gave me a shot of whiskey before he called the doctor. I remember lying there on the couch thinking that I would never be able to use my hand again, that I wouldn't even be able to write. Then I fainted."

"Your patient Doe reminds you of your father in some respects, doesn't he?"

A door inside my thoughts opened — just a crack, but it opened. "In some ways, I guess. He doesn't always seem to be there when I look for him. He seems so distant, untouchable, at least sometimes he seems that way. But other times, I don't know."

"You feel a closeness with him and also a kind of competition," my analyst answered. "It's a feeling of trying to better him in some way, trying to catch his attention and prove something to him. It hides the feeling of closeness."

"Prove something? Prove what? He's just a patient! He doesn't even know who he is!"

"What is it about what I said that makes you angry?"

"I don't know. That interpretation seems so... so intrusive. Everyone seems so goddamn intrusive today. Even Doe. I can't figure out who the hell he is and he acts so damn elusive, but sometimes he digs right into me."

"That play on the words 'elusive' and 'intrusive' — that rhyme — seems important. What about the intrusive part? What does that remind you of?"

The door cracked open another inch. "You mean like my mother? Always intruding, manipulating, expecting something of me. I guess Doe's like that, I don't know."

"You do seem to perceive Doe as having singled you out, as expecting something special from you, as did your mother. And you think you have to comply, to please him, to live up to whatever it is he wants. Your feelings about Doe are complex, quite contradictory and ambivalent. You perceive him as distant, disappearing — but also as intrusive and demanding. He has taken on many meanings for you, many identities."

It made sense. But something was missing. I closed my eyes and focused on a place deep in my thoughts — a place that had not been touched. Outside the window, the wind whistled and a tree branch tapped against the glass pane. Someone whispered to me, at first so softly that I could not decipher it, then louder, clearer:

"It's still running."

The river is cool, deep. I notice, in the distance, something floating towards my canoe. It drifts closer, and closer. It's a corpse. Gently bumping into the side of the canoe, it turns face up in the water. I recognize it. It's me.

"Our time is up." Like a pebble dropped into water, the voice sent ripples through the imagery around me. For a brief moment, some distorted fragments lingered — a cup of coffee, my feet stretched out on a cyclone fence, the mailman delivering a letter — and then, they were gone.

"Thomas, our time is up."

Who calls me Thomas? My mother, sometimes Jon…

I sat upright on the couch. My analyst!

"Did I fall asleep?"

"Yes, you did," he replied.

"I'm sorry. I was on call last night and I, uh — well, I guess I'll see you next week."

He nodded. I got my things together and headed for the door.

"Thomas," he called after me, "think about taking a few days off."

I felt embarrassed. Falling asleep in analysis. Is that resistance or what? I wasn't a very good patient. But I needed the sleep. I was tired, sick. Maybe it was a good thing to fall asleep. But if it was good how come I still felt exhausted and fogged in, even worse than before. No doubt he thought it was therapeutic to let me sleep. Why? A sign of trust on my part, the willingness to let go? Then again, maybe he just assumed that I needed the rest. That was nice of him.

Then I felt angry. What kind of job is it for him to just sit there and get paid while I sleep? It's a waste of my time and money. Why didn't he wake me up and interpret it as resistance, or as progress, or anything. Wouldn't that be more productive?

Ooops! What's this anger about. Transference of some kind?

Confusion set in. I tried to remember exactly what happened in the session, but only bits and pieces came back to me. Doe represents my father and mother? Can one person unconsciously represent both your father and mother? Sounds like Super-Psychoanalytic Psychobabble to me. My mother encouraged me to get good grades in school, to be smart, to be the best. If I got a 99 on a test she would want to know why I didn't get a 100. I could never seem to do it just right for her. So what does that have to do with Doe? Why would I try to please him?

"It's all a lot of crap!" I shouted out the window of my car.

"Me thinks you doth protest too much," replied an old man walking along the road.

Denial as a defense? Is there some truth to this? I remembered the grassy hill, the ocean, a canoe, a woman's face, her eyes — were they blue or brown? The Nova speeds up. As I press down on the accelerator, I notice a plastic cup stuck in the branches of a bush. It's dirty, torn, crumpled. Long ago it had been discarded and forgotten. And now it just sits there, caught on that inconspicuous bush, among hundreds of other bushes, on an obscure patch of land. I'm the only one to notice it. No eyes, no thoughts will ever fall on it again. And eventually I too will completely forget it. This conscious moment will evaporate and disappear forever .

Suddenly something appears in the road ahead of me. I swerve to get out of the way. Thump, thump! My reactions are too slow. I ran over it! In the rearview mirror I spot something lying in the road. What is it? As I try to decide what to do, the thing fades into the distance. Got to stop! I veer the car over to the side of the road, get out, and run back to the scene of the crime. Why didn't I just backup the car!

It's a lump of flattened-out meat, bones, and patches of fur. Steam rises up from it into the cold air. I can't tell for sure what kind of animal it was. Was I the one who first hit it? I want to get closer, to see, but there are other cars coming around the bend of the hill. I stand on the side of the road to watch them approach. Thump, thump. Some of the wheels miss, some don't. Thump, thump. I fall onto my hands and knees, and puke.

CHAPTER 22

~ Tests ~

Jon was wearing a bright orange hunting cap with the flaps pulled down over his ears. The Sears Winter Catalog was propped up on the desk in front of him. I took my foot off the accelerator, intending to coast through the booth without stopping. But when he saw me, he jumped to his feet and waved me down. "Whoooah, Dr. Doom! What's the rush now?"

"Hi, Jon," I replied blandly, "I've got to get back to the unit."

"Say, you look like you've seen a ghost. Was it one of ours, or theirs?" White puffs of crystallized breath chased each word from his mouth.

"All ghosts are one of them, aren't they? So what's with the hat?"

"Ah! Preparation for the snowstorm, of course."

"Oh, right. I forgot."

"Forgot? Forgot the snowstorm? Never lose touch with the weather. It's the very pulse of our psyche. I guess they didn't teach you that in graduate school."

"Psychometeorology wasn't my specialty. Listen, I really have to get back to the unit. See you later."

I stepped on the gas. Jon put his hands to his mouth and called out after me. "Maybe you should consider broadening your current specialization. Meteorology is much more precise."

As I left the car, the cold wind lashed at my bare neck and face. I retreated into my thoughts to escape. I have to check the bathroom and resident's lounge for my journal. But how could it be in either of those places if I found the cover on the unit, assuming that that piece of cardboard was the cover. Possibly someone found the journal in the bathroom or lounge, ripped off the cover, and brought it to the unit. But who? One of the staff? I couldn't imagine any of them doing that. One of the patients? But patients aren't permitted to leave the unit unless they have a pass, and even then they usually are accompanied by a staff member or another patient. Then again, it's possible that one of them had the opportunity to sneak out of unit — to sneak out and steal my journal. Shit! I'm paranoid again, seeing plots everywhere!

"Maybe you need to heal thyself," Hippocrates said in his stony voice.

"That bullshit is getting a bit boring!" I answered as I wearily climbed the stairs. Just because he's the Father of Medicine he thinks he can comment on everything. Those Greeks thought they were so smart. So what that they had half a dozen outstanding geniuses — all of them the equivalent of an Einstein — living at the same time in Athens. That was centuries ago. Civilization has come a long way since then. We're smarter now, more advanced. Aren't we? Maybe not. Maybe we're going in circles. Maybe we're even losing ground. After all, we're slowly destroying the planet with our so-called technological advances? And the Holocaust was only decades ago.

"You're over-intellectualizing again," the librarian said. "Why don't you ease up on the maybe-ing this and perhaps-ing that. You'll feel a lot better."

The computers blinked in agreement.

"If I don't intellectualize, then what do I have left?" I replied angrily, "So mind your own business!" My stomach turned, twisted, growled in pain. More anxiety? No, could be hunger, just an emptiness asking to be canceled out. After all, it's lunchtime. Have to get something to eat. That will soak up some acid and appease my hollow gut.

On the way I stopped off at the resident's lounge. No journal. I stopped off at the men's room. Still, no journal. At the urinal I tried desperately to avert my eyes, to control the compulsion to read the graffiti. But I just couldn't resist the words right there in front of my nose, calling me, teasing me. I just had to read them, as if I were trapped by some hated yet powerfully captivating ritual.

"Jesus saves."

"She blinded me with science."

"Look up, look down, the joke is in your hands!"

But there was a new one there — up high and to my far right, near the corner of the room, too far away to see clearly. I squinted and strained my eyes to read it. Reluctantly, the words came into focus:

"While alive be a dead man."

I blinked — and it was gone.

"Chicken noodle soup," I grumbled to the catatonic kitchen aid with rotten teeth. He held the ladle over my bowl and began pouring ever so slowly. Both of us stared into the gentle flow of noodles and yellow juice. The soup approached the top of the bowl. Locked into his stupor, he showed no signs of stopping. He kept pouring. The soup passed the brim, where surface tension held it for a moment, then spilled down the sides. But he kept pouring. A puddle began to spread across my tray. I yanked myself out of my stare and shouted, "Stop!"

He looked up at me, studied my face. A faint glint of light entered his otherwise deadened eyes. He had noticed something. "Don't say it!" I thought to myself, "Please don't say it."

The mute man finally let some sounds out of his mouth. "You sure look bad," he said.

I reached a new low. Even the walking wounded pitied me.

I tried to avoid the table where Sheikh, Ron, and the med students were sitting, but Sheikh flagged me down. "Come, sit with us!" he called out across the room. By the looks on their faces, I could tell that Ron and the students were not entirely in agreement with Sheikh's decision. "Please, God," the medical students were thinking, "May we never become like him." Of course, I could have been projecting.

All their eyes were on me as I sat down. "I know," I said without looking up, "I look terrible. I'm coming down with the flu, I think, but I'm hanging in there. I'll do my best not to get too close to you, or sneeze on your salad."

The med students giggled. It eased the tension a bit.

"You were on call last night, were you not?" Sheikh asked.

"Yeah, I was. Didn't get much sleep though. I guess that's what triggered this flu."

Ron stuffed his hands into the pockets of his white lab coat. "Actually, research suggests that environmental stresses and deprivations may not have a substantial effect on contracting viral infections."

Everyone ignored him. Sheikh put his hand on my shoulder. "It would be a good idea to take some time off."

"Yeah, I know," I mumbled.

"Believe it or not," Bob Lawrence injected into the quiet, "sometimes I wish I would get sick. In fact, I'm surprised that I haven't so far. I really need a break from the hectic pace of all these rotations. I just finished radiology last month. I've got psychiatry for another two weeks, then oncology and gerontology."

"You were in radiology?" I asked.

"Yeah, last month. Why?"

"Who's that woman who works there, the one with dark hair, attractive?"

"I don't remember there being a woman there."

"Are you sure?"

"Well, I think so." He looked to his peers, "You guys did that rotation too. Do you remember her?"

They just shrugged their shoulders. "We weren't there very long," Bob said somewhat apologetically. "It's possible that we didn't meet all of the staff."

My disappointment must have been obvious. "Never mind."

"Anyway," Bob continued, "even though I haven't finished all my rotations, I think I know what residency I want." The other two med students perked up at the mention of this. Choosing your residency is no small matter. It could determine the rest of your professional life. "What?" they asked inquisitively.

"Psychiatry."

"Is this true?" Sheikh said. He sounded pleased.

"Yeah, though I haven't told too many people yet. I'm a little reluctant to. I've mentioned it to a few friends, and when I do they always look nervous, like they're afraid I'm going to start analyzing them, or something. They always say something like 'Gee, I better be careful now about what I say around you — ha, ha!'"

"It's one of our occupational hazards," I said. "People don't really understand our profession. It's all a bit mysterious to them. Sometimes they worry that we can see right through them, and so they feel uncomfortable around us. And we feel uncomfortable too. We want people to understand us, to understand our work. That's why many psychotherapists mostly choose other therapists to be their friends."

"But it must be nice to give advice to friends who aren't in the profession," Bob said, "if they need help with some problem they're having."

"I guess so. But to tell you the truth, I've found that family and friends often don't listen to my advice, even when they ask for it. They don't want to hear what I have to say — well, at least part of them doesn't want to hear it. They're ambivalent. On the one hand, they know that I'm supposedly knowledgeable about how people behave and they want to hear my ideas. But on the other hand, they don't want to be told something about themselves that they didn't already know. It's a bit threatening. So they try to dispute or ignore what I have to say. Because I'm a friend or a family member, it makes it much easier to discount me. I'm the kid brother, or son, or the old pal from third grade. So why take me seriously? But when they hear the same thing on a talk show, or read it in a book, then they believe it! It kind of upsets me. It makes me feel... forgotten."

I paused to catch my breath, and immediately became paranoid. I was rambling again, although I imagined they were interested in what I way saying. Ron pointed his pen at me, preparing to toss in his two cents, but I beat him to the mark.

"You know," I said more calmly, "we psychologists have our strengths and weaknesses, just like everyone else. We're just normal people too, right?" I punctuated my remark by crossing my eyes and twitching one shoulder. They all laughed, even Ron. For a moment I felt close to them. A surprising sense of well-being washed away some of the stress that had been mounting inside me. I remembered something my analyst had said. God, he was right! I feel so alienated from people. I need to connect.

"So what are you guys thinking," I said to the medical students.

"Is lunch always like this?" Bob replied warily.

We laughed again. "Only when you eat with us shrinks."

"So I've noticed," he replied with a warm chuckle.

I felt lighter, more natural than I had in days. "Say, there's something I wanted to ask you medical guys. I saw this doc yesterday on the other side of the building from the inpatient unit. He was in his fifties, maybe — kind of lanky, with a rumpled suit, carrying a lot of books. Anyone know who he is?"

Ron answered me. "That's Lloyd Williams."

"Lloyd Williams!" I said with surprise. "I didn't know he was here."

"Many people don't," Ron said, "because he doesn't have any formal connection to the inpatient or outpatient staff and he doesn't talk much to anyone. In fact, people rarely ever see him. He's on some kind of special lifetime fellowship to pursue whatever work he wants, although no one seems to have any idea what he's working on."

"Excuse me," Bob interjected, "this may sound a bit ignorant, but I've never heard of him."

"He was very big about ten years ago," I said, "one of those genius types who shot to fame when he was young. He got an

M.D. and Ph.D. from Harvard, worked at Austin-Riggs for awhile, published in the journal *Science* when he was only a graduate student. He was working on reviving Freud's *Project for a Scientific Psychology* that postulated a neurophysiological basis for thinking, emotion, and the unconscious. Freud eventually gave up on the project and never actually published the manuscript himself. Eventually it became hopelessly outdated, just a curiosity in the history of the psychoanalytic movement. But then Williams got hold of it. He won acclaim for reviving and integrating Freud's ideas with current theories about neurology and computer science. They say he would have won the Nobel Prize for psychiatry, if they gave a prize in psychiatry. Then he went on to integrate his ideas with existential phenomenology, and even mysticism. Some people were waiting for that final, seminal book where he'd pull it all together, the neuropsychological and philosophical equivalent of TOE in physics, the Theory of Everything. Other people thought he had gone too far, that he was starting to flake out. Then, suddenly, he stopped publishing and lecturing, and just disappeared. I wonder how he ended up here?"

"No one knows for sure," Ron replied. "The gossip is that his money is from a private source and the medical school simply offered a place for him to work."

"Regarding these people who are geniuses," Sheikh interjected, "before you joined us we were discussing grand rounds with Dr. Stein. It was most interesting, Thomas. You were, I must say, quite outspoken."

"That's putting it nicely. You mean I was rather defiant, maybe even obnoxious. But I figure he deserved it."

Ron revved up. "He's an internationally recognized expert on borderline disorders and schizophrenia!"

"So what, he can still be wrong. And besides, with this patient Doe we're not talking about a borderline or schizophrenic disorder, or even an 'as if' personality. I think Stein is missing the boat with his diagnosis."

"But Fred and Dr. Stein have warned us about such attitudes," Ron replied insistently. "They told us that there's always a tendency to underestimate pathology. Inexperienced clinicians often make that mistake."

That remark made me bristle. "Then you're saying that I'm inexperienced?"

Sheikh interceded again. "I believe that we all know very much at this point in our training, but there is still much that we must learn. Perhaps our most important lesson at this time is to know when our supervisors are right, and when to trust our own intuition."

Ron was still on his own track, and partly deaf. "Dr. Stein also says that there's a tendency for new therapists to get very wrapped up in a particular case and seal themselves off from outside input, especially from the advice of supervisors. It's like being in an isolated cocoon with your patient. You think you know more about your patient than any outsider. You think that you're the only one who really understands that patient. That's when you lose your objectivity. You see things that aren't really there and you fail to see the things that are. You can't tell the forest from the trees. He says that you get too close to the person and tend to underestimate their pathology. In fact, you reinforce it and become part of it."

"Maybe we shouldn't be so concerned about what Dr. Stein says," I replied. "The guy isn't exactly the epitome of mental health himself. He treats us like we're some kind of de-evolved species, and he's as empathic as a post in winter. I think we all tend to underestimate his pathology. But you know, this whole idea about underestimating pathology really bugs me. Throw a rock in any direction and you'll hit some-one who's abnormal by somebody's definition. Remember the Midtown Manhattan Study they did in the 1950s? A team of mental health professionals went door to door doing interviews at all the domiciles in New York. They had a checklist of a whole variety of psychiatric symptoms. After all the results were in, do you know what percent of people in the city were suffering from some significant psychological problem? Take a guess."

"5 percent?" Bob answered hesitantly.

"Try again." I looked at Ron, but he was too nervous about guessing an exact statistic.

"10 percent?" Sheikh said.

"25 percent. That's a lot of people. Now what does a statistic like that mean? The Big Apple is hazardous to your mental health? Only sickos come to live there? Or are we mental health professionals wearing glasses that make use see pathology everywhere? Maybe truly healthy people are indeed in the minority. Maybe they have a secret society somewhere, with a secret handshake and funny little hats. Just take a look at any institution, like this hospital, or any business or company, or any place where there's a group of people working together. It runs rampant with craziness. The backstabbing, the power plays, the simple lack of appreciation or compassion for other people. I'm truly amazed that in any institution productive work actually gets accomplished. By their very nature human beings are kind of crazy. Freud said that all of us are, at best, neurotic. To make the matter even more complex, what's considered sick or abnormal depends on your culture. It's all relative. If Ron here stood up on the table and shouted that he heard voices from the sky, we'd give him a hefty dose of meds and lock him up in Isolation. But if we lived in some traditional Native American tribe, we'd listen with respect because he contacted the Great Spirits. We'd even call him our priest, provide him with a steady dose of hallucinogens, and request that he hear voices on a regular basis. Hell, Richard Mobin might be a hero in such a time and place! Or look at it the other way around. Is competition considered normal in our culture? If Dr. Stein lined us all up and told us to run five laps around the unit — and that the winner would get a 100% pay increase — would we do it? Sure, we'd run our asses off. Not so among the Zuni Indians. Some anthropologists once lined up a bunch of them in a field and asked them to race to a tree at the other end. The winner would get a prize. What happened? They all crossed the finish line at exactly the same time. No one wanted to beat out anyone else. They considered competitiveness wrong and abnormal. But it's a way of life for us, it's our national obsession."

Ron was indignant. "You're saying that there's no difference between normal and abnormal. What good will that kind of relativistic thinking do for psychiatry? It's very clear that abnormality is defined in terms of level of functioning. That holds true across all cultures. If a person's behaviors or symptoms significantly interfere with how they function in their occupation, social relationships, or any of their daily activities, then by definition we say that something is abnormal."

"But that definition doesn't hold in all cases," I replied. "There are people who function very well, are successful, well-liked, the whole ball of wax — but on the inside they are totally miserable. One day they don't come into work, so you go to their house and find them on the bathroom floor with their wrists sliced. Or they're the people who go out one day, buy a gun, and shoot children at the schoolyard. And what does the next door neighbor always say on the 11:00 news? He seemed like such a nice man, kind of quiet, but very polite and friendly. We can't always predict these behaviors, no less explain them afterwards. Our theories are like those prefitted bed sheets. There's always one corner that just won't fit snug."

The medical students looked very uncomfortable, like they were shriveling. Sheikh was puzzled. "Thomas, are you saying that you think John Doe and Richard Mobin are not abnormal?"

"No, yes. I'm not sure what I'm trying to say," I replied as I picked up an empty can of soda and began fidgeting with it. "I just think that we mental health experts sometimes like to think that we know everything about human nature, but we don't. We feel better about ourselves when we can find problems in other people. Maybe we analyze others as a way to avoid looking at our own shortcomings."

With that remark, I realized that my finger — which I had been poking nervously into the soda can — was stuck! The sharp metal hole dug painfully into my skin. I yanked, yanked again. It popped out. Then I sneezed and a tiny dribble of gook ran down my lip. I pulled out a tissue to blow my nose and the result was an embarrassingly loud honk.

"Excuse me, Tom. Am I interrupting?"

Through my watery eyes I made out Peggy — one of the masters degree psychology externs — standing by our table. "Uh, no," I mumbled. I was glad for the distraction. "What's up?"

"Since I have this stuff with me," she said, "I thought I'd give it to you now. It's the results of the test battery on your new patients. I just finished the scoring. Richard Mobin wouldn't give me very much, so I went ahead and gave the battery to your John Doe. He seemed to love it. That's a very dynamic duo you got there. You'll see what I mean when you look at the results. Henry should have a lot of fun with you on this one."

I skimmed through the graphs and tally sheets. The results leaped off the page at me. My heart raced. I jumped out of my seat. "Excuse me, I have to go," I said without looking back.

"That was very impolite," remarked Hippocrates from the other end of the building.

"Sssssssure," agreed the elevator. I felt a pang of regret, but at that moment my primary concern was to find Henry.

Much to my dismay, Ron stepped into the elevator just before the doors closed. I didn't know what to say to him. We both just stood there and stared at the floor indicator. He broke the silence first. His voice was a bit odd. He actually sounded friendly. "You know," he said, "you and I are not all that different."

I wasn't exactly sure what to make of this. Just as I was about to say something, the elevator doors popped open. There, in answer to my prayers, was Henry walking towards us. He waved and as he approached he looked up and down Ron's white lab coat. "Yo, Ronnie!" he called out, "How's the roast beef today?"

"You psychologists," Ron muttered while shaking his head, and then disappeared around the corner.

"Henry, do you have time for a quick supervision?" I asked. "I have the results on the test battery for my new patients."

"Oh yeah, I've heard about them. I'm sorry I missed morning report. Sure, I've got a few minutes. Come on down to my office."

As I followed him down the hallway, I felt some relief. Henry, the only psychologist on staff in the unit, was my primary supervisor for the internship. He always supported and stood up for me. We were in the same boat, or should I say we were both fish out of water, being psychologists in a psychiatric world. In some ways, he had a worse time of it than me. I was a lowly intern, but he was the very first psychologist to work on this unit. He fought tooth and nail for every inch of respect he won for himself and our profession. He was, in his own way, a crusader.

"I hear you're having a bad week," he said as he tossed his short, overweight, but slightly frenetic body into his swivel chair."

"Word sure does get around. Yeah, I'm a little sick and other things are not going well. My depressed patient that I discharged, Elizabeth Baso, died in a car accident yesterday. And my two new patients are real doozies. Fred and Stein interviewed them during grand rounds and in the discussion afterwards Stein attacked me. Get this, he accused us psychologists of being feeble-brained because we talk about the concept of secondary gain."

His neck and round face suddenly reddened and puffed out. "Damn! Hold on a second," he said as he reached into the bottom drawer of his desk, pulled out a bottle of Maalox, and took a deep swig. "He can be such a jerk! If he'd just look at his patients for a minute and stop using them as material for his damn books, maybe he'd learn something. The guy is all intellectualizations and no common sense, especially about people. Don't tell anyone I told you this, but he had this girlfriend a few years ago. Never talked about her to anyone. So one day she shows up on the unit looking for him. She's got hair teased straight up to the ceiling, bright red lipstick, a low cut blouse, and a mouth like a drunk sailor. Everyone who met her swore that she was a borderline. And I'd be willing to bet that he never even knew it. He's a genius, but that's how out of it he can be sometimes."

We both laughed.

"But listen to this," I said. "In the middle of grand rounds, my patient Doe pointed out to Stein that he had dog shit on his shoe. You should have seen Stein's face.

He ran out of the room like people had seen him with his pants down."

Henry rolled back into his chair, threw his wiggling arms and legs up into the air, and squealed "Wheeeeh! Wheeeh! That's great! Oh lord, I can't wait until I see him in the mail room. 'Excuse me, Dr. Stein, do you smell something funny?' Wheeeh! I can't stand it! This patient Doe is great! Let's see his test data."

We spread the sheets onto Henry's desk. While he scratched his beard and looked over the data, I sat back, tried to relax, and waited.

Henry was an expert at test interpretation. He generated big bucks for the hospital when he created the testing program, which was why the psychiatrists had a hard time finding a justification to block his promotion to associate professor with tenure. Historically, psychologists first entered psychiatric hospitals as administrators and interpreters of psychological tests. Psychiatrists knew nothing about it. They also knew nothing about experimental research methods — an ignorance that eventually became a burden once medical schools started to require empirical research as a criterion for promotion. So, many of them relied on psychologists to design the research studies for them. Henry was constantly being badgered by the psychiatrists to take them into his projects so they could put their name on his publications, even when their only contribution to the project was stapling papers. He flatly refused and they resented it. They resented the fact that he was so bright and capable. They also resented the fact that he continually fought for the rights of psychologists beyond doing testing and research — for the right to be actively involved in making diagnoses and conducting psychotherapy, activities reserved exclusively for the medical staff in the old days. It was a constant battle and it took its toll on Henry's stomach. But he never let them know. In fact, in his own unique hypomanic style, he persistently kidded them about their pomposity, made faces at their demands, and sometimes even got them to laugh at themselves.

"Holy moly," Henry exclaimed, "this guy Mobin is a real hurtin' soldier! His refusal to take the tests clearly indicates paranoia. He even tried to rip some of the pages out of the MMPI. Be on the lookout for violence, Tom. The few responses he gave to the Rorschach are also bad news — poor form, poor affect control, deviant thinking. On card 2 he said it was blood gushing out of a crack in the universe. And here on card 6, the bear skin rug, he says it's a knife stuck up the asshole of the universe. Both are pathognomic signs of schizophrenia. Jesus, this guy is psychotic up the wazoo! That remark about the knife is a sign of homosexual conflict and the one about blood gushing out of a crack suggests intense hostility towards women. Very strong underlying rage in this guy. It's completely disorganized his identity structure. Even his gender identity is fouled up on a very primitive level. Watch him carefully. Has Fred looked into transferring him over to the state hospital?"

"Yeah, but right now there are no beds."

"OK, keep an eye on him. So, let's take a look at Doe. On the WAIS he scored a 115, so he's slightly above the average range of intelligence."

"But look at the pattern of right and wrong answers, Henry. On all the subscales, he gets a right answer followed by wrong answers, but exactly the number of wrong answers allowed before that subscale is terminated — and then he gives another right answer, almost as if he knew that if he got one more wrong answer in a row the test would be ended. It's like he was familiar with the WAIS and was playing games with it. His IQ is probably a lot higher."

"Hm, interesting," Henry answered, "but you may be reading too much into it. The scatter of right and wrong answers is typical of patients with attention and memory deficits, including those deficits caused by schizophrenia. Peggy has a note here that some of his responses were bizarre. Let's see, here for instance, in response to 'Why do we pay taxes' he says 'Because we have to die.' And here, in response to 'What are the apocrypha' he says 'Bedtime stories.' Sure sounds like psychotic thinking to me. But let's take a look at the MMPI before we jump to any conclusions. Remember, we're always looking for converging evidence across all the test data that confirms our diagnosis. On the MMPI he has an 8-6 profile two standard deviations above normal on the schizophrenia and paranoia subscales. That clearly indicates psychosis and paranoid thought processes."

"But couldn't those elevations also mean eccentric or creative thinking," I added, "or an acute sensitivity to the environment, especially social events."

"Yeah, there's some of that here. But it's more typical of a schizophrenic profile. Here again Peggy has a note indicating that some of his answers were clearly abnormal. For instance, he answers true to both 'I hear voices in the wind' and 'My soul sometimes leaves my body.' And on the Rorschach he shows mostly poor form responses. He just doesn't see the shape of the inkblots like most people do, which is another sign of psychosis. Also, there are a lot of special scores and other idiosyncratic responses. Now, what's interesting in terms of the content of his responses is that he often perceives the inkblots as being masks. It's his primary response on cards 1, 3, and 5, and on card 6 he says it's either a flattened out animal or a mask. That preoccupation with masks might confirm Stein's ideas about an as-if personality, but I'd still rely more on the diagnosis of schizophrenia. He puts on a mask for people, probably a very normal looking mask, but underneath he's psychotic. He also gives many white space responses. Rather than telling you what the inkblots look like, he tells you what the white spaces look like. Essentially, he subtly defies the instructions of the test and does just the reverse of what you are asking. He's oppositional, stubborn, and has a lot of buried anger."

"Look what he does on card 10, Henry. He balances it on the tip of his finger, spins it, and gives the response 'The center disintegrates and the world flies apart.' What does that mean?"

"It means he has exquisite motor control," he said with a laugh, "but in its own psychotic way, it's beautiful. I can see why you might find this guy creative and intelligent. That card is filled with different colors and shapes. It's very difficult for even a normal person to pull it all together into one coherent image. It requires a cohesive sense of self, which Doe doesn't have. For him there is no sense of a center to his intrapsychic world. It really is flying apart. What's fascinating about the guy is that he finds a way to express that so vividly."

"Yeah," I replied, "but isn't it possible that there's more going on here than just schizophrenia? There's something about Doe that gets to me. He seems to be aware of things that I'm not. He... sees things."

Henry threw me a quizzical look. "Hmmm, well, schizophrenics do sometimes have access to things that we may miss. It's called schizophrenic insight. It can be fascinating and very enticing to tap into their experience. But it requires a lot of ego strength on the part of the clinician to explore that stuff — and Tom, I'm not sure you're up to it right now. You're stressed out, you're sick. I think it would be a good idea for you to slow down a bit. It's just a job, right? That's a free piece of advice," he said as he reached over and put his hand on my shoulder, "and as we all know, free advice is worth twice what we pay for it."

CHAPTER 23

A Finger

I FELT A BIT BETTER AS I left Henry's office and walked towards the elevator. But a bit didn't seem like enough. As usual, Henry was on target with his observations. It was just that something was missing, or not quite right — something that poked at me from the inside.

"Maybe it's parallel process," My Biographer said. "Remember? What happens in one relationship gets played out in another."

"Please, mind your own business!" I replied.

A figure down the hallway waved his arms at me. It was Sheikh. "Quick, Thomas!" he called out. "You must come to the unit. Mobin and Doe are fighting!"

"You mean they're arguing?"

"No, I mean they are FIGHTING!"

All my thoughts and blood sank to my feet. I ran.

The unit was reverberating with anxiety. Some of the staff were talking to the patients, offering explanations and comfort, while the others were gathered around four security officers. Doe and Mobin were not anywhere in sight. I pulled Carole aside. Even she looked upset. "What happened?" I asked.

"I'm not exactly sure," she replied. "Doe was in Center Circle, standing in this funny position. He had his legs spread apart, like he was riding a horse, and his arms out in front of him like he was holding a big ball. It looked very odd. He said he was gathering the universe into his belly, or something like that, and he refused to move when we asked him. So we just let him be. It didn't seem to be doing any harm. But then Richard Mobin came out of his room and began circling around and around the unit, the whole time staring at Doe. He got very agitated. We tried talking to him but he wasn't listening, almost as if he were in a trance. Then he just lost control and attacked Doe."

"Was anyone hurt?"

"No, in fact it was interesting what happened when he went after him. It looked like Mobin was going to pounce all over the guy, but Doe just side-stepped him at the last instant. And when Mobin went after him again and again, he just kept slipping away, like he was disappearing right under Mobin's grip. It almost looked like they were dancing, except Mobin got more and more infuriated. Thank God security got here quickly and helped us put them both into Isolation."

"Where's Fred?"

"He's on the phone trying to find out where we can transfer Mobin."

"Could you give me the key? I want to talk to them."

"Doe's door is open. Richard's is locked."

"Right. Can I have the key?"

She hesitated. "Well, I don't know if it's a good idea to disturb him now."

"Please, Carole," I pleaded. "You've got to give me a chance to do something here. He's my patient!"

"Well, all right," she said reluctantly as she handed over the key. "I hope you know what you're doing."

"I hope so too," I replied over my shoulder.

My heart pounded as I walked towards the Isolation rooms. They stood side by side — one door open, lights on, the other door closed, lights off. I knew they were waiting for me.

Someone once said that all of psychotherapy boils down to just two basic principles. You try to get patients to understand themselves, so rather than being pushed around by their unconscious, they can make clean, free, fully informed choices about their lives. But even more important than that — regardless of all the interventions and insights — it's your relationship with the patient that heals.

Keep that in mind, Dr. Holden. Keep that in mind.

Before opening the door to Mobin's lair, I decided first to peek through the small wire-meshed window. It took a few seconds for my eyes to adapt to the dark. Inside, Mobin was pacing back and forth. He was agitated almost to the point of being wild, reciting incoherent incantations to himself. His psychotic, tumultuous energy ricocheted off the walls. In his acute paranoid state, he instantly noticed my movement at the window. "Never! Never!" he shouted at me, his rage piercing right through the walls. Our eyes locked. He raised his blubbery arm, pointed his finger at me — and then collapsed to the floor, disappearing from view.

Where the hell did he go? I stood on my tippy-toes, straining to see through the tiny window, but he was gone. Had he rolled to the side of the room? Did he pass out? It was too dark inside to tell. As quietly as I could, I unlocked the door and pushed it open just a crack. There was no sound or movement inside. Too spooked to enter, I slid my hand in and groped along the inside wall for the light switch. I couldn't find the damn thing! "Shit!" I mumbled to myself. I kept fumbling until finally my fingers touched a cool metal plate. There it is!

But terror froze my hand right where it was. Like some monster rising up from below, Mobin's face appeared in the window. He pressed himself against the glass, warping his fat face into a grotesque shape. "Now you're mine!" he howled as he grabbed my hand.

I panicked. Frantically I pulled my arm hard to get my hand out, but his hold was tight. He leaned his weight against the door. It was closing on me. I threw myself against it to counter him. I managed to drag most of my hand from his fist, leaving only my index finger in his grip. Stretched to its limit and aching, it straddled the ever-shrinking space between the door and the frame. I could see his sweaty, blubbery hand wrapped around it. Grunting like some hungry animal, he pushed even harder. The door started vibrating from the force of our bodies meeting head on. My strength was giving out. I couldn't hold any longer. I knew with certainty the door would slam onto my finger and most likely snap it right off. "Help!" I gargled, and at that moment my finger popped out of his sweaty hand, the door slammed, and I landed squarely on my ass.

I jumped back to my feet as quickly as I could. Across the unit, Carole caught my eye. I read her lips. "You OK?" she said. Apparently she hadn't noticed what happened. Oddly, no one did. "Fine!" I called back. I leaned against the wall and tried to calm my pounding chest. My whole body was shaking. I wanted to run as fast as I could and as far away as I could.

But I didn't.

I cradled my throbbing finger in my other hand. Well, if I couldn't reach Mobin, then I had to try again with Doe. The lights were on in his room. I walked in and found it empty. Fear welled up inside me — not the kind of terror that Mobin just offered, but an eerie dread. Where the hell is he?

"Ah, it's the Ripe One — welcome!"

I turned around. He was right behind me, sitting cross-legged against the wall. "What happened with you and Richard Mobin?" I asked.

"I sent him to an empty place," he answered.

"What's that supposed to mean?"

"It supposes nothing."

"You know, talking to you is like talking to a brick wall."

"Like this, like that, everything is like this and that. A shiny new pair of shoes too tight to fit. When will you see that I'm not like a brick wall? I am the brick wall."

"You're crazy, that's what you are, or you're just pretending to be. In either case, there's something wrong with you. And all I'm trying to do is help. That's all I've been trying to do since you came here. It's my job. If you would just help me out a little then I could do that job. All I ask is that you tell me about yourself, what you're thinking and feeling, what happened out there with Richard, anything — just talk to me in a way that makes some sense, if you can."

"You want talk."

"Yes, talk. How else can I reach you? But maybe you don't want that. Maybe that's the whole point. I don't know. I just wish I knew what the story is with you."

"Story? This story is as old as the hills, a variation on a theme. There's nothing new here. Or it's everything new. Depends how you look at it. But if you want a story, if you need talk, here's some. It's actually a puzzle. What happens when you're dangling over a bottomless pit, hanging only by your teeth clenching the root of a tree — and a tiny mouse starts to gnaw away at the root. What do you do?"

"This really isn't the time for riddles."

"Whether you like it or not, the time is here."

"You know, if you don't want my help, you don't have to stay here. You can leave against medical advice. I think you already know that. So why do you stay?"

"Who is it that asks?"

"Me! Your doctor, Dr. Thomas Holden, in case you've forgotten that too."

"Show me this Thomas Holden."

"I've had enough," I answered with a sigh of exasperation. I headed towards the door. "I'm out of here. If you want to talk, let me know."

"Dr. Holden!"

"Yeah!" I spun back around to face him.

"There it is!" he said.

"There what is?"

"Never mind."

Something blinked on inside my head, then blinked off again — too fast to catch. My exasperation melted away to reveal something deeper, something beneath my doubts about Doe and everything else. It felt like a plug.

"You turn to others for help," Doe continued, "but when there is no one there, who is there left to turn to?"

"I... I..." I wanted to say something, but I didn't know what it was, or how to get it out of my mouth. My throbbing finger kept time to the ebb and flow of the plug as it tried to wiggle loose.

"Yes, you're close," Doe injected calmly. "You almost have the answer to the puzzle, don't you?"

"Wha... What?"

"You shout your name."

Suddenly Doe somehow changed. His new face looked familiar, very familiar. I knelt down next to where he was sitting on the floor and looked straight into his eyes. "Who are you?" I whispered. I wasn't sure he even heard me. He closed his eyes. All expression left his face. He instantly slipped into a deep catatonic state. I waited, hoping some inspiration would help me find a way to pry him back open — but none came to me. As I looked at him, an urge to touch his face overcame me. I reached up. An awful pain shot through my finger. It was so stiff and swollen that I couldn't move it. "I give up," I muttered as I dropped my hand to my side. Frustrated, tired, I stood up and stumbled towards the door.

"Dr. Holden."

I turned. With his eyes wide open, Doe was looking straight at me, a warm smile stretched across his face. He raised his index finger into the air — and wiggled it.

CHAPTER 24

– More Tests –

S HOUT YOUR NAME.

My finger hurts. I should go to the emergency room. Shout your name.

My knock sounded tentative, sapless.

There was no answer, but I could see a light under the door. I knocked again, this time with more persistence. A chair squeaked, feet scuffled — then silence again.

"Who's there?" a voice crackled.

"Uh, excuse me for bothering you, Dr. Williams," I said to the door. "My name is Thomas Holden. I'm a psychology intern on the psychiatric inpatient unit. I'd like to talk to you about something, if you have a few minutes."

"I don't do lectures anymore."

"That's not what I wanted to ask you. It's about one of my patients. I'd like your advice."

"I don't do supervision anymore either."

"I'd really appreciate your help. I'm sort of, uh, desperate."

The door opened a notch, just wide enough so he could peer out the crack. He looked me up and down. "You look terrible," he said.

"I know." I waited, hoping he would let me in, but he still seemed wary of me.

"I doubt that I can be of any help to you," he said.

"I really would appreciate any thoughts you might have on the case. I'm feeling very... alone on this one, Dr. Williams."

For a moment, the suspicion melted from his face. "Very well," he answered, "but I can't guarantee anything."

As I entered his office, I felt nervous and awkward. So did he. I was an intruder into his space, a possibly untrustworthy interloper who had managed to invade his sanctuary. Neither of us knew what to expect. Once he sat down behind his desk, he relaxed a bit. The tall, chaotic piles of books and papers formed a safe bulwark around him. I had no such advantage. Among the countless stacks of journals, books, and papers scattered across his otherwise empty office, I felt lost, anomalous. There also was no chair for me to sit in.

"So what do you want from me," he said as he bit on his already bitten-down nails.

"Well, this patient of mine — he doesn't know who he is. He can't remember his name or his past or anything about himself. It seems like total amnesia, even though many of his mental functions are intact and there aren't any other obvious symptoms. He side-steps any attempts I make to understand him. He just doesn't fit the typical dissociative diagnoses. It's like his identity has been wiped clean away, and he doesn't care. Either that, or he's just faking, even though there doesn't seem to be any reason why he should be malingering. So, how can I tell whether he is or isn't faking?"

"Whether he is or isn't doesn't matter. In either case there is a secret, a secret he keeps from others, and from himself. It's the secret that's the kernel of his identity, that forms his self boundary. It's the secret that marks the distinction between inside and outside, knower and unknown. This patient is all patients distilled down to the one essential common denominator."

"Uh, I'm not sure that I understand."

"Tell me this," he continued, now with more confidence, "why is it so important for you to know who he is?"

"I have to know who he is in order to treat him, don't I? Or, I mean, the goal of the treatment is to know who he is."

"Why… why is it important to know that, or anything else for that matter?"

His remark surprised me. Was he going to play games too? I was hoping that Lloyd Williams, of all people, would understand, but now I was beginning to think I had make a mistake. "I still don't know what you mean," I said as politely as I could.

He picked up a book from his desk. "What is this?"
"A book."

"But is that what it really is? Is it simply a book?"

I looked at its title. "Well, it's a book on epistemology."

"But is that all that it is?"

"I don't understand."

"Is that really what this thing is trying to tell you that it is?"

"I don't get it. It isn't trying to tell me anything."

"Exactly. It isn't trying to tell you that it's a book. YOU are trying to tell it that it's a book, or I am."

He seemed pleased with himself. I, on the other hand, was not pleased at all. "I don't understand. I'm lost," I replied with obvious irritation. But he seemed completely unaffected by my tone of voice.

"I know, that's the problem."

"You don't seem to understand what I'm trying to say."

"I understand that you really need to understand, but you don't understand that there is nothing that you can understand — and all my understanding won't help."

My irritation bubbled up into outright anger. "Will you please stop talking in riddles like Doe! I came here for help and all you're doing is playing games with words. I need help with this patient!"

"There's nothing I can do that will help you. I'm sorry."

"You've got to help me. I'm at my wits end. I'm trapped. I can't move ahead and I can't run away. It's like I'm damned if I do and damned if I don't!"

Sadness settled onto his face. "I know," he answered solemnly, "Believe me, I really do. But I'm sorry. There's nothing I can do."

The sound of the door closing behind me echoed down the dead-ended hallway. I felt stunned. There's nothing he can do? All his goddamn papers and books and awards and there's nothing he can tell me about Doe! He should have been given the Nobel Prize for Ineptitude.

That book in his hand.

Why is it so important for me to know?

Shout my name.

I knock.

No answer.

Shout my name.

I knock again.

Still no answer. Henry isn't in.

My finger was still throbbing. My head and throat hurt. My congested sinuses ached. I fumbled through my knapsack for some Tylenol, and while I was in there I grabbed some more decongestants. There was a water fountain down the next hallway, but I didn't bother to walk the extra distance. I just swallowed the pills dry — all of them in one gulp. They stuck in my throat. I couldn't breathe. I was choking. I coughed them up into my mouth, wiped the tears from my eyes, and swallowed them again. This time, thanks to the extra saliva, they went down.

Why is it so important for me to know?

I knock.

No answer.

I knock again.

No answer. Marion isn't in either. No one is in.

"I'm still here," My Biographer said.

"A lot of good you do me. Your type always waits until we're dead to say anything helpful."

"Well, who's left besides me? You have no alternatives."

"There are always alternatives."

"Ssssssssure," interjected the elevator doors.

My dog Rags, he loves to play.

Why is it so important?

The guy behind the desk wore glasses as thick as the textbook he was reading. He didn't hear me walk in. I shot the words at his ear. "Is this radiology?" He nearly jumped out of his seat.

"Yes — that's what the sign says on the door, doesn't it?"

We both turned to look. There was no sign on the door, just a rectangular patch of clean paint where a sign used to be. "Uh, oh yeah, I forgot," he said, "we're getting a new one. Is there something I can help you with?"

"Yeah, can you tell me where the woman is who works here?"

"What woman?"

"The one who works here, in radiology."

"There is no woman who works here."

"Yes there is," I answered with persistence, "I saw her in the cafeteria. I have her exposure badge right here." I tossed my knapsack onto his desk and began rummaging through it, but I couldn't find the badge. "Damn!" I blurted.

"Uh oh!" My Biographer said, "Next you're going to lose your head."

"Believe me, sir, there's no woman here."

"I know there is! There's got to be!"

"Listen, maybe I should call security and they can help you."

"Never mind! Just forget it," I muttered, and stumbled out of the room.

"Maybe you should've had your finger x-rayed while you were there."

"Please, shut up!"

I kick the wall and stubbed my toe.

"Two digits down."

"Dr. Holden!"

Now who's calling me? I looked up from the cracks in the floor tiles. It was Dr. Stein coming straight at me. I pretended not to hear. I willed him to disappear, but he didn't.

"Dr. Holden," he says as he passes by, "you made some good points during grand rounds today. Keep up the good work."

That didn't just happen. Ignore it.

Shout your name.

There's nothing he can do to help. I'll just have to do it myself. Is everyone on the unit looking at me, or is it just my imagination?

"Carole, I want to take Doe off the unit for a while."

Her eyes nearly pop out her head. "You can't take a patient in Isolation off the unit!"

"I'm taking him off the unit, just for a half hour. It'll be good for him."

"We have to speak to Fred about this."

"I did. I'll be with Doe the whole time. I'll take full responsibility."

"You spoke to Fred?"

"We'll be back in half an hour."

"But —"

"We'll be back in half an hour."

One isolation room closed, lights on — one room open, lights off. I should have done this a long time ago.

"How would you like to go for a little walk," I said to Doe. He was still sitting cross-legged against the wall, right where I left him.

"If that's what you want," he replied. He's not surprised. Nothing surprises him. Together we strolled off the unit and down the hallway. Almost like a couple. He seemed to know where I was taking him. He made some of the turns before I did. Who is leading whom?

"Psychophysiology laboratory," Doe read off the door plate. "Now that's a mouthful!"

"Yes, Descartes would have been proud," I replied as I unlocked the door. "Come on in. Are you in the mood for a few tests?"

Doe calmly passed his eyes over the multi-thousand dollar array of computers and polygraphs. "You mean, am I in the mood for a duel?"

"Well, let's not think of it that way. Come on into this chamber. You know, once the door is closed, it's completely soundproof in here. A very nice place to relax. You can sit down in that chair over there. I'm just going to run a few tests on you," I said as I started to paste up the electrodes, "you know, get some data on heartbeat, respiration, blood pressure — stuff like that."

When I looked up, I saw Doe playing with the video camera. He had slipped it off the mounting on the chamber wall and was staring intently right into the lens. "Hello in there," he said, "Is that you?"

"What are you doing?" I asked.

"Running my own tests, but there's a better one. Come with me." He carried the camera out of the chamber, snaking the long cord behind him, and pointed the camera into the video monitor seated next to a polygraph. The image on the TV monitor was striking. An infinite regression of TV screens, like a series of picture frames one inside the other, spiraling off into a bright white light that glowed eerily in the distance.

"Visions within visions within visions," Doe said. "Now THIS is what you should be testing."

"Please, come back into the chamber. This won't take long." I steered him inside and sat him down onto the reclining chair. After repositioning the video camera on its mount, I attached all of the electrodes to him — EEG, EKG, GSR, arm and forehead EMG, as well as the automatic blood pressure and respiration cuffs. It's not often that you use all the psychophysiology measures at the same time, but I didn't want to leave any stone unturned. I stepped back to marvel at my masterpiece. With electrodes and wires radiating out from his head, arms, hands, and leg, he looked like the Bionic Patient — a modern age Frankenstein's monster.

"Mourning becomes electric," Doe said, unruffled.

"None of this is going to hurt," I said. "These wires will just be measuring some basic physiological processes — like heart rate, brain waves, and muscle tension. All you have to do is sit here and relax for a while, and in few minutes I'll give you some instructions over the intercom."

I didn't tell him that I intended to use the psychophysiological measures as an objective, quantifiable means of probing his thoughts and emotions — that I intended to bring to bear all the tools of modern technology to enter his internal subjective world.

"Remember," Doe said as I closed the chamber door, "there is nothing on the inside and nothing on the outside that you can grasp."

"Ssssssure," I whispered to myself and shut the door to the chamber.

I turned on the polygraph, calibrated it, and checked the computer interface. There's an odd sense of security in pushing buttons, pulling levers, and turning dials. It all seems so definite.

"All you have to do for the next few minutes is sit back and relax so I can get a baseline," I said into the intercom. On the video monitor, Doe appeared calm, even peaceful. Some people panic in there.

No activity registered on the computer screen. Just flat lines. Did I forget to turn something on? I checked the equipment. Everything was as it should be. What the hell? Is something broken? I banged my fist on the top of the computer.

Nothing. Damn!

"Are you OK," I said into the intercom. "Are you asleep?"

"Perhaps you are?" Doe's voice replied through the speaker.

"How do you feel?"

"Usually with my hands, but often with all my skin."

"Listen, I'm not getting any recordings out here. Did something come unplugged in there?"

I looked at the video monitor. Staring quietly up at the ceiling, Doe had settled back into a reclining position. Suddenly, the levels on the computer screen sprang to life. All biological functions normal. Funny. Must have been a loose connection.

"OK I've got it," I said. "What I'm going to do now is play a series of tones over the loudspeaker in there. You don't have to do anything. Just sit there and listen to them."

I started up the tone generator and watched his physiological responses. In response to each tone, his galvanic skin response jumped and his heart rate decelerated then accelerated — the typical orienting reactions to a new, moderately loud sound. At least I knew his nervous system acted like that of normal people. Over time, his responses would diminish in volume as he became used to the tones. "Habituation," I mumbled to myself. "Habituation."

But he didn't. Tone after tone, he showed the exact same magnitude of response. I waited — ten, twenty, thirty trials — and still no change. The levels looked like exact copies of each other. He reacted to each tone as if he were hearing it for the first time. His EEG showed slow wave delta patterns indicating deep sleep. The respiration recording fell to a nearly flat line. It didn't make sense.

"Enough of this bullshit," I said to myself. "Time for the real stuff." I pressed the intercom button. "OK, let's try something different. I'm going to ask you some questions, and you just answer yes or no. How does that sound?"

"Like you have many questions," Doe replied.

"I do."

And I was determined to get some answers, even if it meant resorting to lie detection techniques. Better start off with easy, non-threatening inquiries. "Here's the first question. Do you live in this state?"

"No."

There was little if no physiological reaction, indicating no noteworthy emotional response. People show the arousal of anxiety when they lie. He must be telling the truth.

"Did you come here from the north or south."

"No."

No physical reaction. Good, I'm narrowing down the possibilities.

"From the west?"

"No."

"Then you must come from east of here, correct?"

"No."

Still no physiological reaction! He hasn't lied yet? How could he not come from any direction? Something is wrong here. Try something else.

"Does your last name start with any letter between A and M?"

"No."

No reaction.

I was almost afraid to ask the next question. "Does it start with any letter from N to Z?"

"No."

Again no reaction. How can this be? This just isn't working. All this equipment and technology is garbage. I closed my eyes and wracked my brain for another question to ask, but nothing came to me. My concentration drifted. I felt dizzy. Blackness billowed up below my feet. Where am I? Shout my name. By the power of fear and sheer determination, I yanked myself out. "Who are you!" I implored through the intercom.

No answer. The computer screen showed all flat lines. No recordings at all. I looked up at the video monitor. The seat in the soundproof chamber was empty. EMPTY! Where was Doe? I jumped up, unlocked the chamber door. He wasn't there — just the wires and electrodes placed neatly across the armrest.

CHAPTER 25

Fire, Snow

MY HEAD ON A SWIVEL, I run frantically down the hallways, breaking to a halt at each intersection. He's not there, or there, he's not anywhere. "Boy, it's really coming down now," says the woman by the window. "I wonder if we can get home," replies the man.

Doe must have gone back to the unit. Move! My legs and heart start pumping. What will I tell Fred? What if Doe isn't there? Shit, oh shit! The doorknob spins uselessly in my hand. Goddamn it! Not now!

"Did you really think it would be easy?" it remarks. I jerk it hard until something snaps and the door opens. A wall of smoke envelops me. People are shouting.

"Get the extinguisher!" someone yells as silhouetted figures run to and fro. The flickering light of bright flames puncture the smoky haze. One of the library cubicles is on fire.

"Someone give me a hand with this!" Fred calls out. I run to his side and take the metal canister from him. "Upside down, you have to turn it upside down," he shouts. Foam sprays over the books and water pours down from the ceiling sprinklers. Refusing the onslaught of the clamor around me, my mind searches for an escape. It fixes onto something in the corner of the library cubicle — paper burning under a slow flame, the pages from a spiral notebook.

A loud crash transcends all the commotion in the room and wrenches my guts. Someone screams. "He's out! He's out!" Fred spots the danger first. "Holy shit!" he utters in horror.

There in Center Circle, with smoke swirling upwards around his body and water cascading downwards, is Richard Mobin. Fierce insanity oozes from his bloodshot eyes and twisted grin. He's clutching something in his fist, something shiny, metal. What is it? My eyes focus. SCISSORS.

"Someone call security," Fred cries out and then turns to whisper to me. "Tom, you circle around to his left. Make sure the patients stay away. Let's try to maneuver him back into seclusion." My instincts tell me otherwise. They tell me to run, to run away as fast as I can, but fear saps the strength from my legs.

Slowly, Fred approaches him. "Richard, I want you to put down those scissors. Can you hear me? Just drop them onto the floor."

But Richard doesn't hear. He hears only the madness within. He raises the weapon above his head and bellows from deep inside his deranged world, "Now I spear YOU!"

His scream paralyzes me. I can do nothing to help as he lunges forward and stabs Fred in the shoulder. Fred falls, blood oozes onto his white shirt.

"Do something!" My Biographer says.

"I can't! I can't!" I plead pathetically.

A goose in a bottle.

There's nothing I can do.

Richard raises his arm to strike at Fred again. I see life and all reason collapsing before my eyes.

There's nothing I can do.

Shout your name!

Wiggle that finger!

Shout your name!

The knots inside me snap apart. Without thought or feeling, I quickly climb onto the countertop, launch my body through space, and land squarely onto Richard's back. Screaming, bucking, and flailing his arms, he tries to throw me off. I won't let go. I won't. My legs and arms hold tight as he runs through the smoke and water towards the exit. Back first, he plows through the doors. The blow dislodges me. I fall to the floor.

"Let go!" the doorknob interjects.

After him!

Why is it so important?

After him!

I sprint down the hallway as fast as I can. Confused, frightened people step aside. They hide between the rows of book shelves.

"Are you sure you want to do this?" the librarian asks.

"Stop, go," blink the computer screens.

After him!

My feet tumble confusedly down the stairs. "Do you really think this is therapeutic?" Hippocrates inquires.

After him!

The blinding snow whips into my face. I look to the left, and right. He's nowhere in sight. But there are tracks in the snow. A voice calls from the tree line. "Shout your name." Without hesitation, I follow it, past my snowbound car, past the oak tree that points its beckoning fingers into the wintry sky. Behind me the building disappears into the blustery haze.

Staggering and stumbling, I run down the slope, further and further into the woods. Something sucks one of the shoes off my foot, but I keep running.

There's someone up ahead, waiting for me.

Why is it so important?

I trip over something, my ankle twists. I fall head first into the ground. When I try to stand up pain shoots through my leg. I fall back down. A profound exhaustion sweeps through me. I can't move. I lie there, staring at the bumper of a car jutting up out of the snow that gathers around me. I look up into the sky, into the blowing wind and snow, knowing I've lost, knowing there is no hope left. The icy wind penetrates my clothes. My feet are wet, cold. What will Mobin do to me if he finds me? And if he doesn't, will anyone find me?

"Sorry," My Biographer says, "there's nothing we can do."

A figure appears above me. "Where did you go?" I ask.

"You say that I've gone, but I've been here from the very beginning."

* * *

The wind dies down, a ghostly quiet settles around me. Looking up into the twilight sky, I watch the drifting snowflakes weave in and out of elaborate patterns that blend, separate, and rejoin with incomprehensible rhyme and reason. They whisper to me. They speak of ceaseless changes with no beginning and no end, of ease and simplicity — of that which remains forever eternal. With awe and compassion, I surrender to it, letting mind and body fall away. Slowly, gently, the tapestry of time and space unravels. When the last thread is gone, there remains a peaceful stillness, an emptiness, that overflows with infinite possibility and unborn beginnings.

CHAPTER 27

– Down –

Tᴵᴹᴱ ᵀᴼ ᶜᴼᴹᴱ ᴮᴬᶜᴷ.

I hear talking in the distance. I make no effort to discern what they are saying. My awareness rests gently on the tone and rhythm of their voices, on the warm air moving across my face and the soft cushion beneath me. It all feels comforting. It all feels right.

I open my eyes. It's a cozy room — dimly lit, with a pastoral painting on the wall and an EKG monitor tucked into the corner. Bright but soft fluorescent light gently spills in from the hall. I listen carefully as thoughtful, gracefully paced footsteps approach. A silhouette of a woman appears in the doorway, her face hidden in a halo of light.

"How are you doing?" she asks warmly.

"As good as new, I guess. But, uh…"

"You're in obstetrics. The emergency room is packed with people. All sorts of accidents today. We're right next door, so they moved you in here for a while. You had some adventure out there, didn't you? A twisted ankle, mild concussion, and a bad sprain to that finger. You're lucky you didn't get too deep into the woods, otherwise no one might have seen you. There's almost two feet of snow out there. You also threw up quite a few decongestants. You really should go easy on that stuff. But you'll be fine."

"Yeah," I answer, "I believe so." I still can't see her face, but I know she is smiling. I wonder what color her eyes are.

"Oh," she says, "there are some people here for you." She steps aside to let them enter, lingers a moment, then waves goodbye.

Fred, with his arm in a sling, and Marion walk into the room.

"Hey, cowboy," Fred says cheerfully, "how're you doing?" Marion stands beside my bed to rest her hand on my shoulder.

"Fine, Fred. How're you?"

"Well, it'll be tough writing progress notes with my left hand, but I'll survive."

"Maybe we both could use a few days off."

He laughs. "Right! That was some heroic act you pulled up there — stupid, but heroic."

"It seemed right at the time. Is Mobin OK?"

"He's fine. They found him in the library, pulling magazines off the shelves and stuffing them into his pants. We're shipping him out tonight. A bed opened up at the state hospital. We're just still trying to figure out how that fire got started, whether he had something to do with it."

"And what about Doe?"

"He's gone. He disappeared sometime during the fire. In the middle of the confusion, the nut actually took the trouble to sign himself out AMA. God knows where he got the presence of mind to do that. We alerted the police and they'll be on the lookout for him. Anyway, don't worry about it. He didn't seem to be suicidal or homicidal. Just an oddball character disorder with an identity disturbance to boot. It's not unusual for dissociative types like him to just disappear at the drop of a hat, especially during a crisis situation."

It doesn't seem important to disagree. I just smile.

"Anyway," Fred continues, "they say you should stay here for the night. Tomorrow the roads will be clear and you can go home. How does that sound?"

"Just right, Fred, just right. And by the way, thank you. Both of you. Thanks a lot."

"Thanks for what?" Fred answers quizzically.

"Thanks for helping me, for tolerating me... for being here now. I appreciate it."

"Hey, it's my pleasure!" Fred says jokingly. "It's my job!" Without saying a word, Marion pats me on the shoulder, looks into my eyes, and nods. She knows. I reach up to take hold of her hand.

"Well, we better be going," Fred interjects as he moves towards the door, glancing at his watch. "It's time to cure some mental illness. You take care of yourself. Take the day off tomorrow. Enjoy life, for one day that is, then you gotta get back to work." He chuckles as he slips out the room. Marion follows, more slowly. Before passing through the doorway, she stops and turns back to face me.

"Enjoy life," she says, almost with a question in her voice. "That sounds like a good idea."

"I think so," I reply.

She smiles, and leaves.

I lay back in bed. The wind-blown particles of snow tap lightly against the small window high in the corner of the room above my head. I quietly listen to them, then reach for the phone. The tones I tap out sound more familiar and comforting than I ever remember them being.

"Hello?" she says.

"Hello, Mom."

"Thomas! How are you? I'm so glad you called. It's funny, I was just thinking about you," she pauses, as if uncertain about continuing, "and about your father."

"Me too."

Outside the perimeter of the parking lots, the snow forms a smooth, crystalline blanket that covers the wooded landscape. Jon's booth pops up among the plowed banks of snow like a hermit's hut on the edge of civilization. I coast in and toot the horn. He's reading *Scientific American*.

"Good morning, Jon!"

"My word, if it isn't the ox-herder himself," he exclaims. "You're getting to be something of a legend around here. Say, how's that ankle of yours?"

"Not too bad — a little tricky working the clutch, but I'll manage. Fortunately, I wasn't seriously hurt."

"Fortunate is the word. You're looking mighty good all around. What's your secret?"

"Well, Jon, it goes something like this. I used to think that trees were trees and hills were hills. But then trees no longer seemed like trees, and hills no longer just hills. Now I'm back where I started. Trees are trees and hills are hills. Only they look different. They look NEW."

"Very curious logic, dear doctor. But that reminds me. An old dude came by here yesterday. He mentioned you. Can't remember what his name was, but a very interesting fellow. He was looking for the way to somewhere."

"The way where?"

"Hmm, you know, he never made that clear. He didn't walk down the road, though. He cut right across the woods over there, towards the highway, I think."

I stretch my neck to see. "Are you sure, Jon? I don't see any tracks in the snow."

"I guess the drift must have covered them over."

"Did he say anything about where he was going?"

"No," Jon answers thoughtfully, then picks up an envelop from the counter. "But he left this. He told me to give it to the first person who asked where he went. You must be the lucky winner."

It's sealed, and feels rather light. When I open it, there's nothing inside except a single blank sheet of lined paper that was cleanly cut from a spiral notebook.

"What is it?" Jon asks.

"A new entry," I answer, smiling.

"An entry to what?" He's straining to see inside the envelop.

"Now that's a good question," I reply. "Say Jon, when you're done with that *Scientific American,* can I borrow it for a while?

"It would be my pleasure."

"Thanks. See you later."

I gently gas the Old Nova to the edge of the hill, shift into neutral, and begin coasting down.

About the Author

JOHN SULER IS A writer, scholar, clinical psychologist, and Professor of Psychology at Rider University. Internationally recognized as an expert in emerging fields of psychology, he has published widely on topics related to eastern philosophy, psychotherapy, and cyberspace, including the books *Contemporary Psychoanalysis and Eastern Thought* (State University of New York Press) and, his groundbreaking work, *The Psychology of Cyberspace*, one of the first and most widely cited online hypertext books. Suler's popular websites include *Zen Stories to Tell Your Neighbors* and the innovative guide *Teaching Clinical Psychology*. Most recently, his lifelong passion for photography and the role of images in identity expression has led him to develop Photographic Psychology as a way to study how people create, share, and react to images.

John Suler's work has been translated into a dozen languages and reported widely by national and international media, including the New York Times, The Wall Street Journal, the BBC, CNN, MSNBC, US News and World Report and The Chronicle of Higher Education. Much of his work is available online, including his most recent publication, *Photographic Psychology: Image and Psyche*. The author currently lives with his wife, two daughters, and ancient border terrier in Bucks County, Pennsylvania.